THE GUIN SAGA Manga

The Seven Magi

Volume 1

ILLUSTRATED BY

KAZUAKI YANAGISAWA

STORY BY

KAORU KURIMOTO

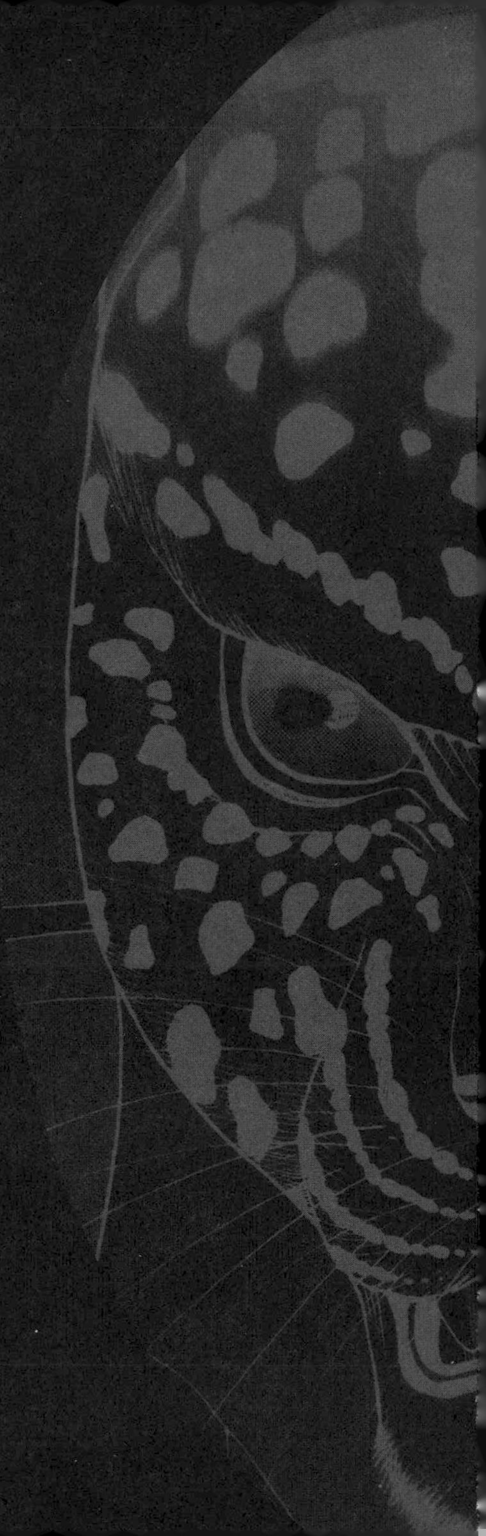

VERTICAL.

Translation—Ishmael Arthur
Production—Hiroko Mizuno
Ayako Fukumitsu
Shinobu Sato
Grace Liaw

First published in Japan in 2001 by MEDIA FACTORY, Inc.

Published by Vertical, Inc., New York

Originally published in Japanese as *Guin Saga: Shichinin no Madoushi,*
with a story adapted from the eponymous novel by Kaoru Kurimoto.

ISBN 978-1-932234-80-0

Manufactured in the United States of America

Vertical, Inc.
1185 Avenue of the Americas, 32nd floor
New York, NY 10036
www.vertical-inc.com

The Seven Magi

Volume 1

CONTENTS

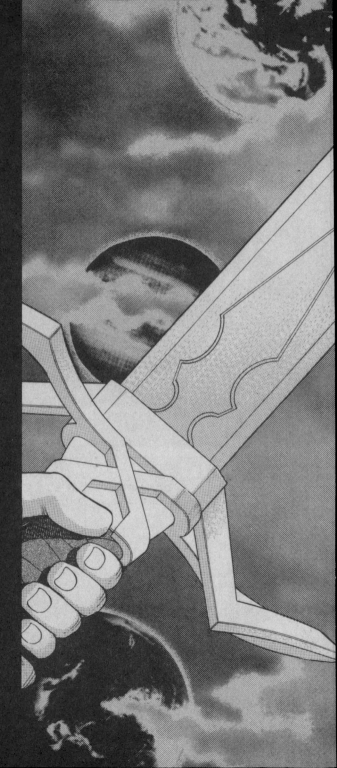

CHAPTER 1

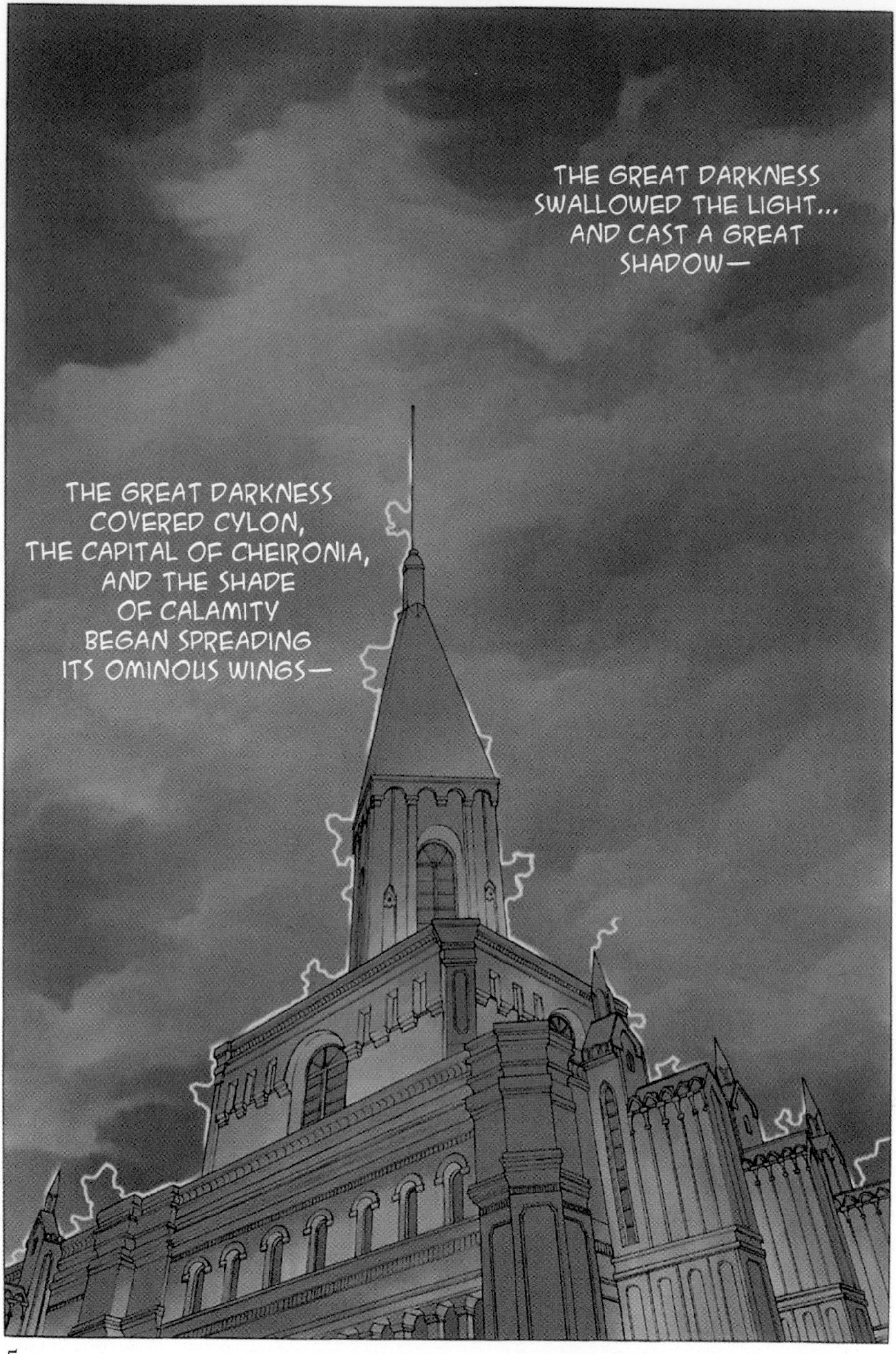
THE GREAT DARKNESS SWALLOWED THE LIGHT... AND CAST A GREAT SHADOW—
THE GREAT DARKNESS COVERED CYLON, THE CAPITAL OF CHEIRONIA, AND THE SHADE OF CALAMITY BEGAN SPREADING ITS OMINOUS WINGS—

Chapter 1

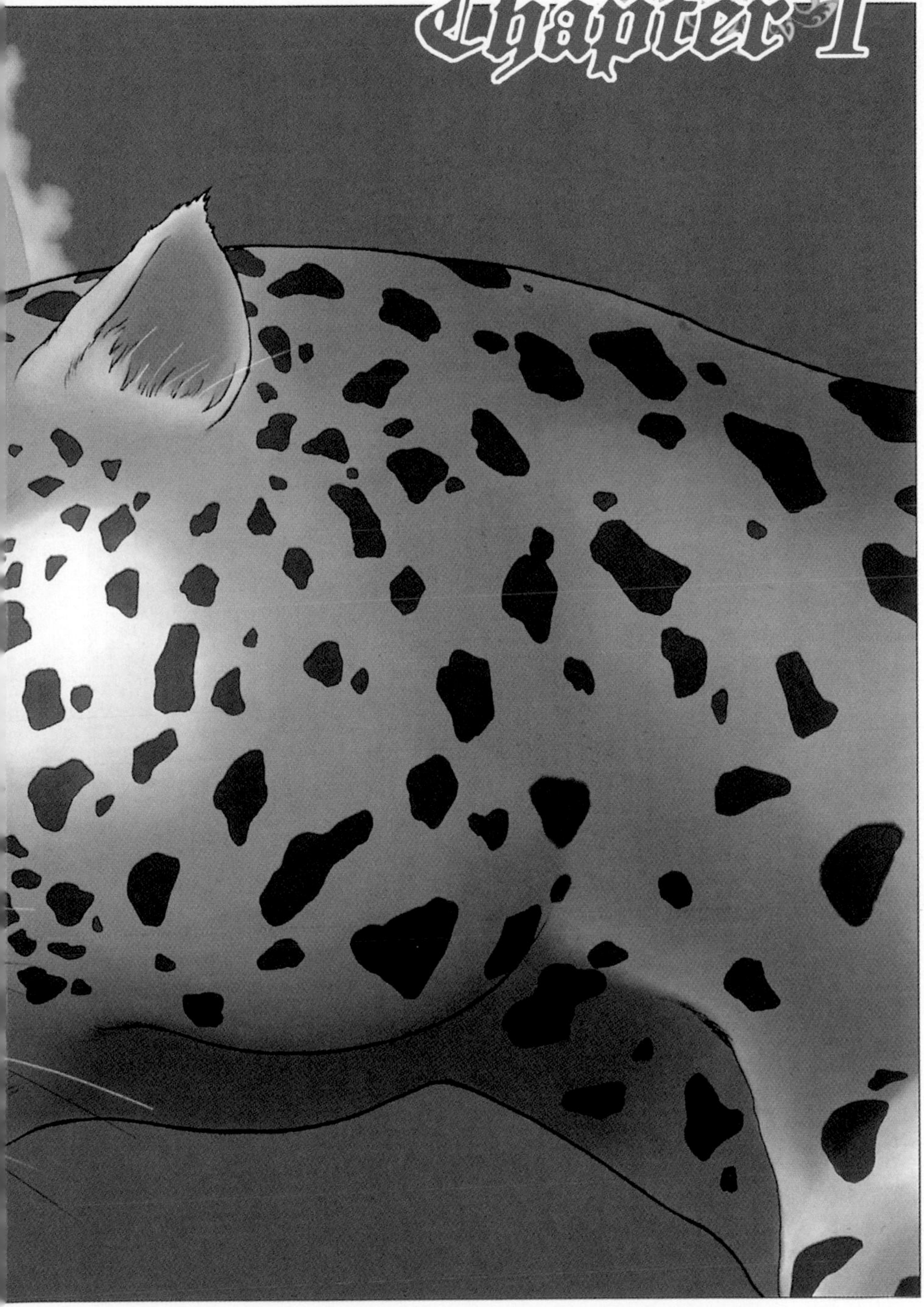

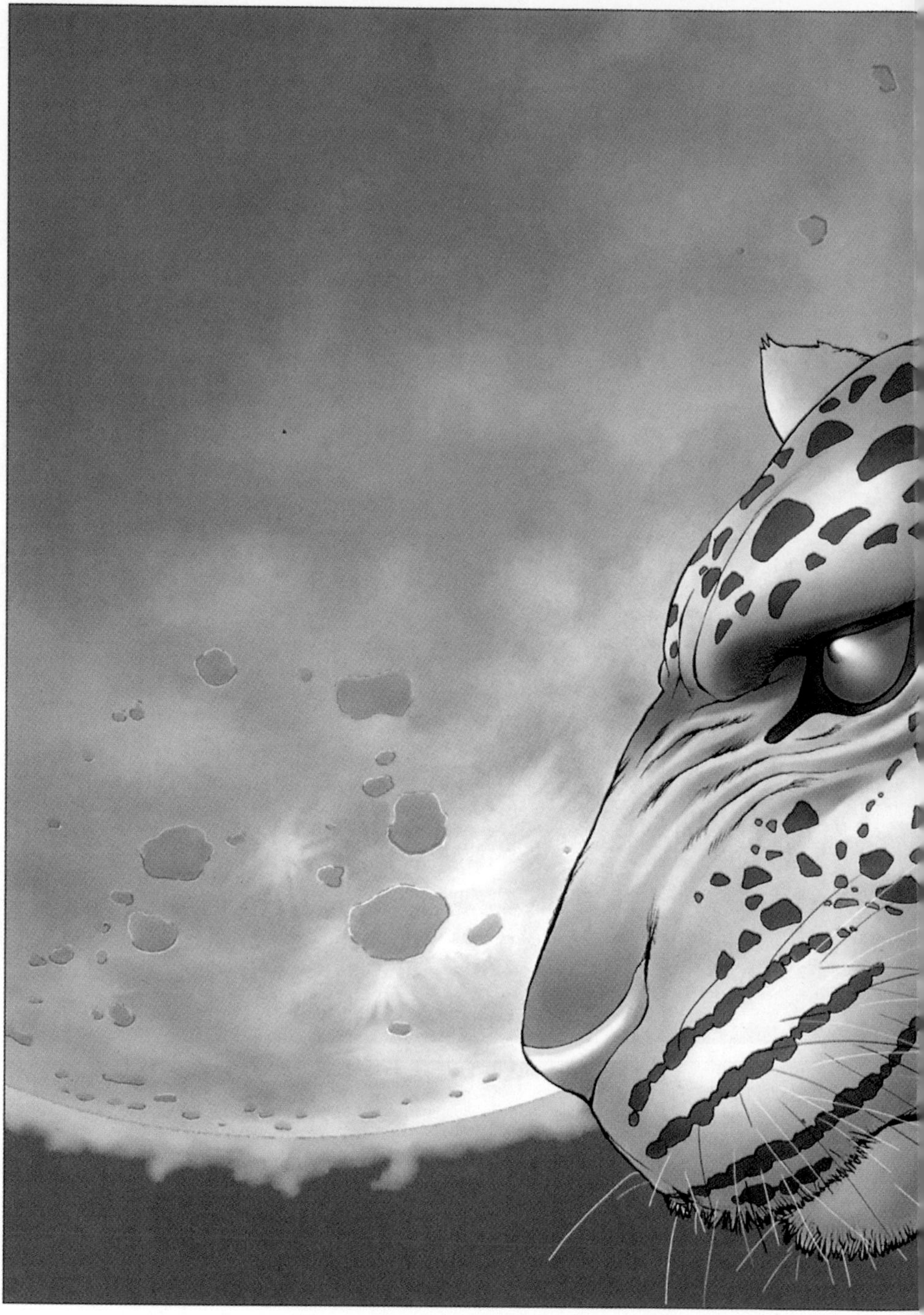

THE YEAR OF
THE CAT—

EARLY IN
THE BLUE MONTH—

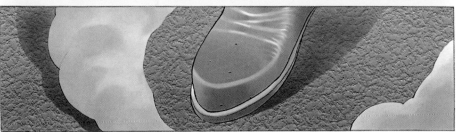

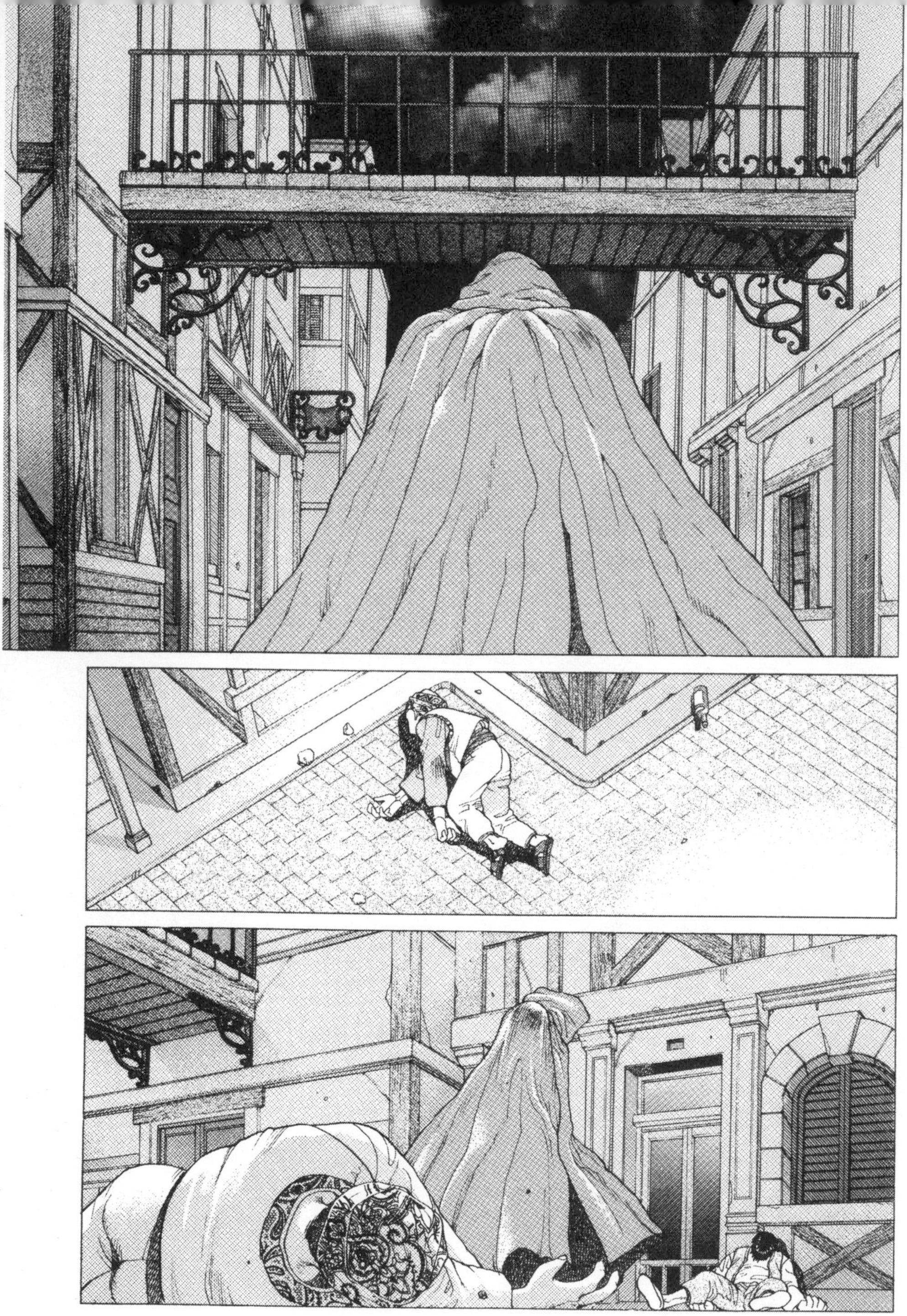

PRAISE THE BLESSINGS OF MILOCH, FOR WE WERE BORN TO LOVE ONE ANOTHER. CAST AWAY THY ARMS, KILL NOT, HUMBLY LIVE AS THE SALT OF THE EARTH.

WHEN THE DARKNESS COVERED ALL...

MONSTROSITIES DREW NEAR.

P-HA

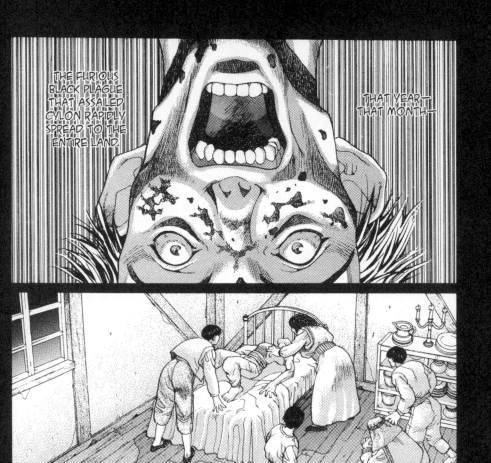

THE FURIOUS BLACK PLAGUE THAT ASSAILED CYLON RAPIDLY SPREAD TO THE ENTIRE LAND.

THAT YEAR— THAT MONTH—

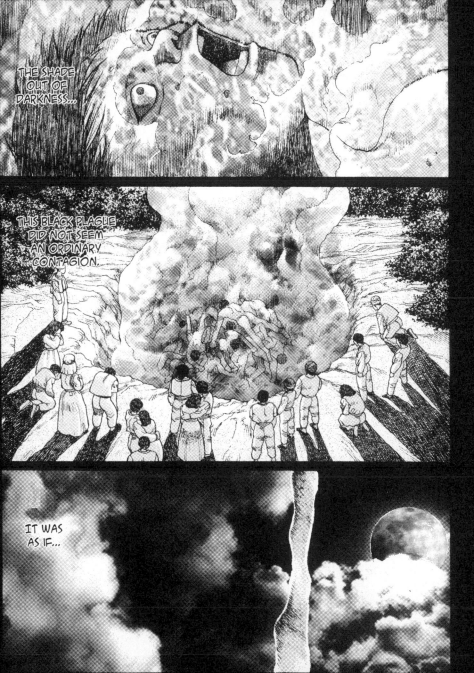

THE SHADE OUT OF DARKNESS...

THIS BLACK PLAGUE DID NOT SEEM AN ORDINARY CONTAGION.

IT WAS AS IF...

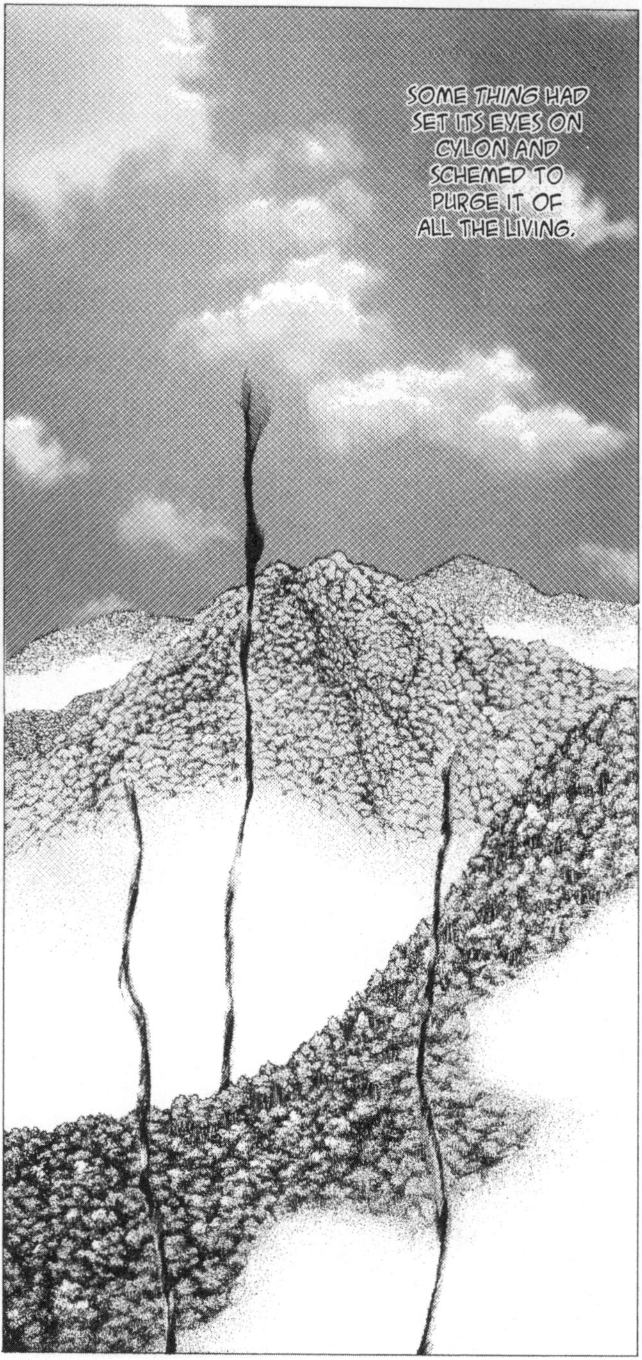
SOME THING HAD SET ITS EYES ON CYLON AND SCHEMED TO PURGE IT OF ALL THE LIVING.

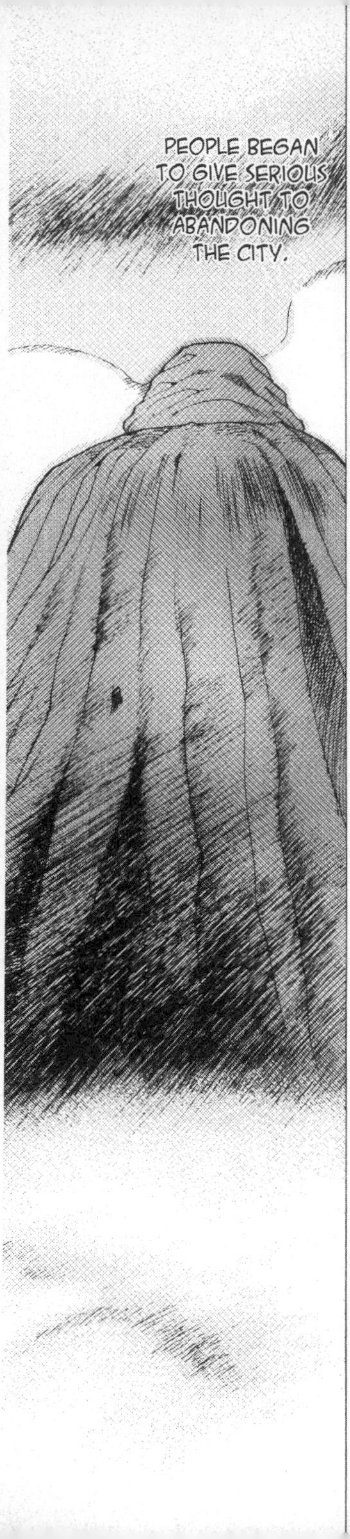
PEOPLE BEGAN TO GIVE SERIOUS THOUGHT TO ABANDONING THE CITY.

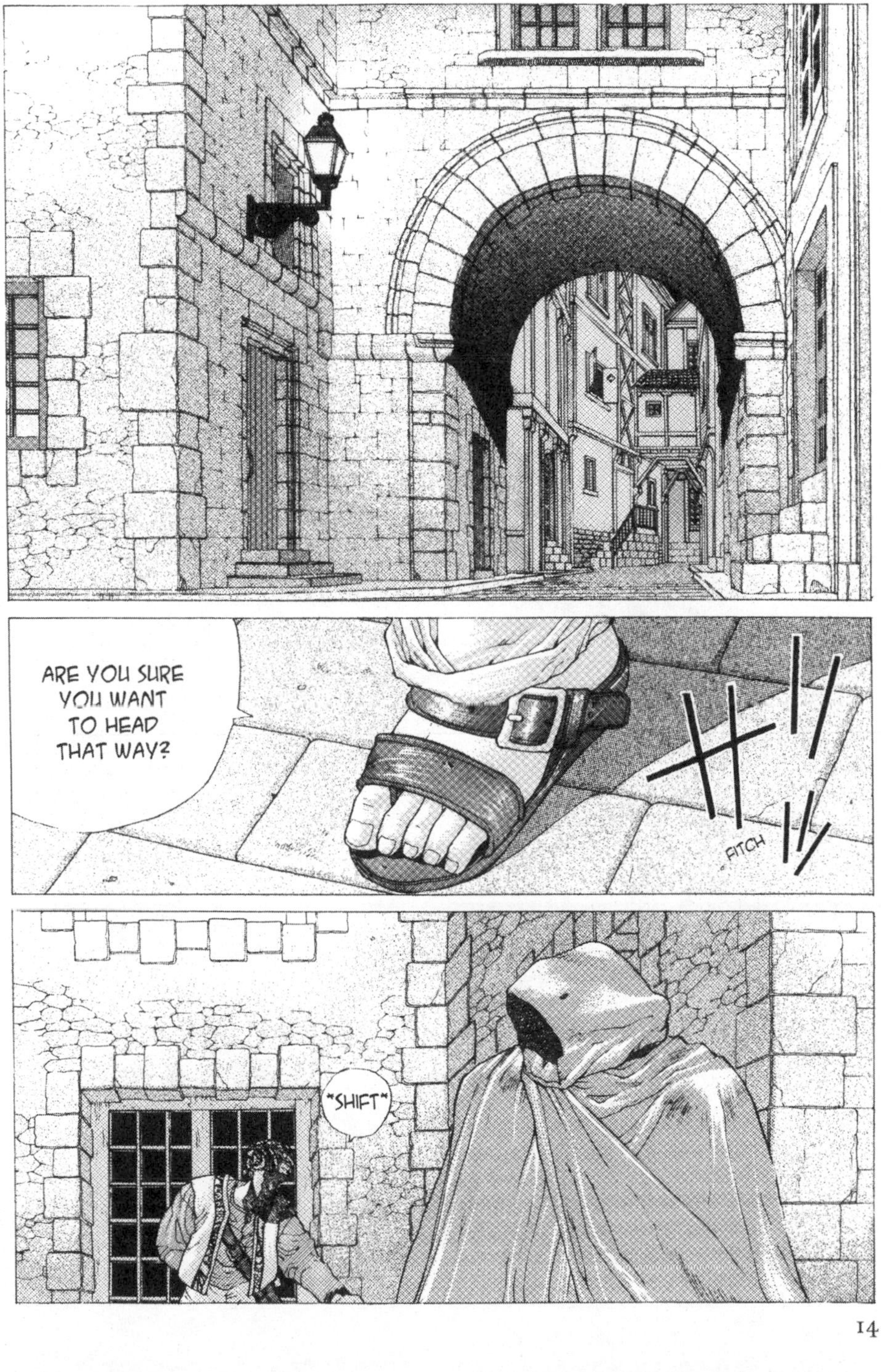
ARE YOU SURE YOU WANT TO HEAD THAT WAY?
FITCH
SHIFT

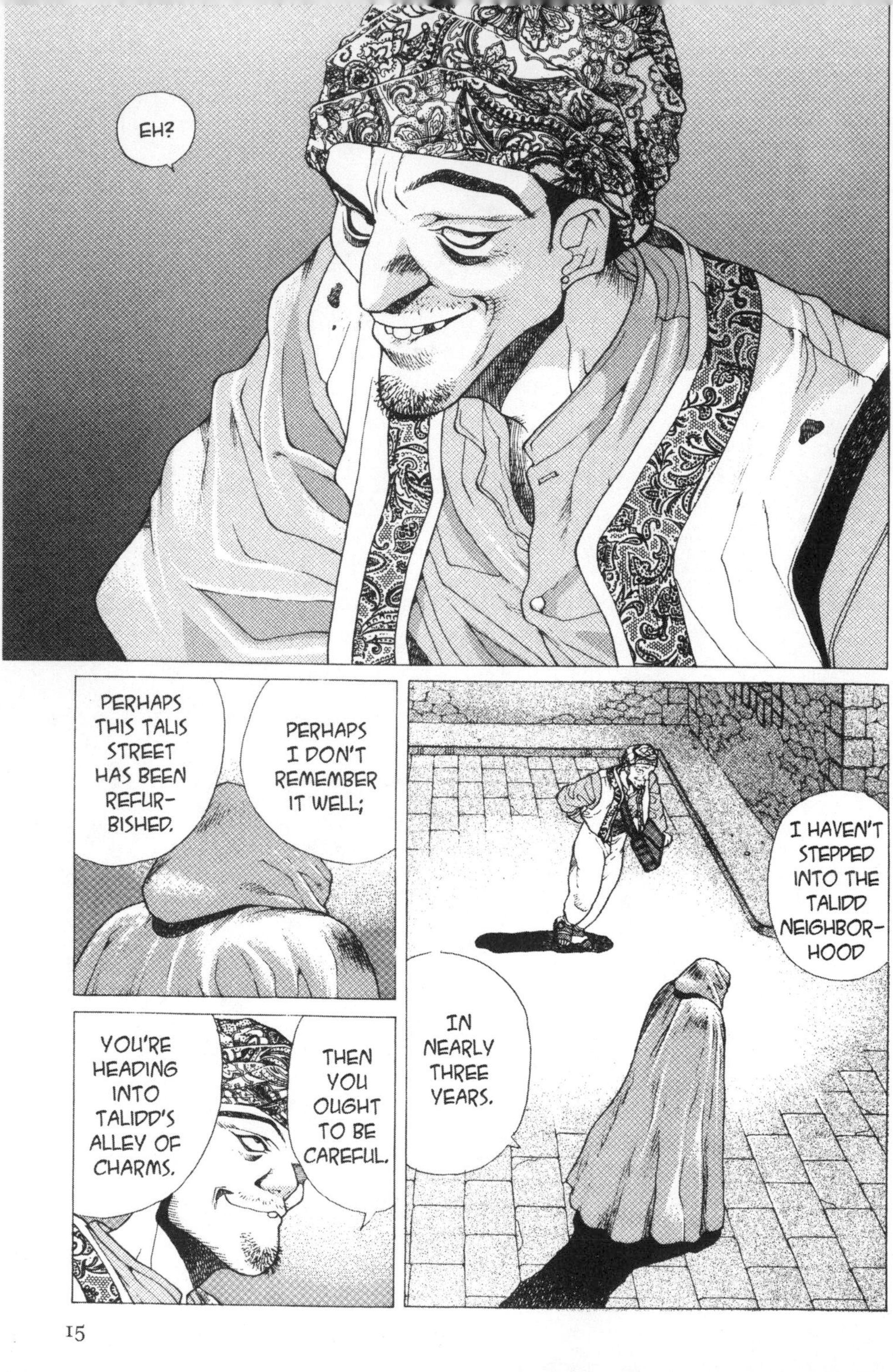
EH?
I HAVEN'T STEPPED INTO THE TALIDD NEIGHBOR-HOOD
IN NEARLY THREE YEARS.
PERHAPS I DON'T REMEMBER IT WELL;
PERHAPS THIS TALIS STREET HAS BEEN REFUR-BISHED.
THEN YOU OUGHT TO BE CAREFUL.
YOU'RE HEADING INTO TALIDD'S ALLEY OF CHARMS.

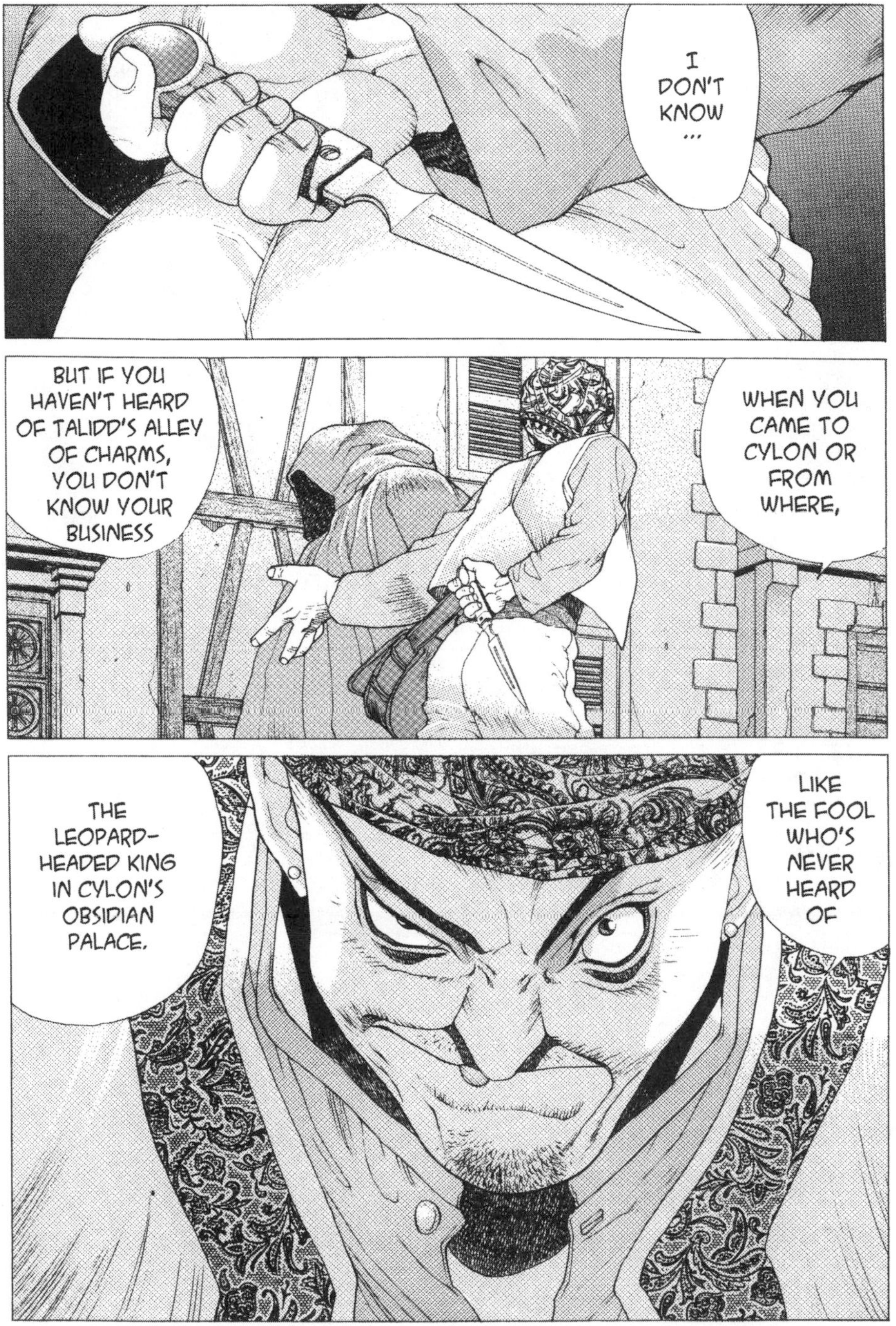
I DON'T KNOW ...
WHEN YOU CAME TO CYLON OR FROM WHERE,
BUT IF YOU HAVEN'T HEARD OF TALIDD'S ALLEY OF CHARMS, YOU DON'T KNOW YOUR BUSINESS
LIKE THE FOOL WHO'S NEVER HEARD OF
THE LEOPARD-HEADED KING IN CYLON'S OBSIDIAN PALACE.

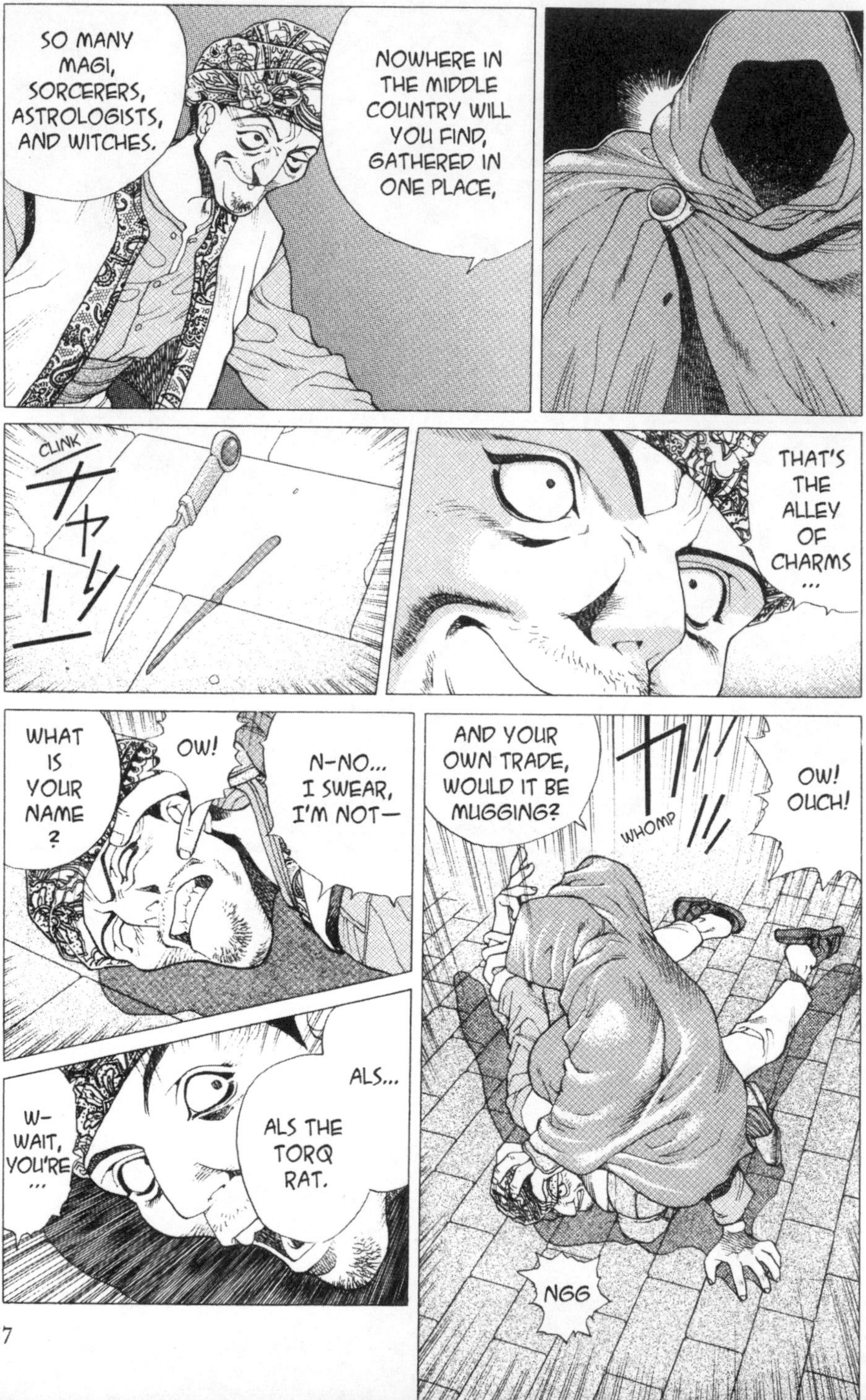
NOWHERE IN THE MIDDLE COUNTRY WILL YOU FIND, GATHERED IN ONE PLACE,
SO MANY MAGI, SORCERERS, ASTROLOGISTS, AND WITCHES.
THAT'S THE ALLEY OF CHARMS...
CLINK
OW! OUCH!
AND YOUR OWN TRADE, WOULD IT BE MUGGING?
WHOMP
NGG
N-NO... I SWEAR, I'M NOT—
OW!
WHAT IS YOUR NAME?
ALS...
ALS THE TORQ RAT.
W-WAIT, YOU'RE ...

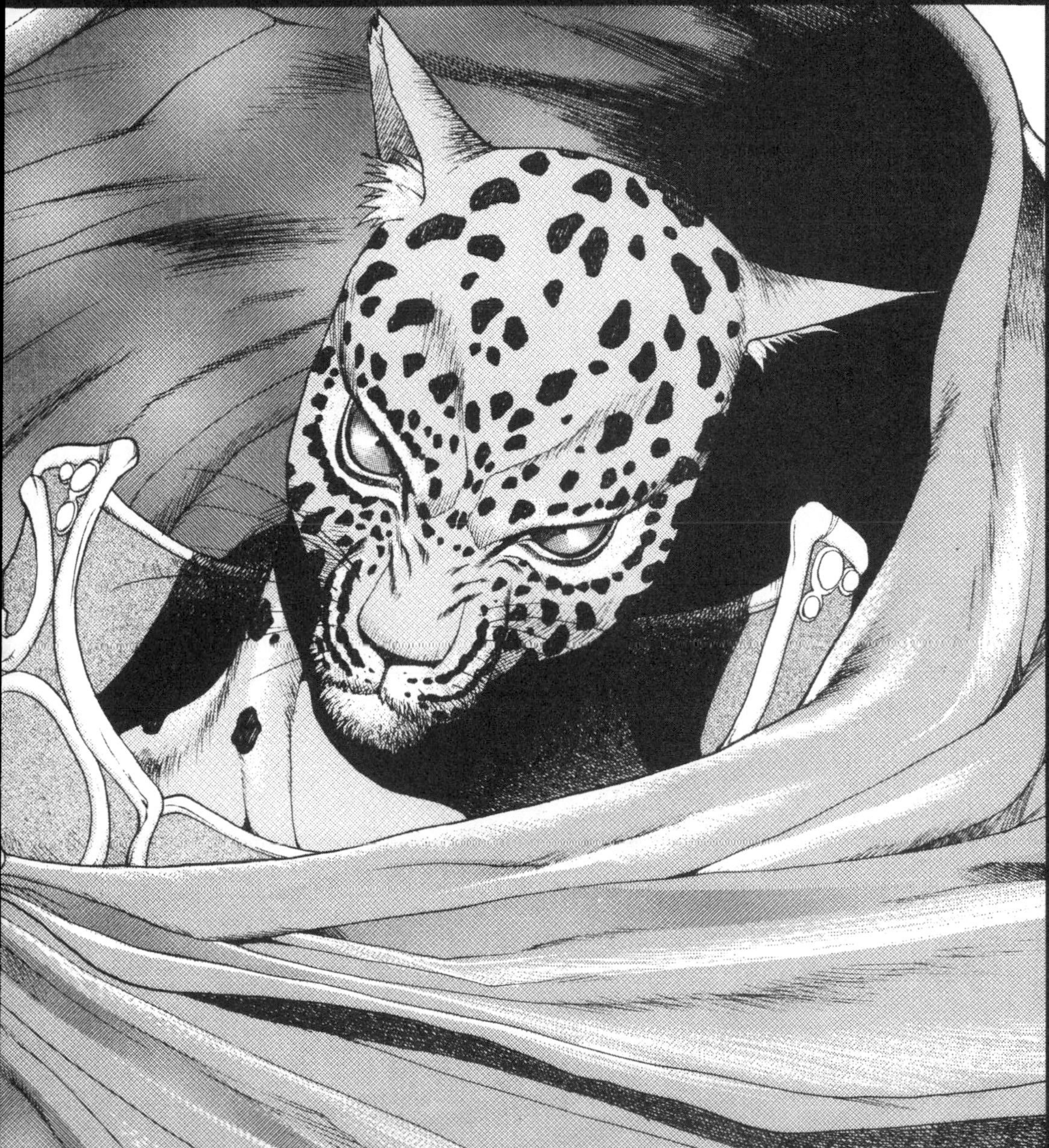

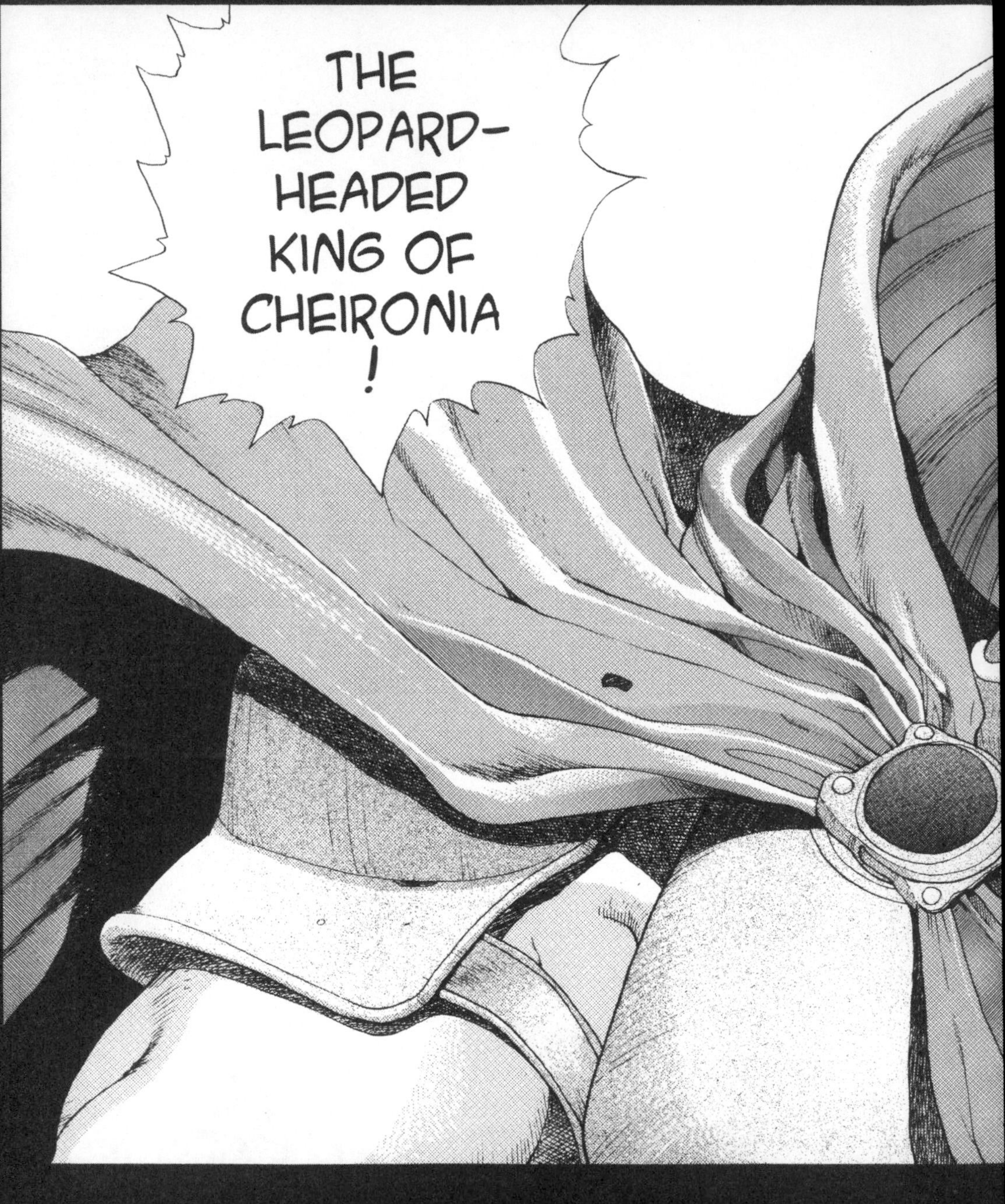
THE LEOPARD-HEADED KING OF CHEIRONIA!

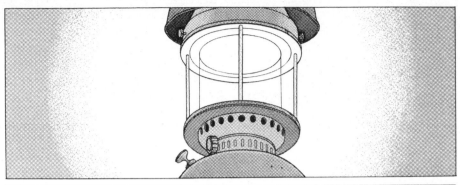

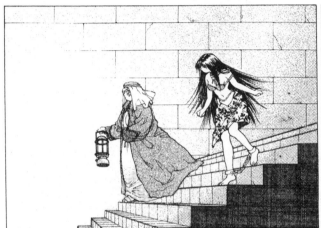

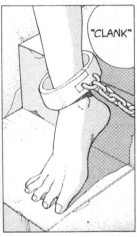

CLANK
MADAM ARACHNE ...
TODAY WE HAVE A TOP-TIER CLIENT.
DO NOT DISPLEASE HIM.

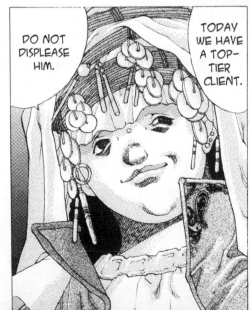

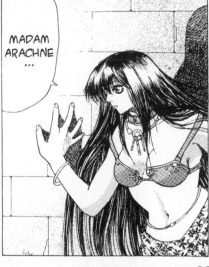

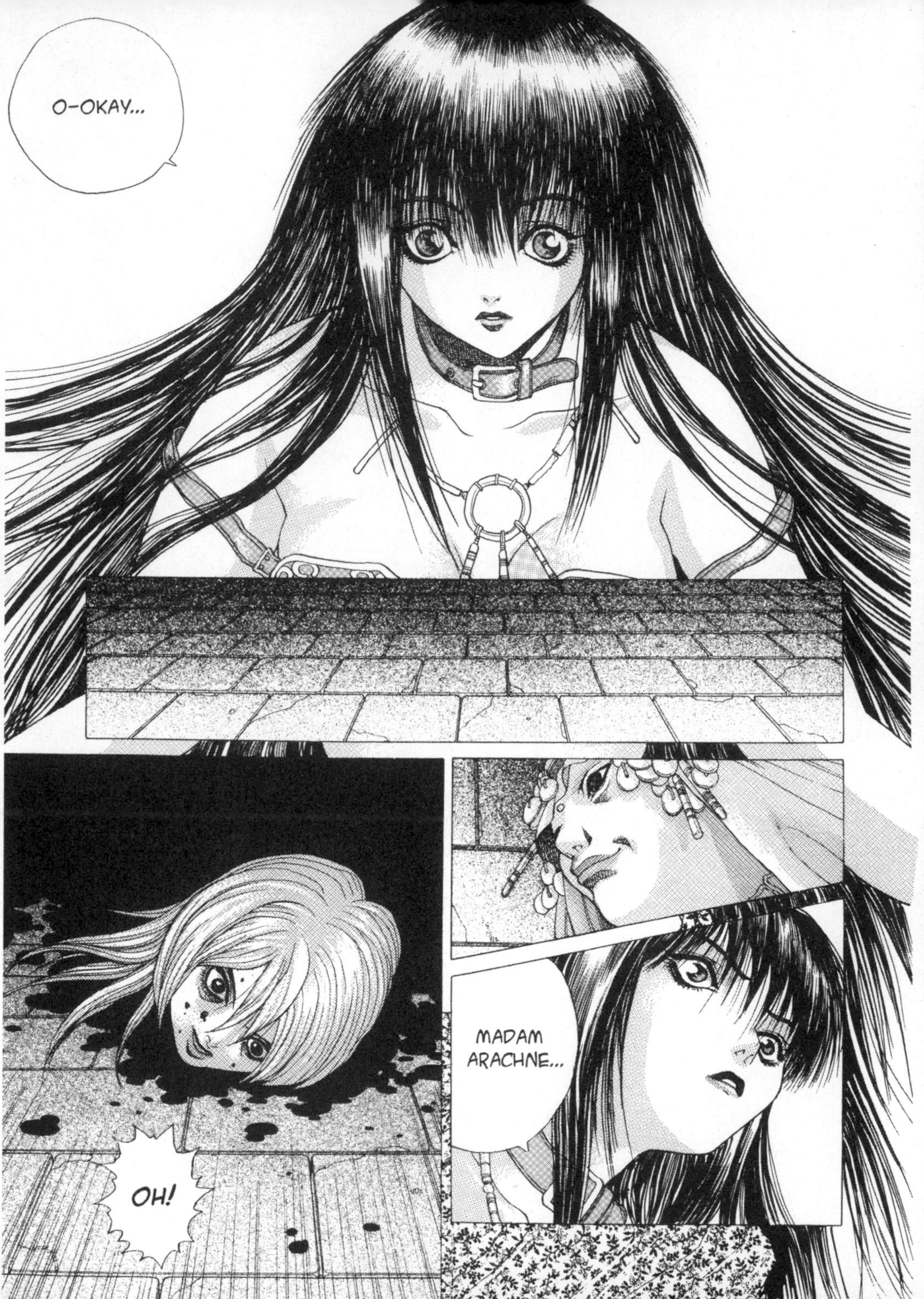
O-OKAY...
MADAM ARACHNE...
OH!

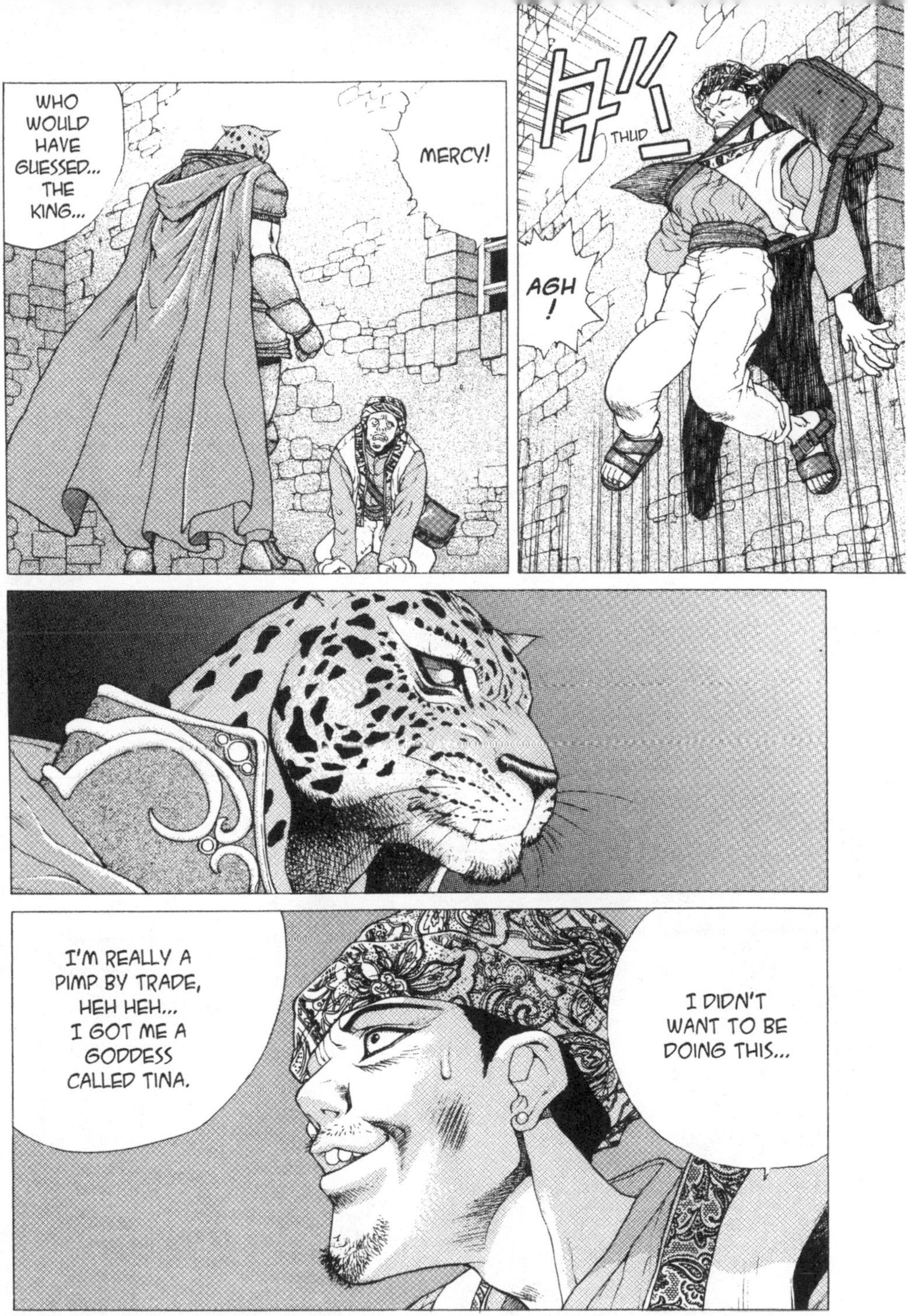
THUD
AGH!
MERCY!
WHO WOULD HAVE GUESSED... THE KING...
I DIDN'T WANT TO BE DOING THIS...
I'M REALLY A PIMP BY TRADE, HEH HEH... I GOT ME A GODDESS CALLED TINA.

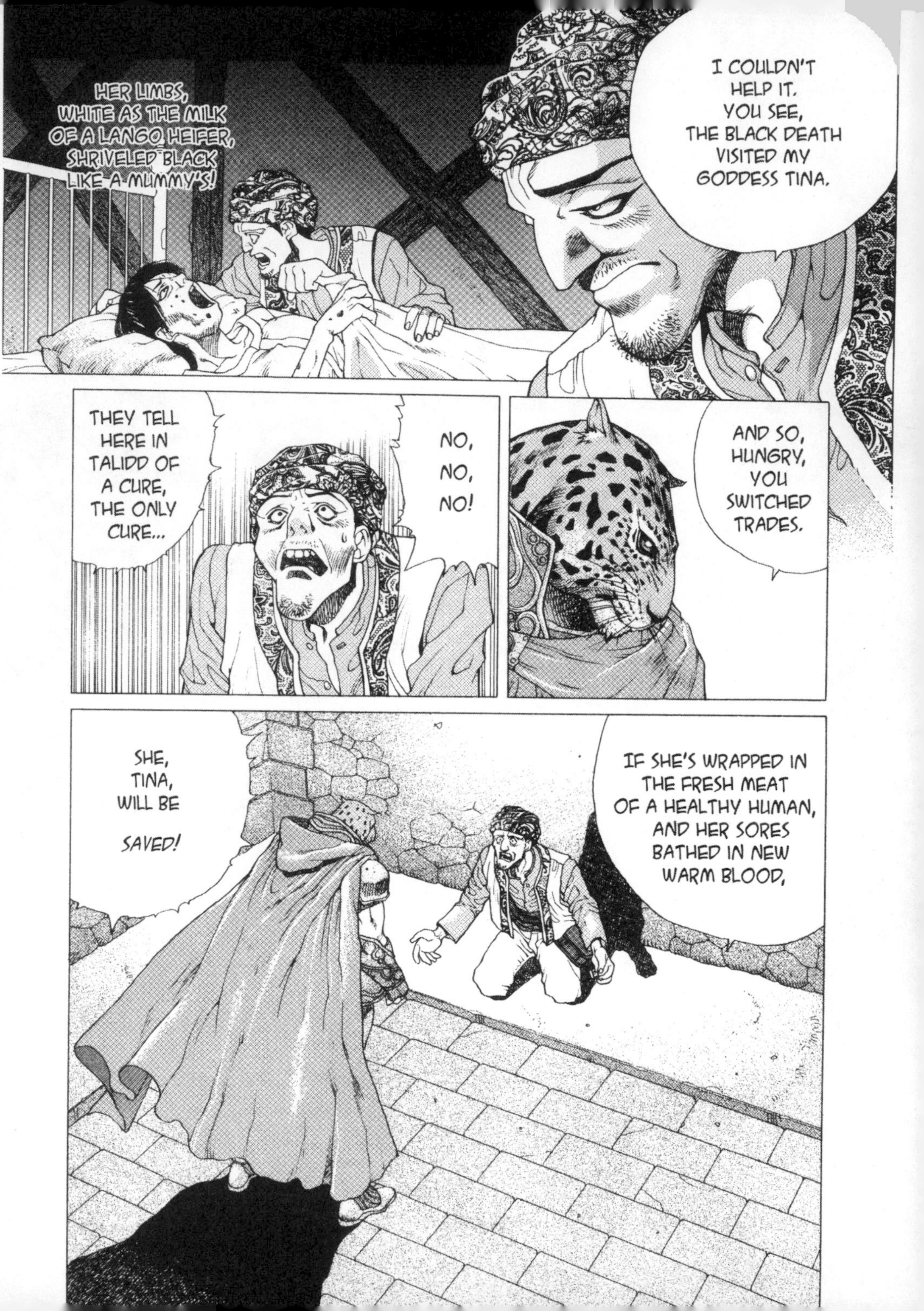

I COULDN'T HELP IT. YOU SEE, THE BLACK DEATH VISITED MY GODDESS TINA.
HER LIMBS, WHITE AS THE MILK OF A LANGO HEIFER, SHRIVELED BLACK LIKE A MUMMY'S!
AND SO, HUNGRY, YOU SWITCHED TRADES.
NO, NO, NO!
THEY TELL HERE IN TALIDD OF A CURE, THE ONLY CURE...
IF SHE'S WRAPPED IN THE FRESH MEAT OF A HEALTHY HUMAN, AND HER SORES BATHED IN NEW WARM BLOOD,
SHE, TINA, WILL BE *SAVED!*

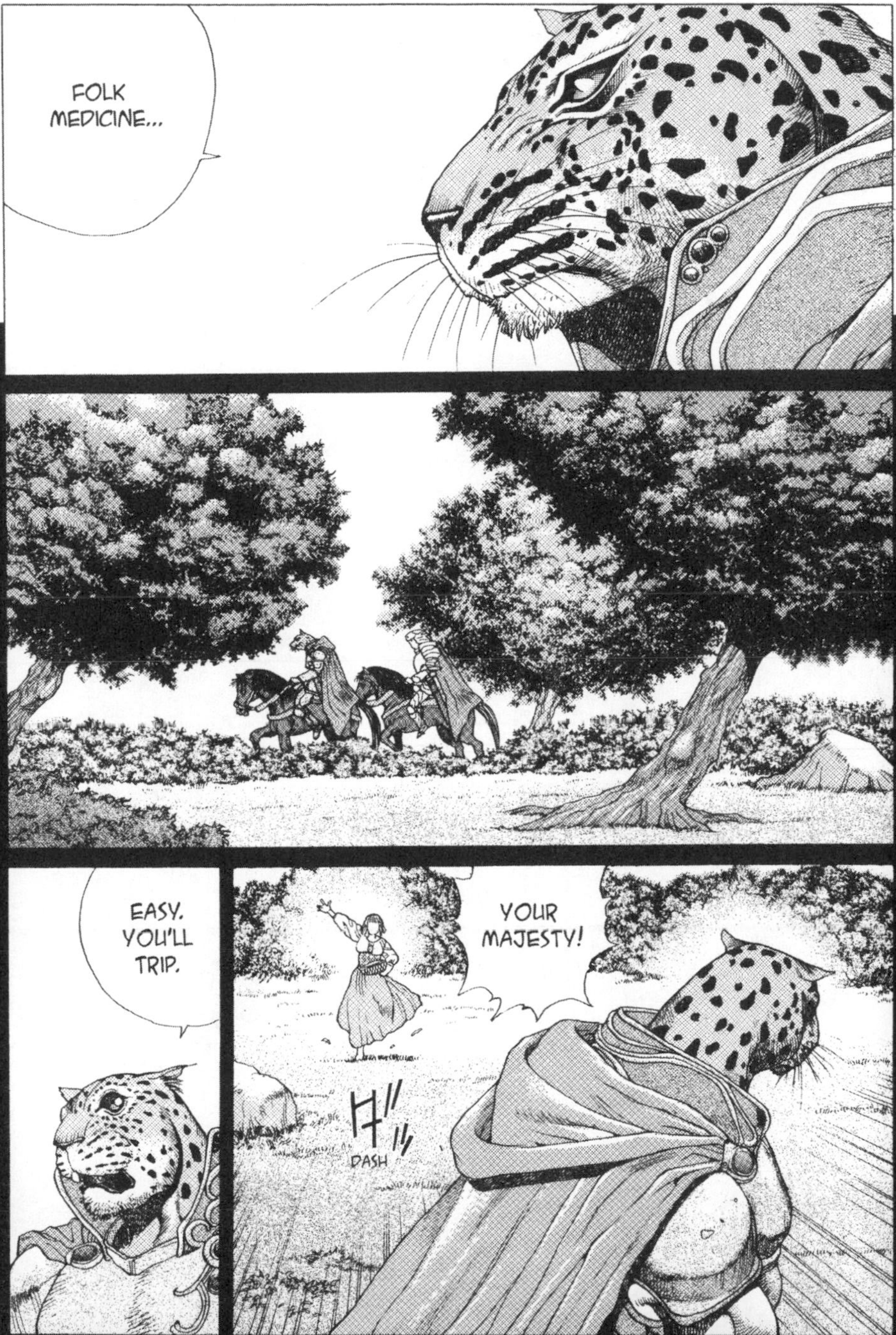
FOLK MEDICINE...
YOUR MAJESTY!
DASH
EASY. YOU'LL TRIP.

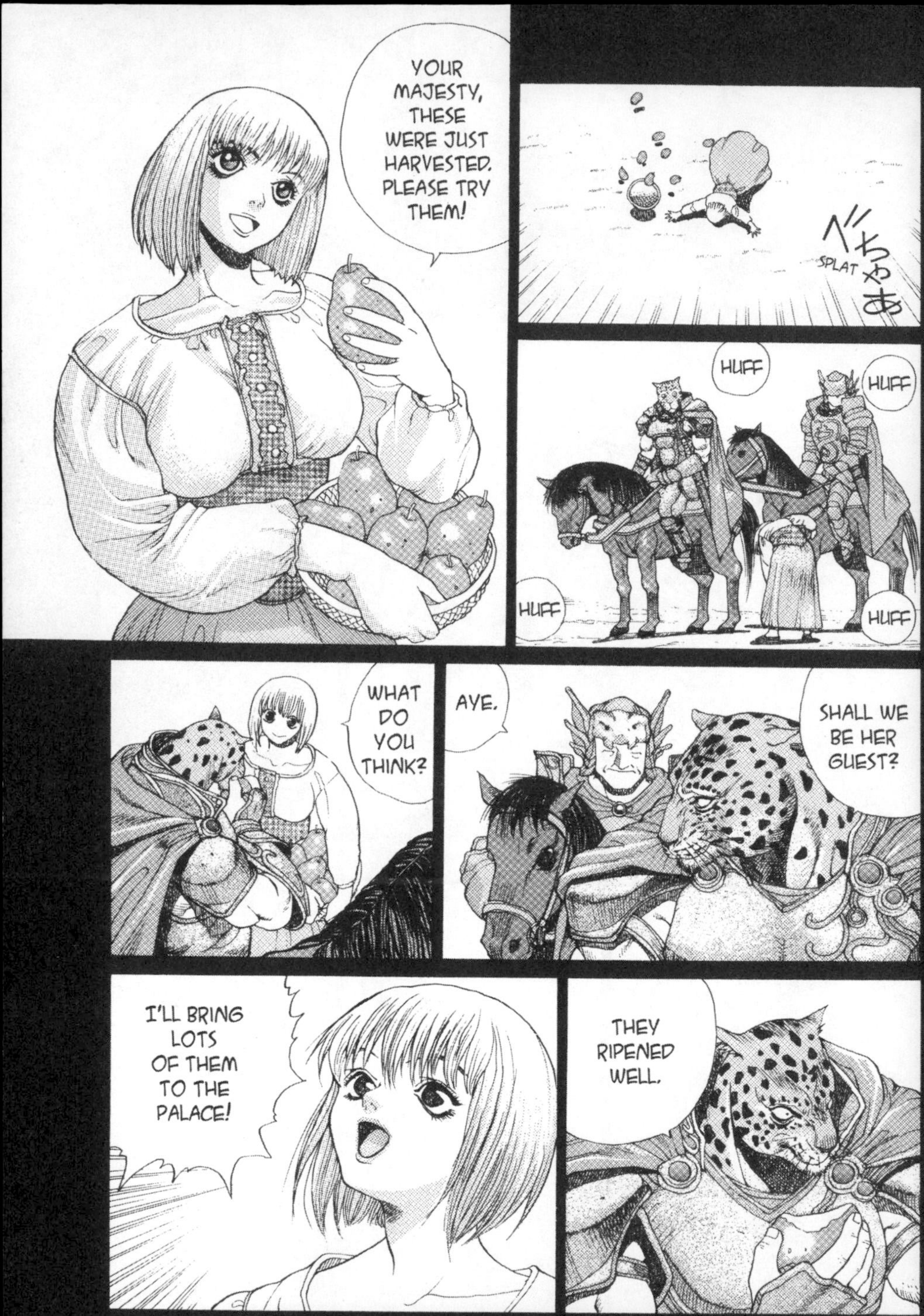
べちゃあ
SPLAT
HUFF
HUFF
HUFF
HUFF
YOUR MAJESTY, THESE WERE JUST HARVESTED. PLEASE TRY THEM!
SHALL WE BE HER GUEST?
AYE.
WHAT DO YOU THINK?
THEY RIPENED WELL.
I'LL BRING LOTS OF THEM TO THE PALACE!

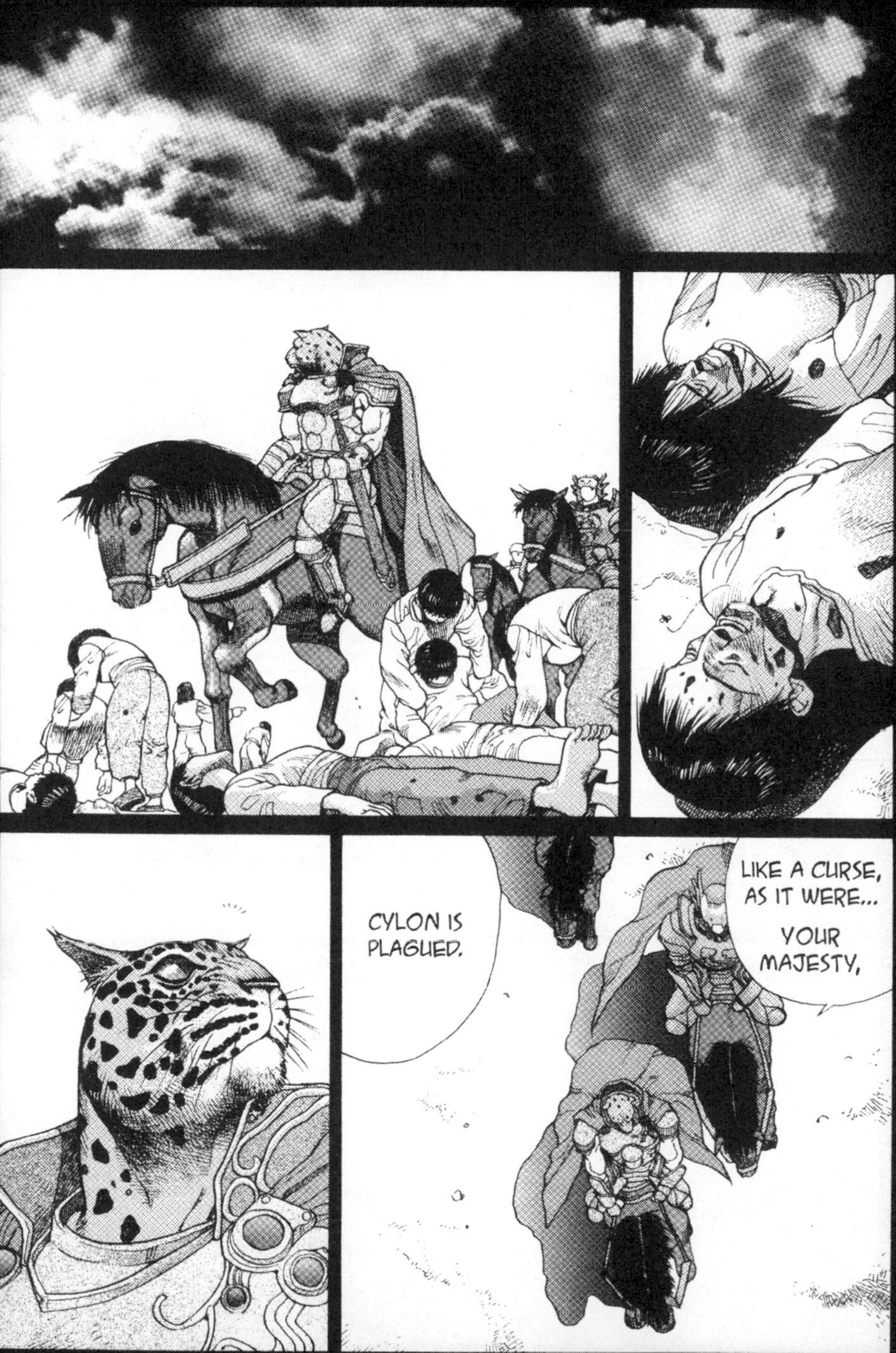
LIKE A CURSE, AS IT WERE...
YOUR MAJESTY,
CYLON IS PLAGUED.

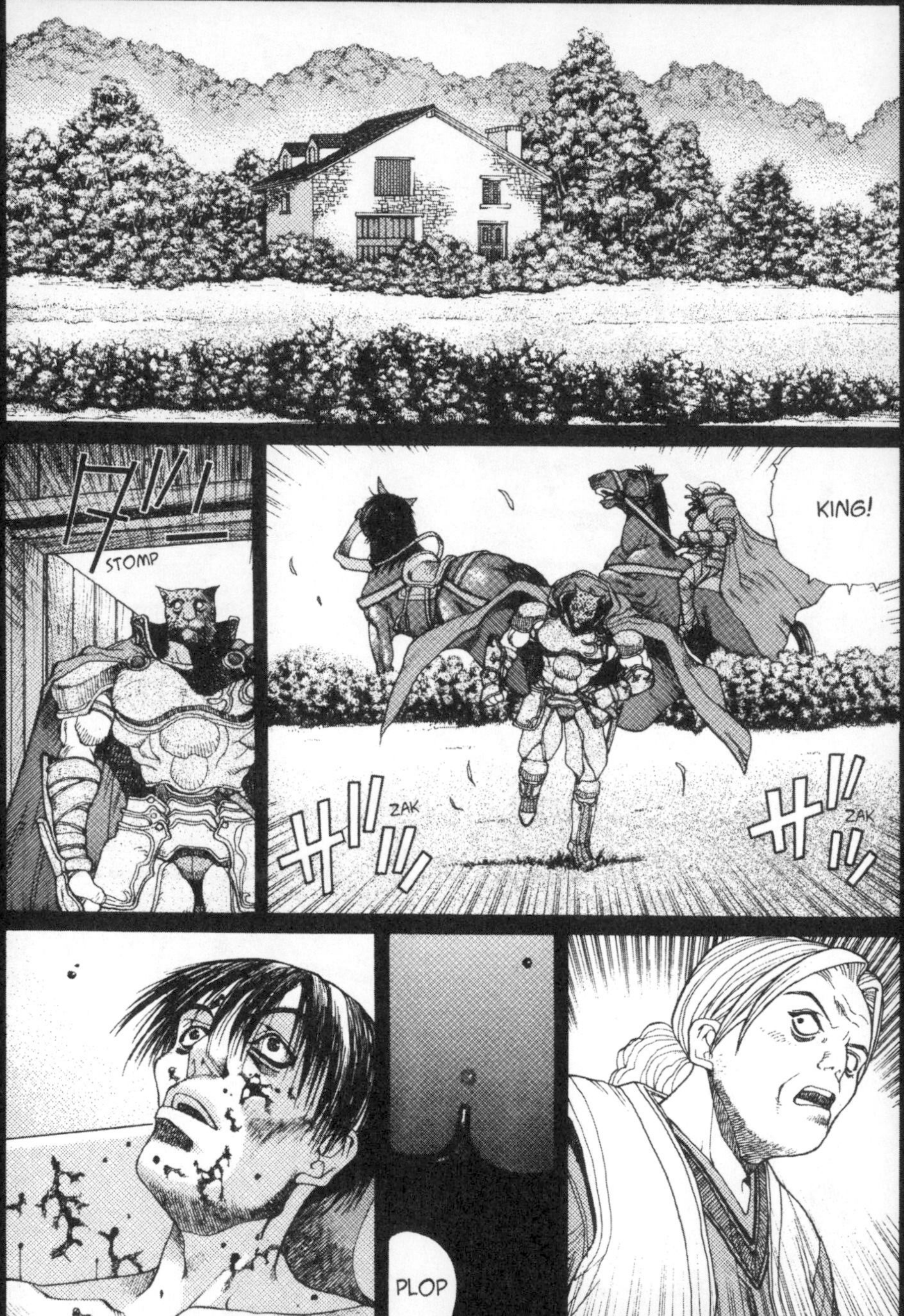
KING!
ザッ
ZAK
ザッ
ZAK
ダッ
STOMP
PLOP

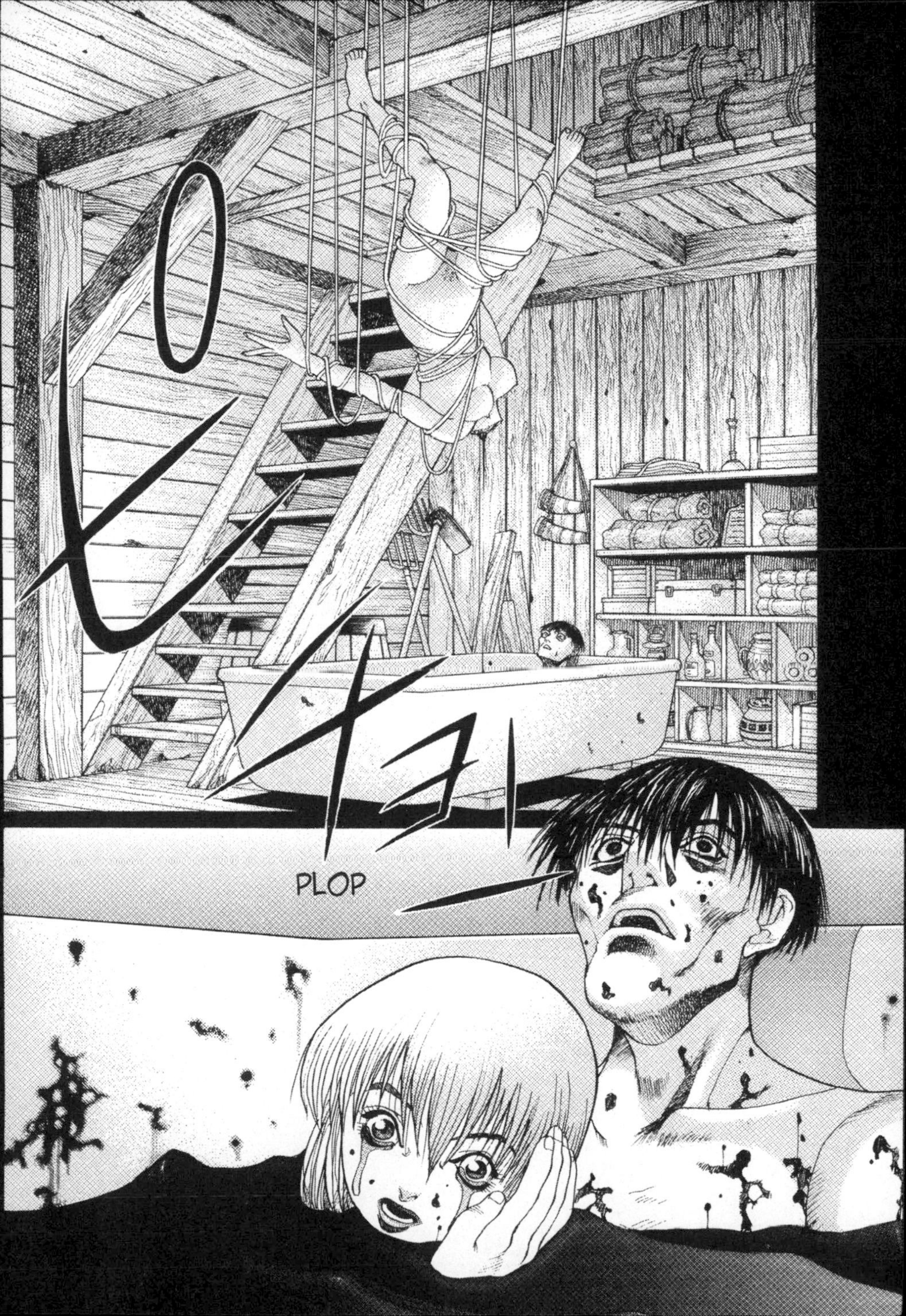
PLOP

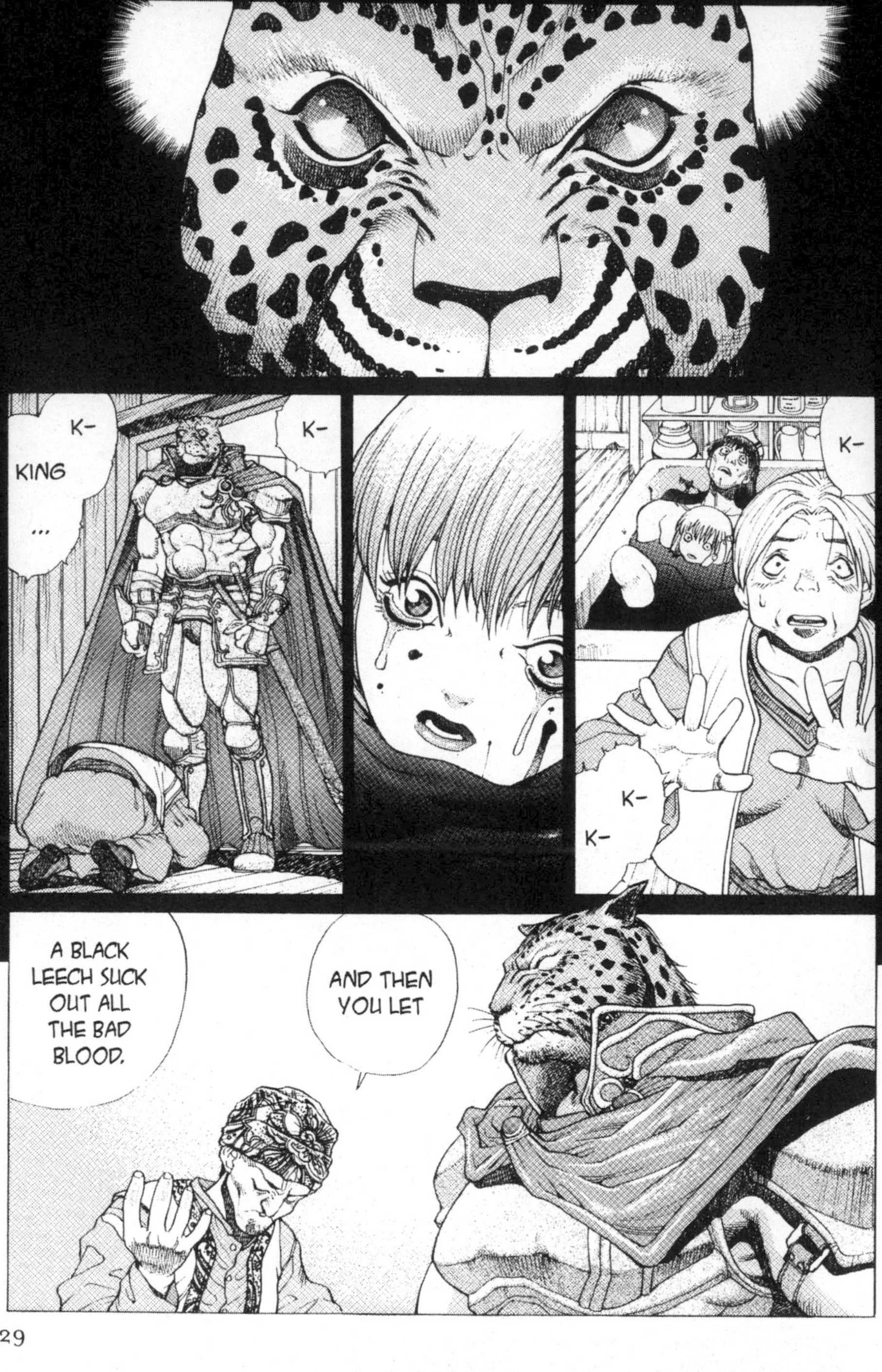
K-
K-
K-
K-
K- KING ...
AND THEN YOU LET
A BLACK LEECH SUCK OUT ALL THE BAD BLOOD.

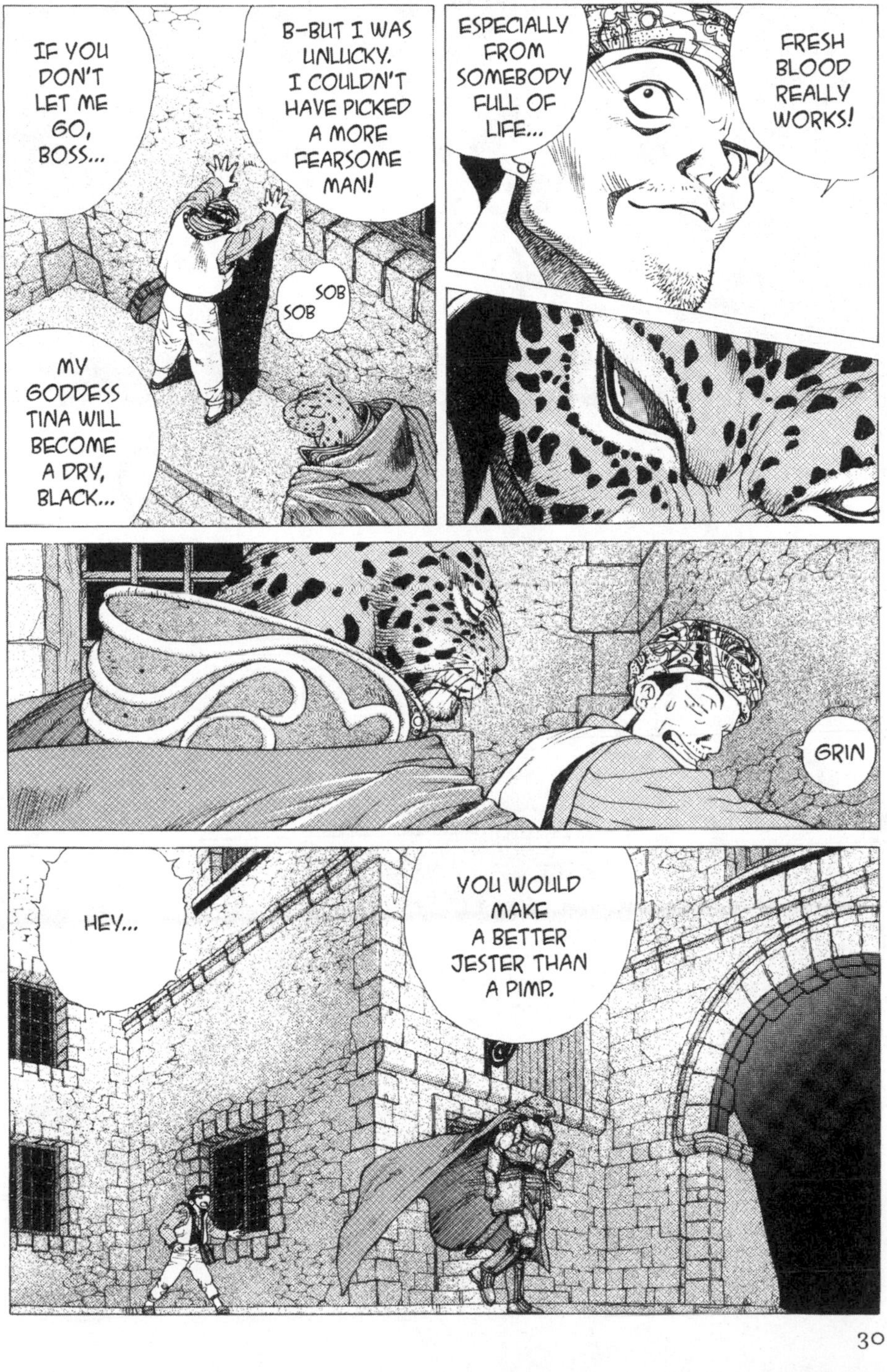
FRESH BLOOD REALLY WORKS!
ESPECIALLY FROM SOMEBODY FULL OF LIFE...
B-BUT I WAS UNLUCKY. I COULDN'T HAVE PICKED A MORE FEARSOME MAN!
IF YOU DON'T LET ME GO, BOSS...
SOB SOB
MY GODDESS TINA WILL BECOME A DRY, BLACK...
GRIN
YOU WOULD MAKE A BETTER JESTER THAN A PIMP.
HEY...

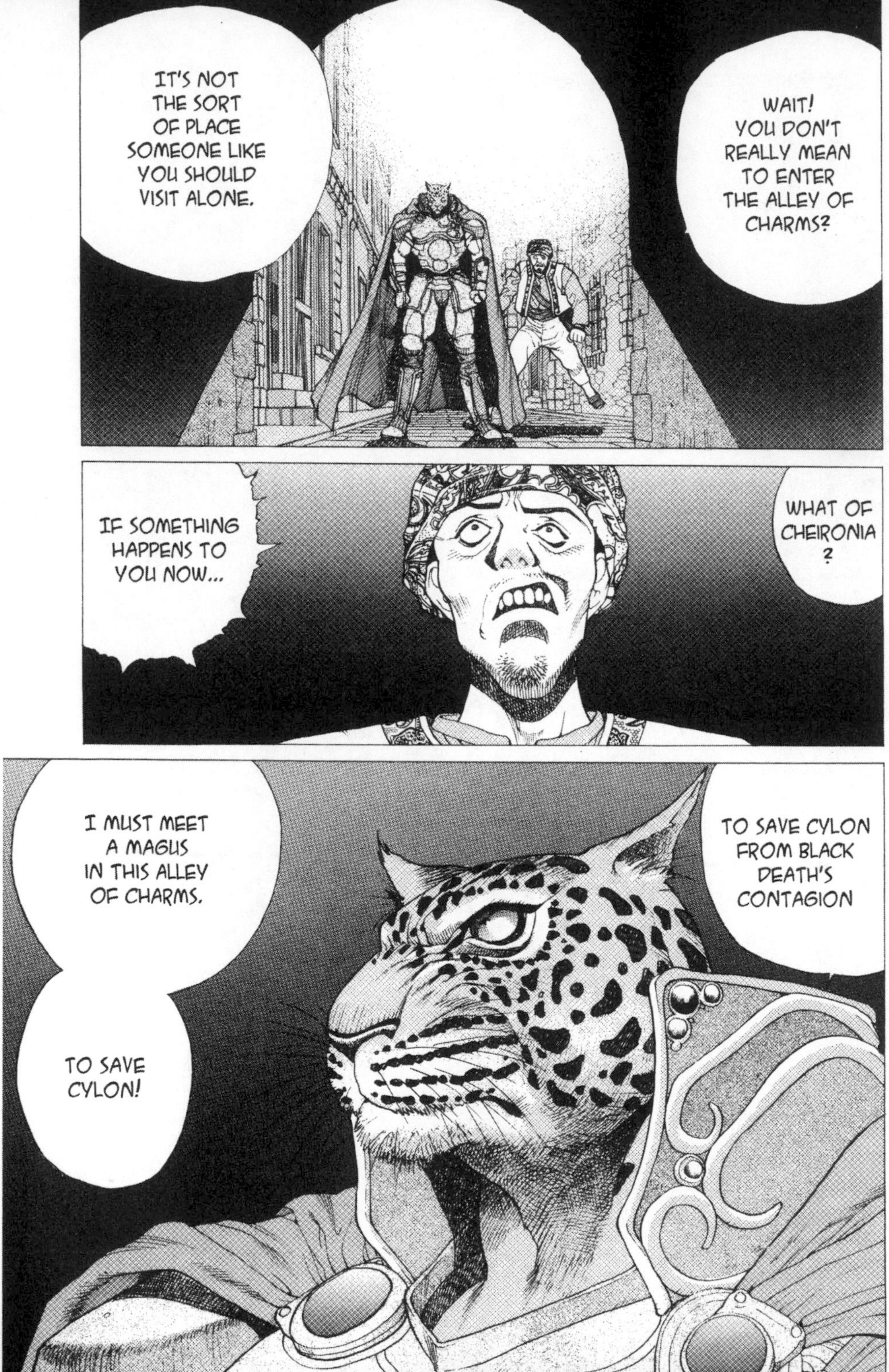
WAIT! YOU DON'T REALLY MEAN TO ENTER THE ALLEY OF CHARMS?
IT'S NOT THE SORT OF PLACE SOMEONE LIKE YOU SHOULD VISIT ALONE.
WHAT OF CHEIRONIA?
IF SOMETHING HAPPENS TO YOU NOW...
TO SAVE CYLON FROM BLACK DEATH'S CONTAGION
I MUST MEET A MAGUS IN THIS ALLEY OF CHARMS.
TO SAVE CYLON!

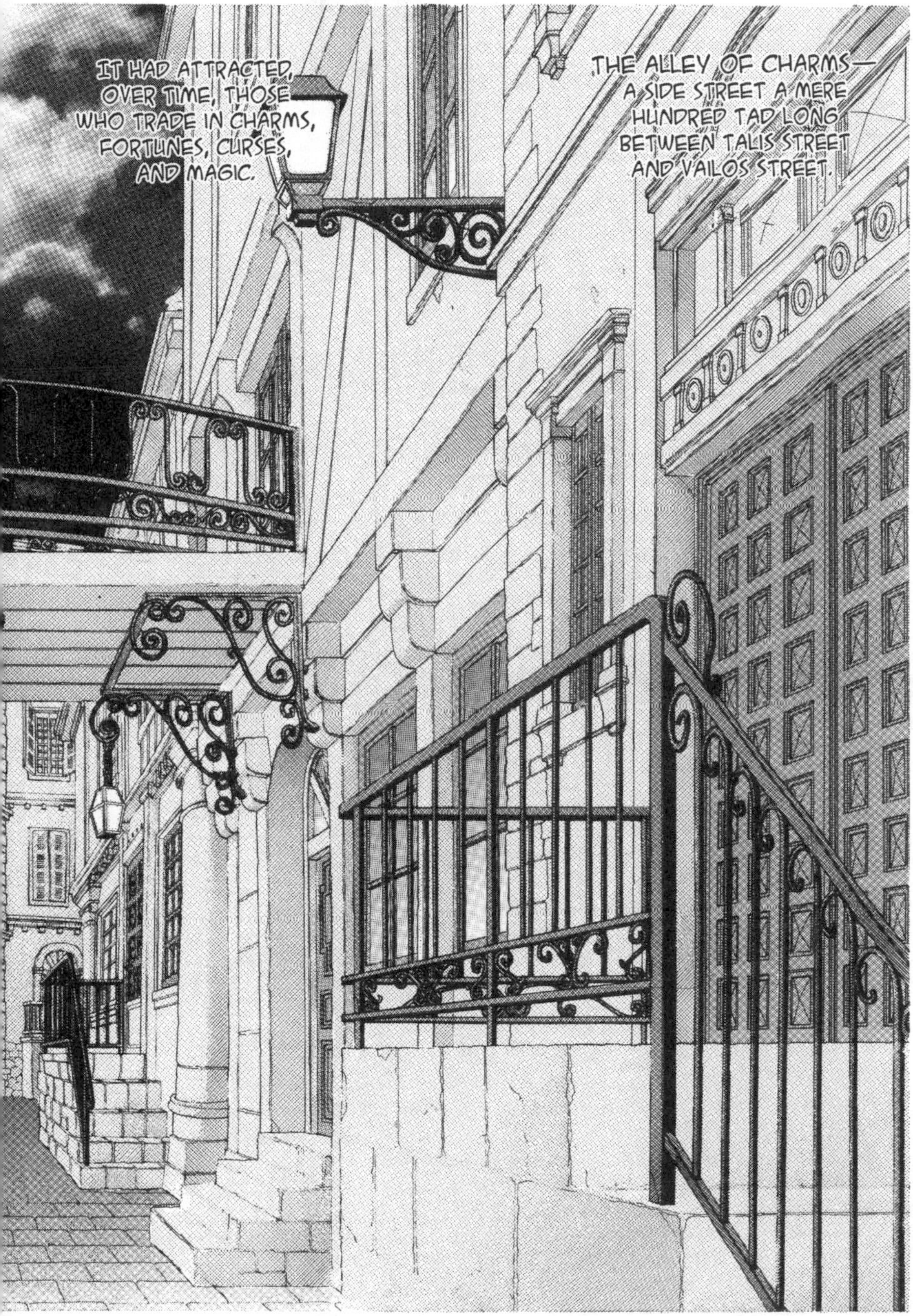
THE ALLEY OF CHARMS—A SIDE STREET A MERE HUNDRED TAD LONG BETWEEN TALIS STREET AND VAILOS STREET.
IT HAD ATTRACTED, OVER TIME, THOSE WHO TRADE IN CHARMS, FORTUNES, CURSES, AND MAGIC.

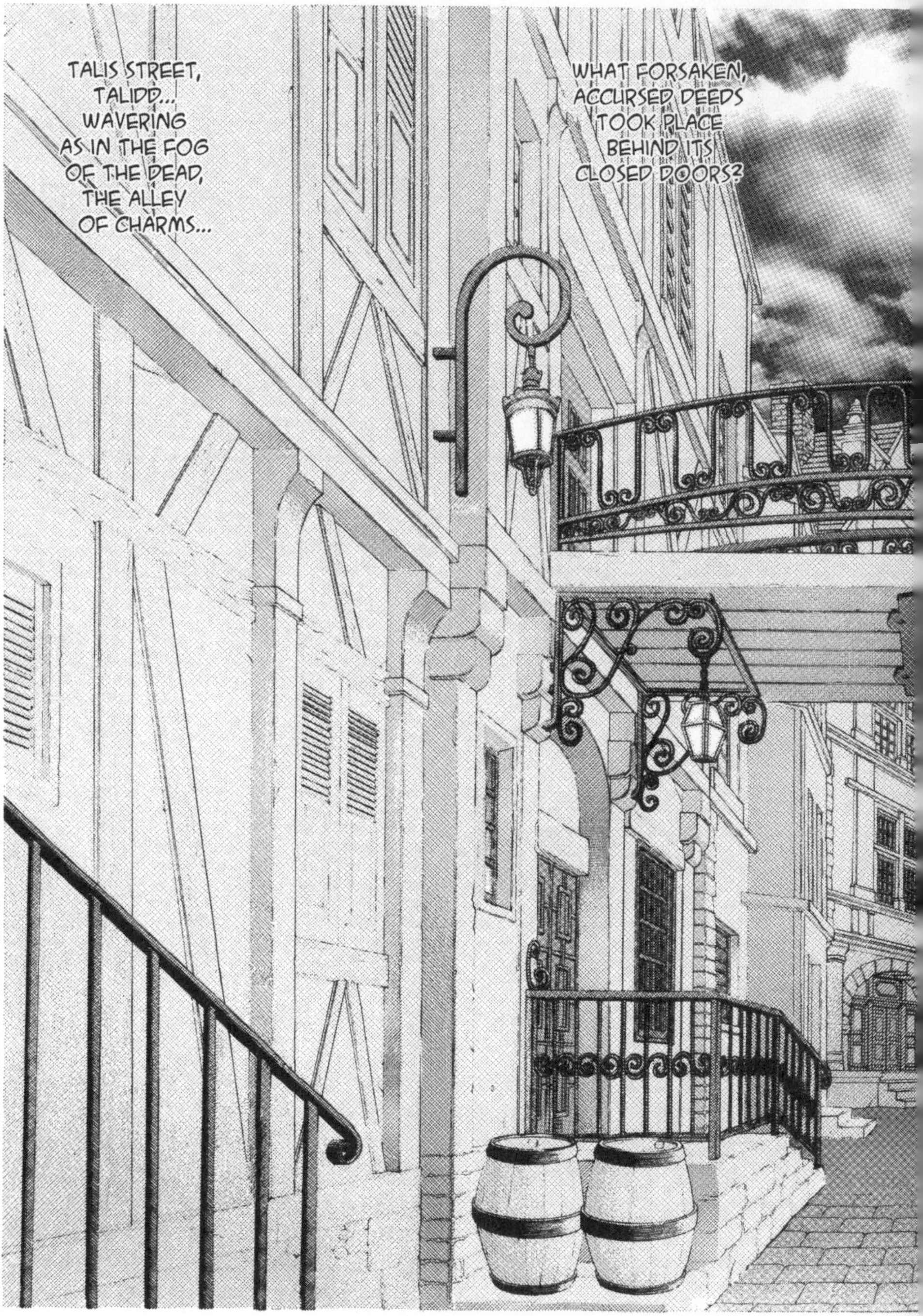
WHAT FORSAKEN, ACCURSED DEEDS TOOK PLACE BEHIND ITS CLOSED DOORS?
TALIS STREET, TALIDD... WAVERING AS IN THE FOG OF THE DEAD, THE ALLEY OF CHARMS...

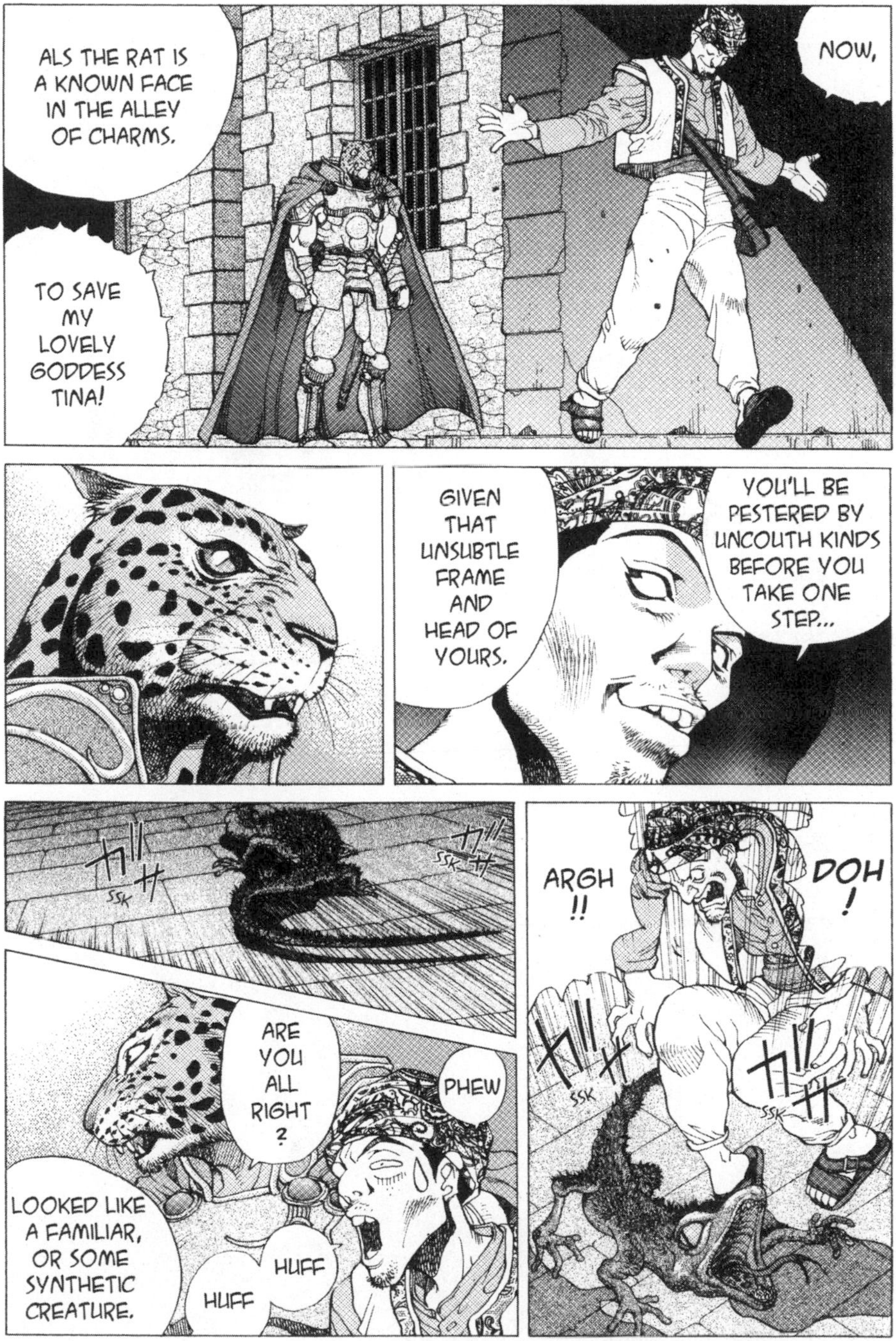
NOW,
ALS THE RAT IS A KNOWN FACE IN THE ALLEY OF CHARMS.
TO SAVE MY LOVELY GODDESS TINA!
YOU'LL BE PESTERED BY UNCOUTH KINDS BEFORE YOU TAKE ONE STEP...
GIVEN THAT UNSUBTLE FRAME AND HEAD OF YOURS.
DOH!
ARGH!!
SSK
SSK
SSK
SSK
PHEW
ARE YOU ALL RIGHT?
HUFF
HUFF
LOOKED LIKE A FAMILIAR, OR SOME SYNTHETIC CREATURE.

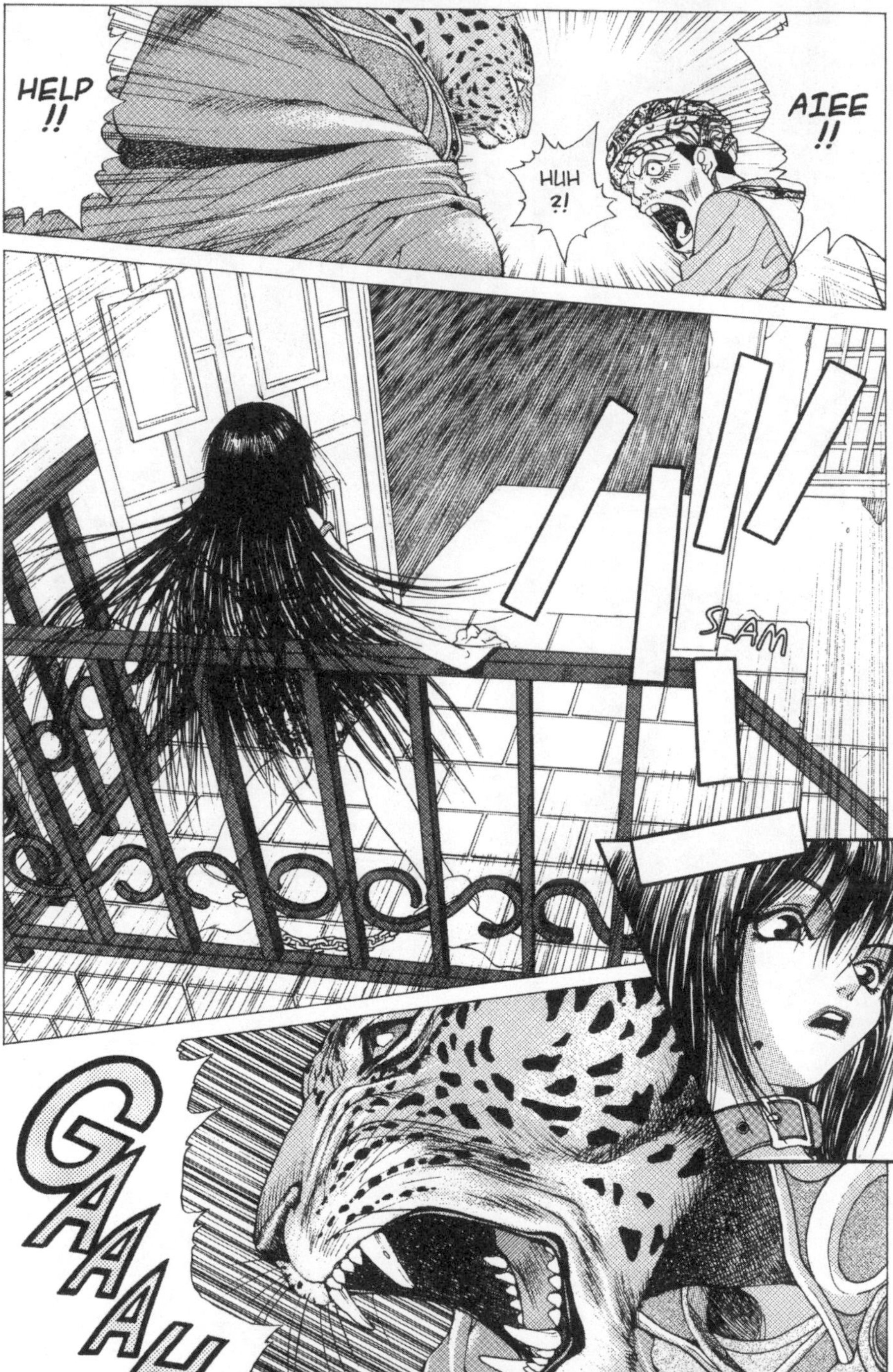
AIEE !!
HUH ?!
HELP !!
SLAM
GAAAAH

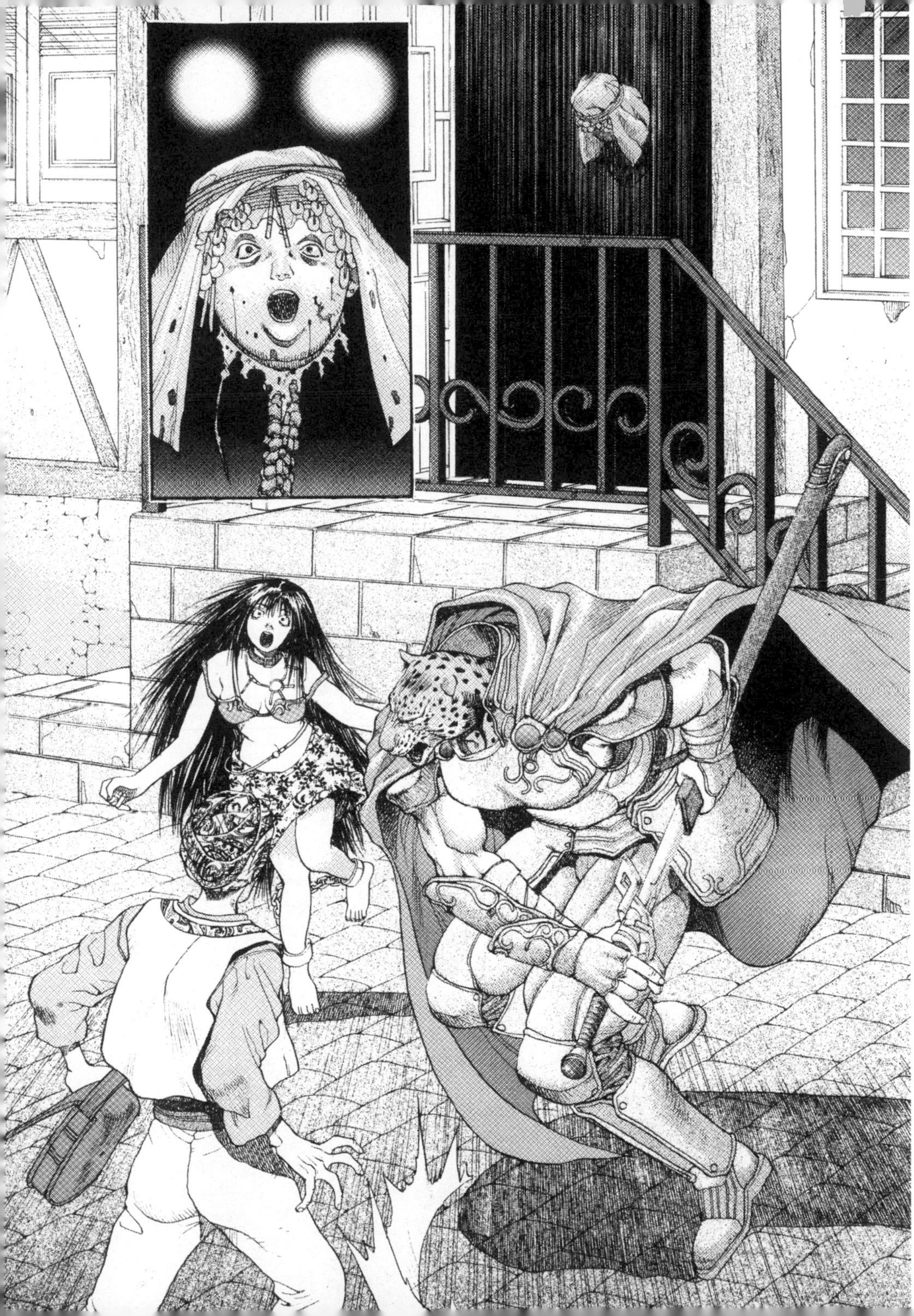

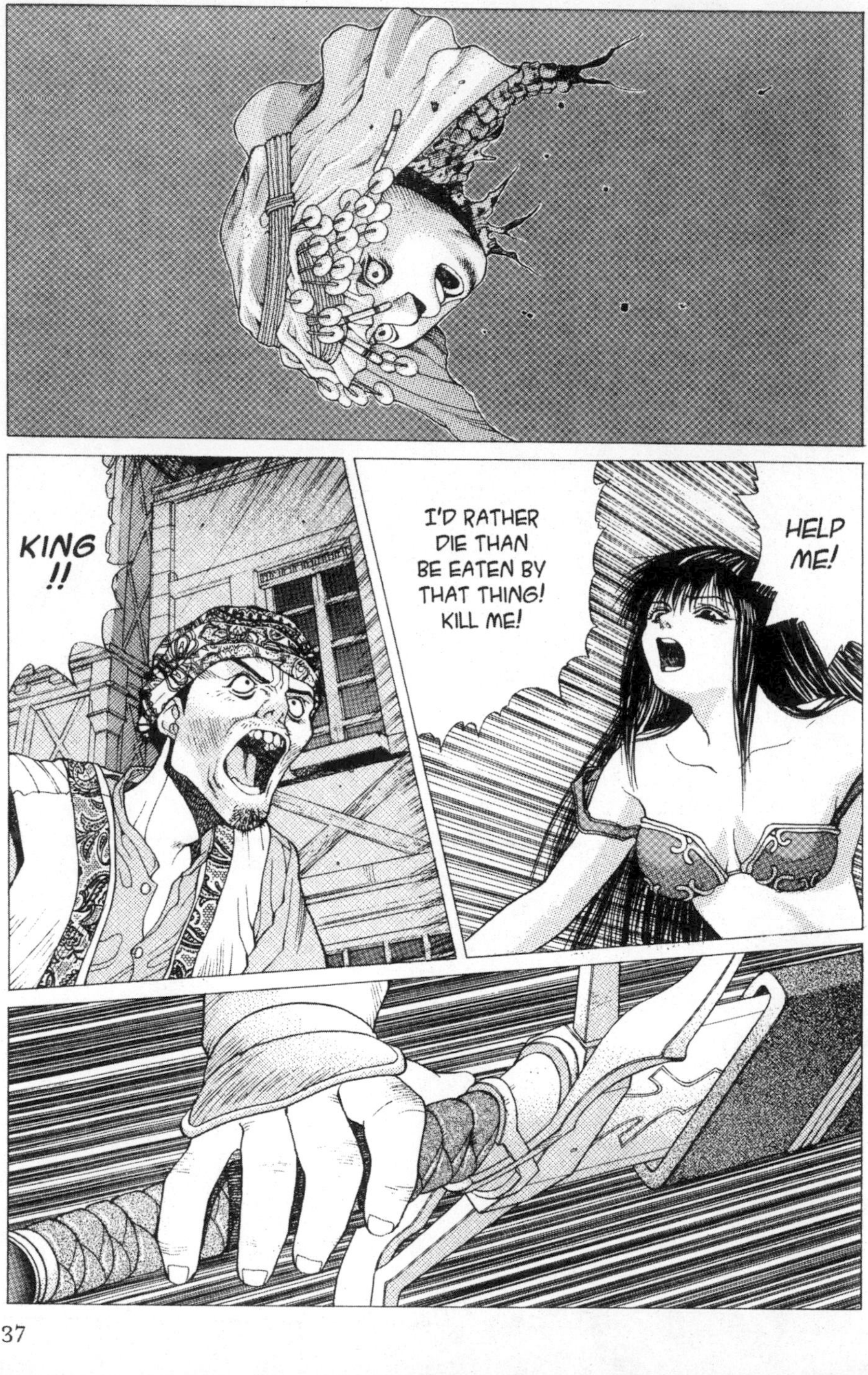
HELP ME!
I'D RATHER DIE THAN BE EATEN BY THAT THING! KILL ME!
KING !!

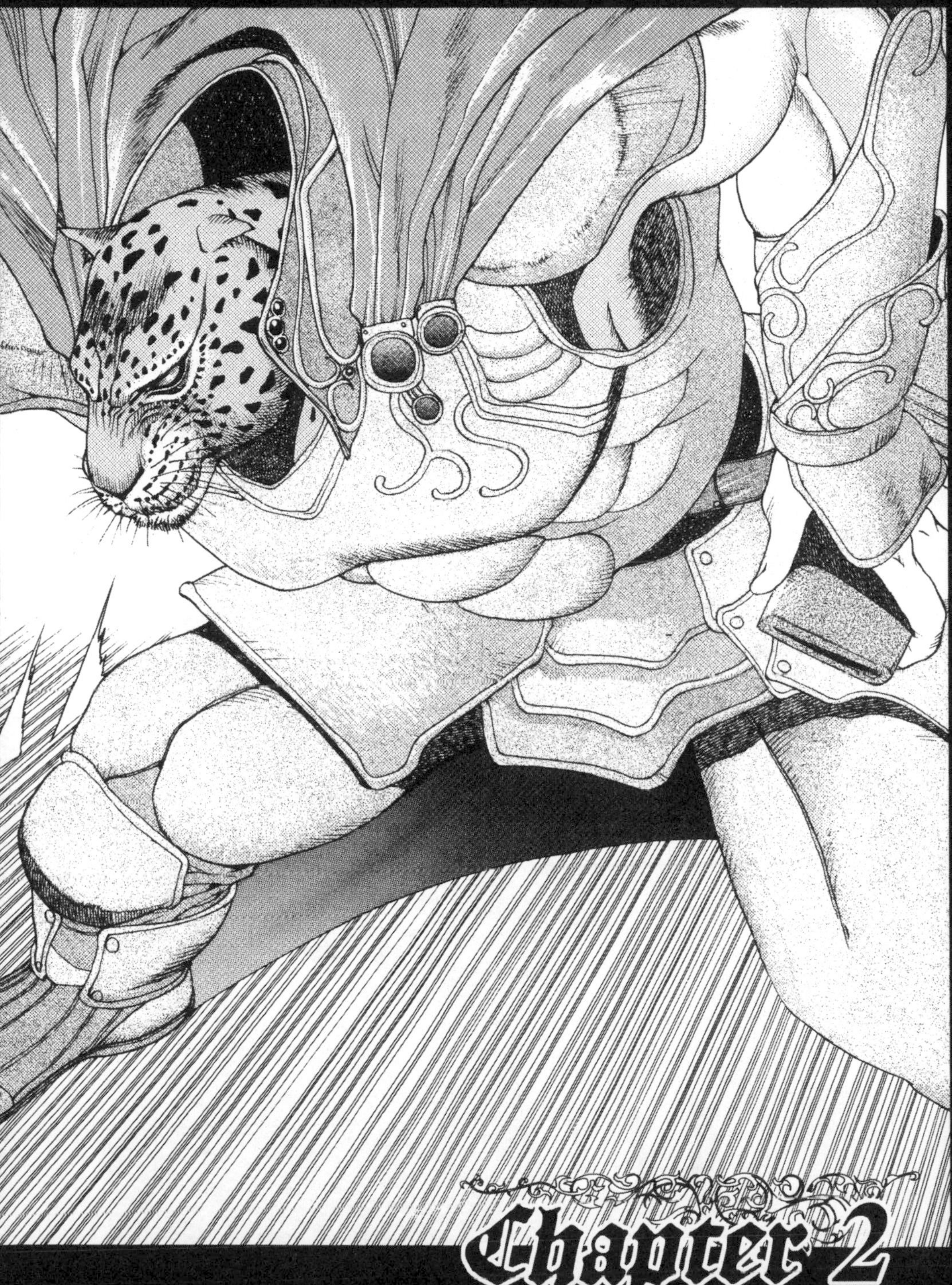
Chapter 2

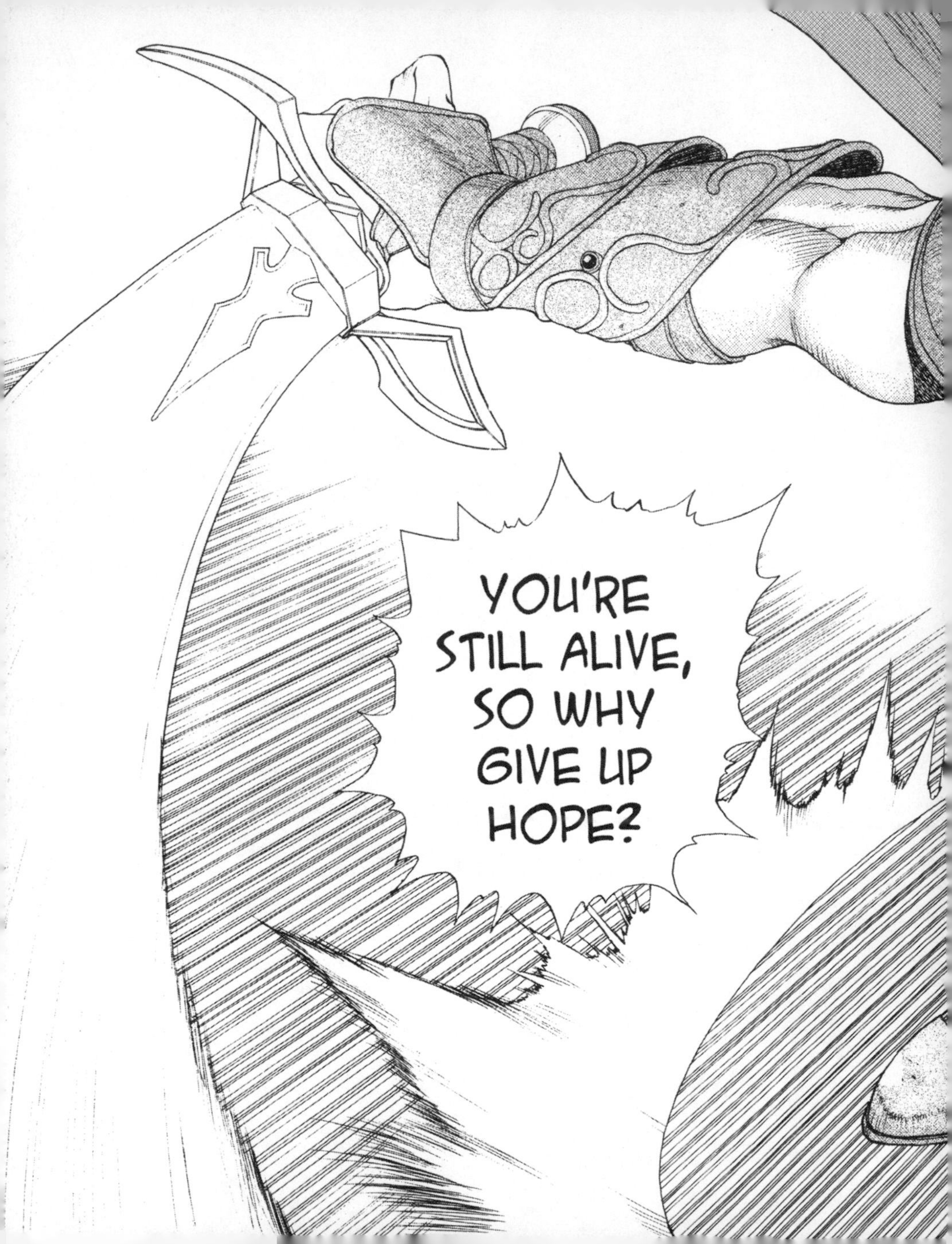
YOU'RE STILL ALIVE, SO WHY GIVE UP HOPE?

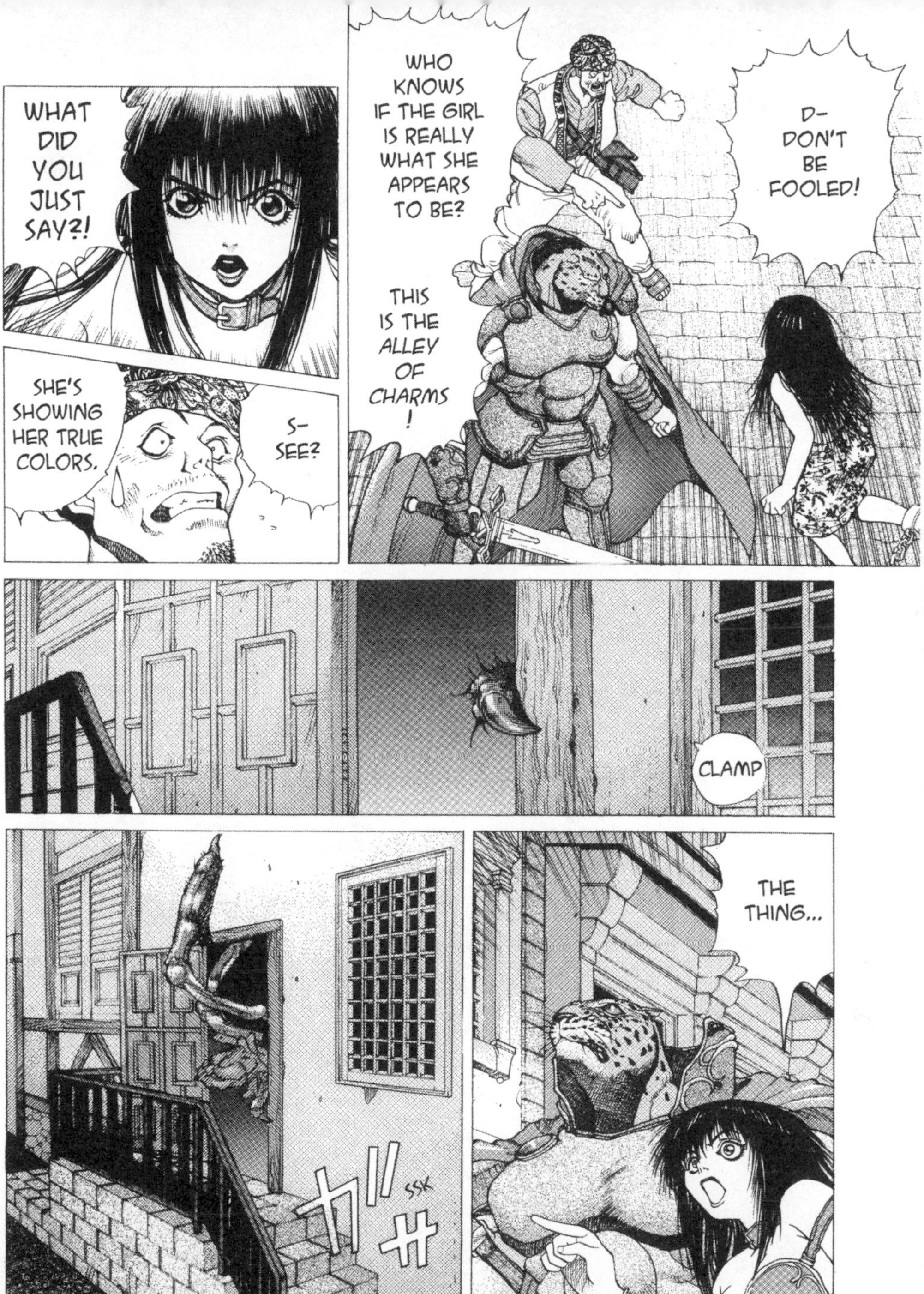
D-DON'T BE FOOLED!
WHO KNOWS IF THE GIRL IS REALLY WHAT SHE APPEARS TO BE?
THIS IS THE ALLEY OF CHARMS!
WHAT DID YOU JUST SAY?!
S-SEE?
SHE'S SHOWING HER TRUE COLORS.
CLAMP
THE THING...
SSK

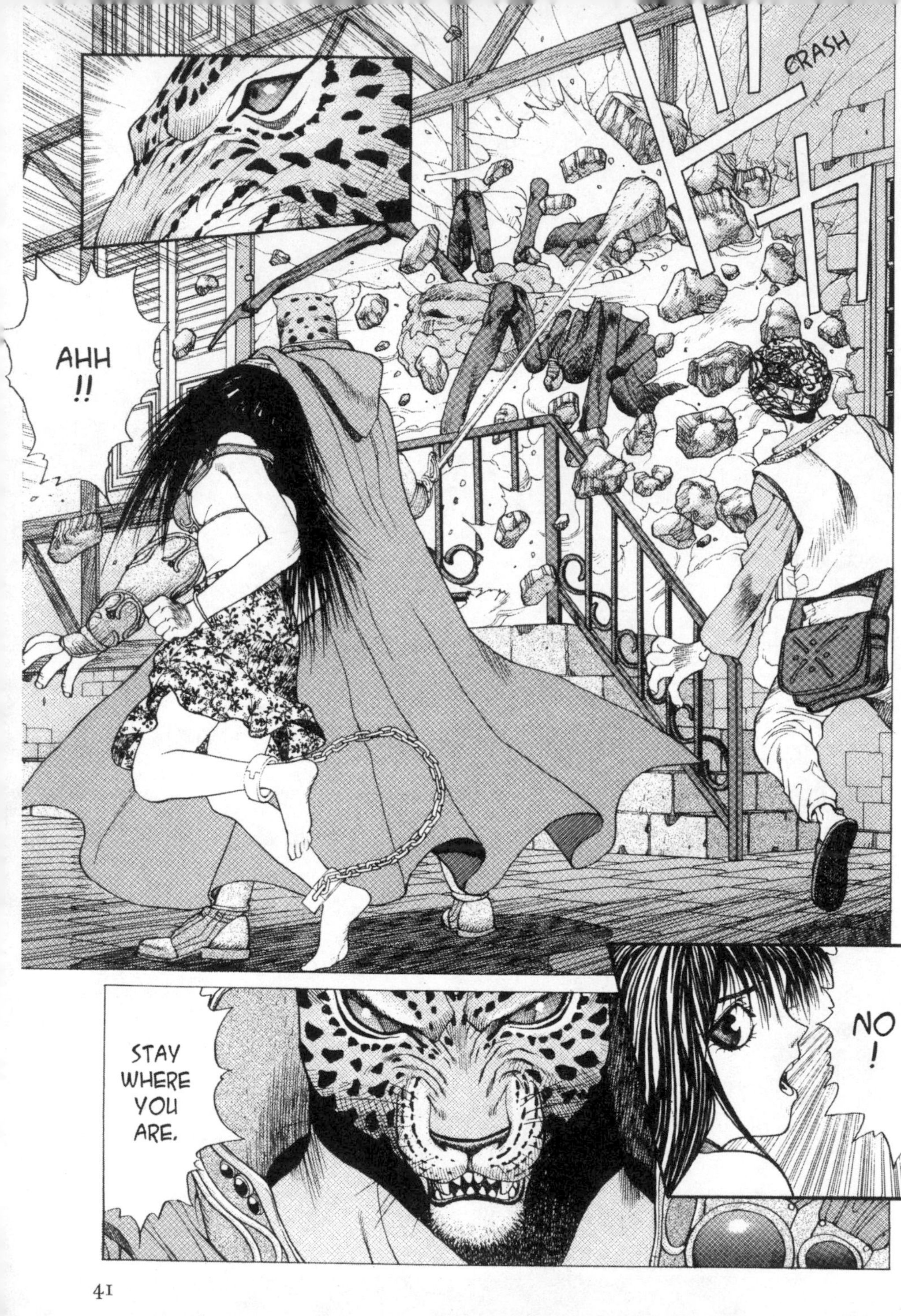
CRASH
AHH !!
NO !
STAY WHERE YOU ARE.

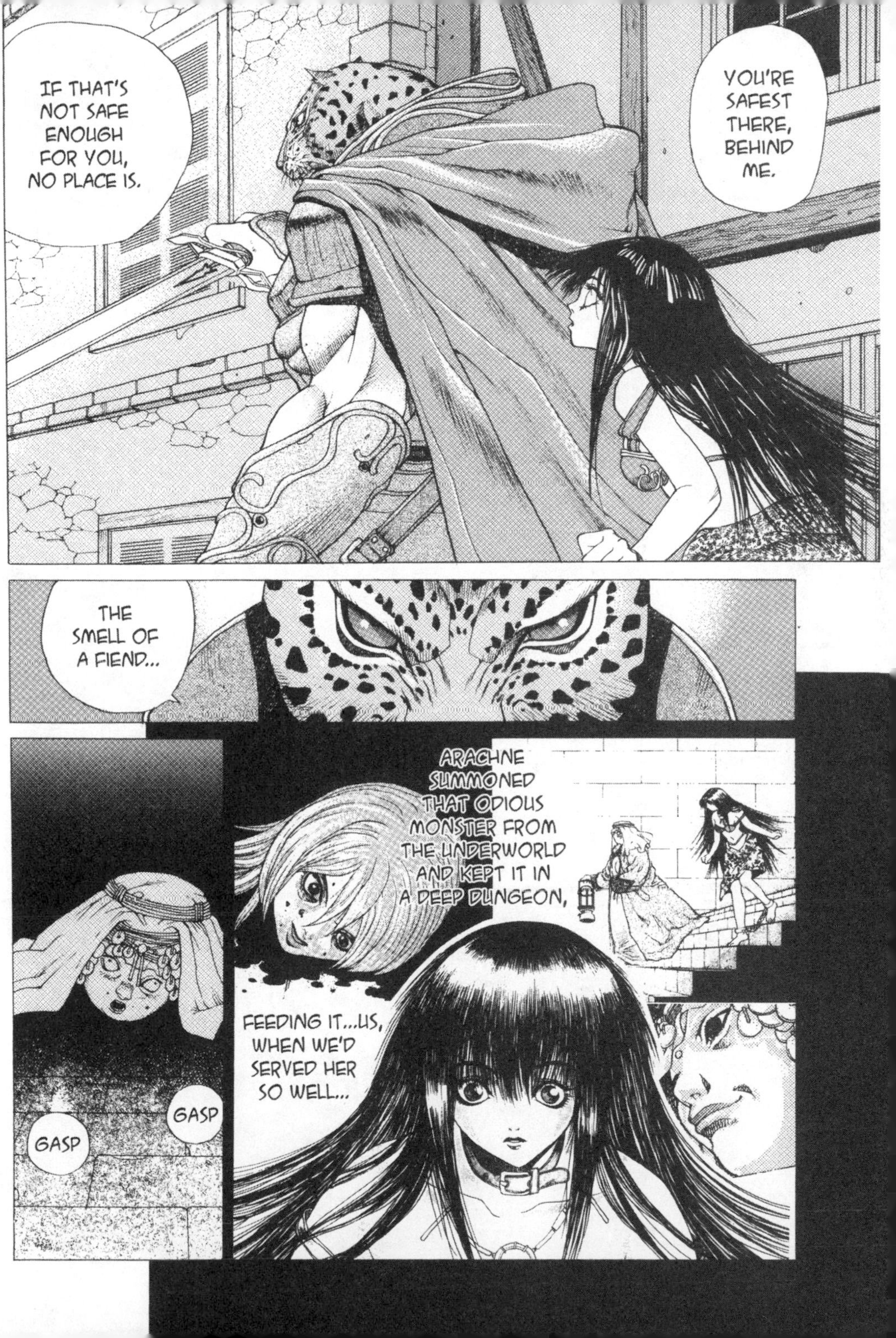
YOU'RE SAFEST THERE, BEHIND ME.
IF THAT'S NOT SAFE ENOUGH FOR YOU, NO PLACE IS.
THE SMELL OF A FIEND...
ARACHNE SUMMONED THAT ODIOUS MONSTER FROM THE UNDERWORLD AND KEPT IT IN A DEEP DUNGEON,
FEEDING IT...US, WHEN WE'D SERVED HER SO WELL...
GASP
GASP

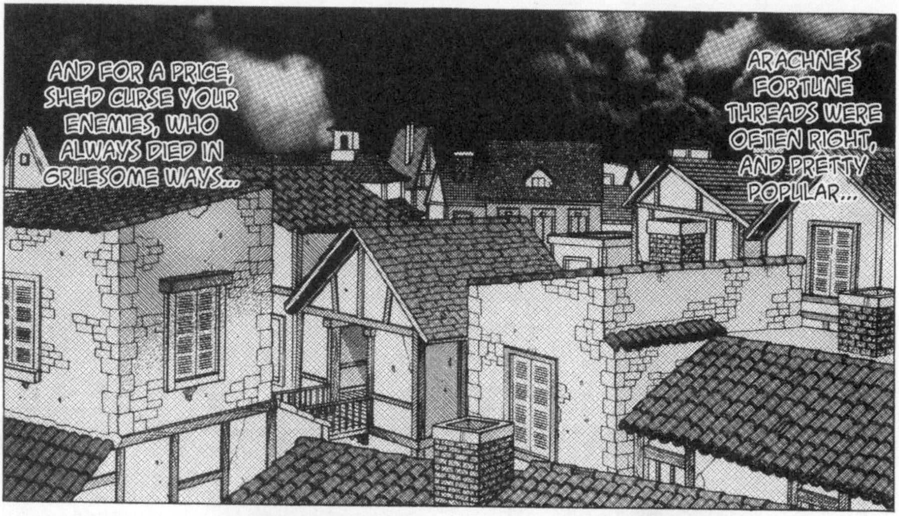
ARACHNE'S FORTUNE THREADS WERE OFTEN RIGHT, AND PRETTY POPULAR...
AND FOR A PRICE, SHE'D CURSE YOUR ENEMIES, WHO ALWAYS DIED IN GRUESOME WAYS...
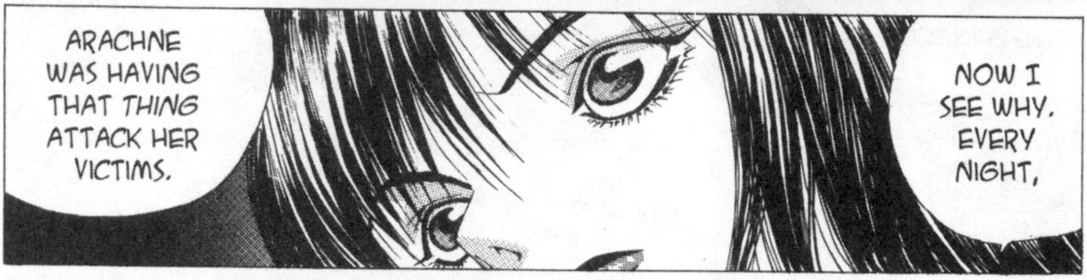
NOW I SEE WHY. EVERY NIGHT,
ARACHNE WAS HAVING THAT *THING* ATTACK HER VICTIMS.
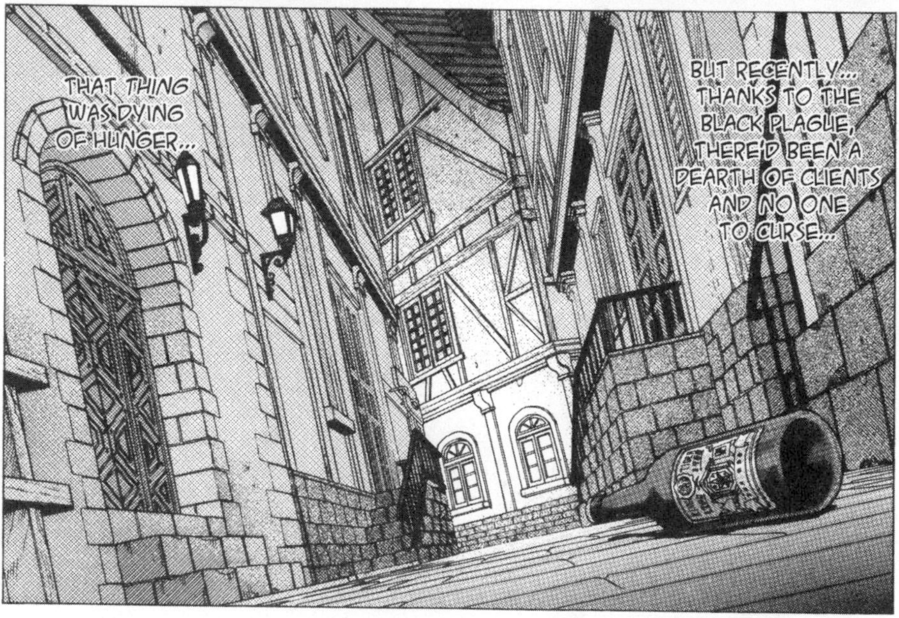
BUT RECENTLY... THANKS TO THE BLACK PLAGUE, THERE'D BEEN A DEARTH OF CLIENTS AND NO ONE TO CURSE...
THAT THING WAS DYING OF HUNGER...

AND SO...
SHE DECIDED TO FEED IT DUELLA AND ME—WHEN WE'D DONE SO MUCH FOR HER.
AH, BUT THIS THING CHOSE TO
FEED ON ARACHNE AS WELL.
HA HA HA... I CAN SEE...
THE BLACK PLAGUE... IS ONLY... A HARBINGER...
GASP
GASP
ARACHNE
CHEIRONIA DESCENDS THE ROAD OF RUIN...
SPLAT

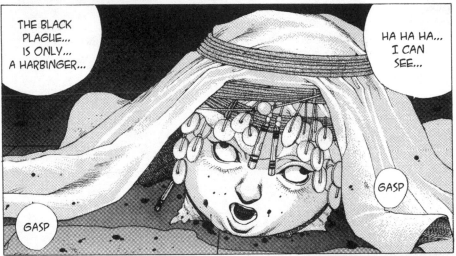

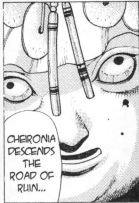

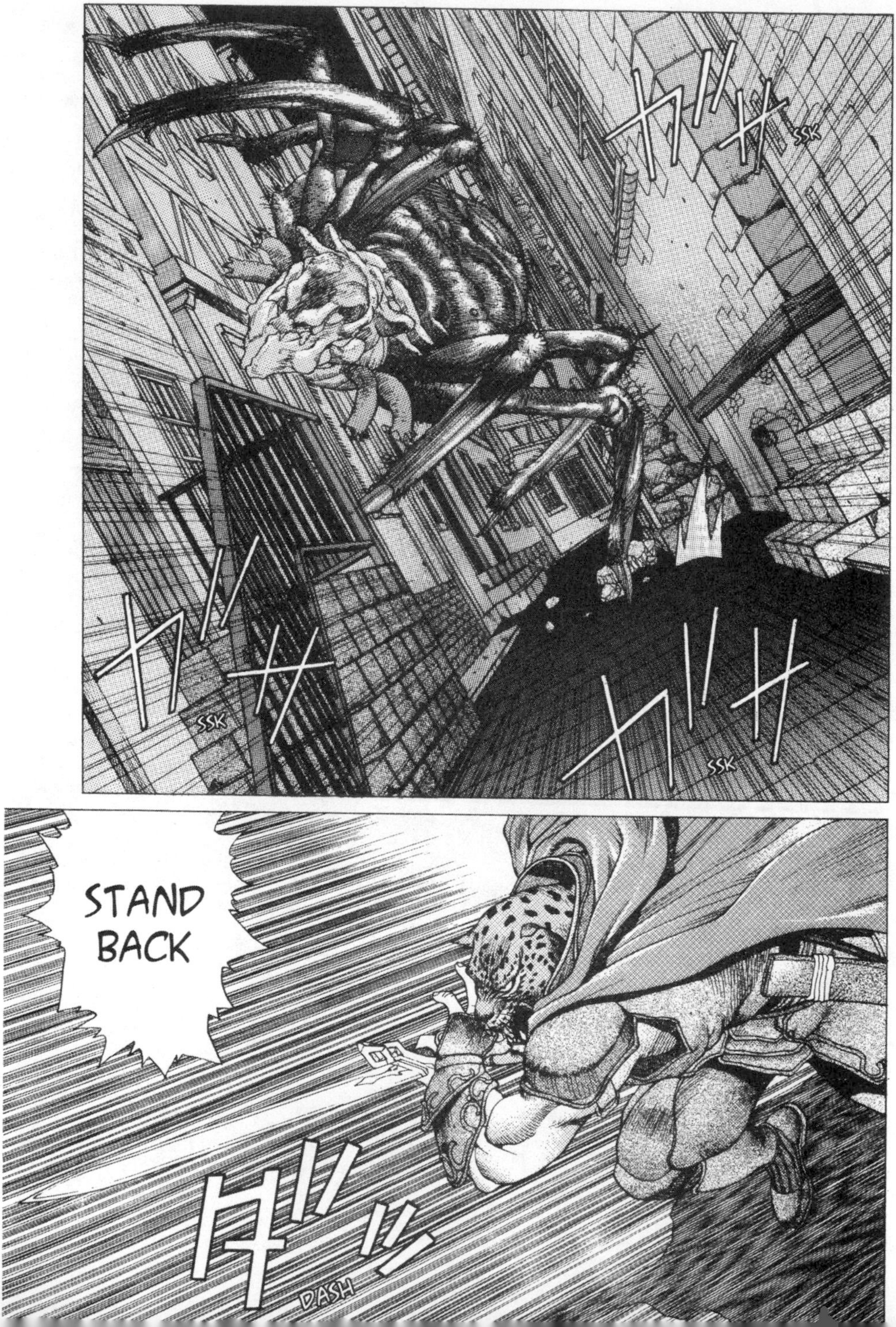
SSK
SSK
SSK
STAND BACK
DASH

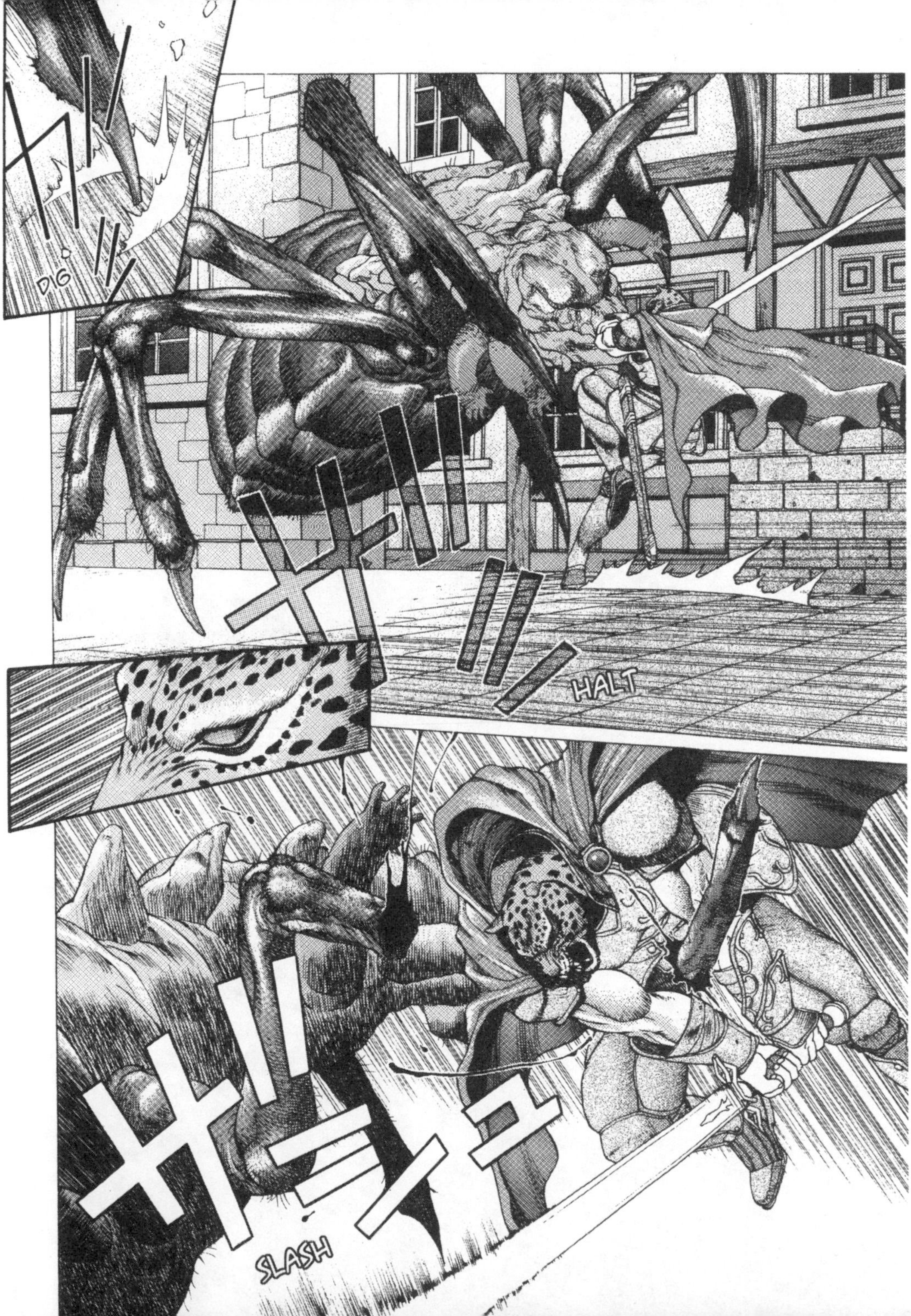
HALT
DIG
SLASH

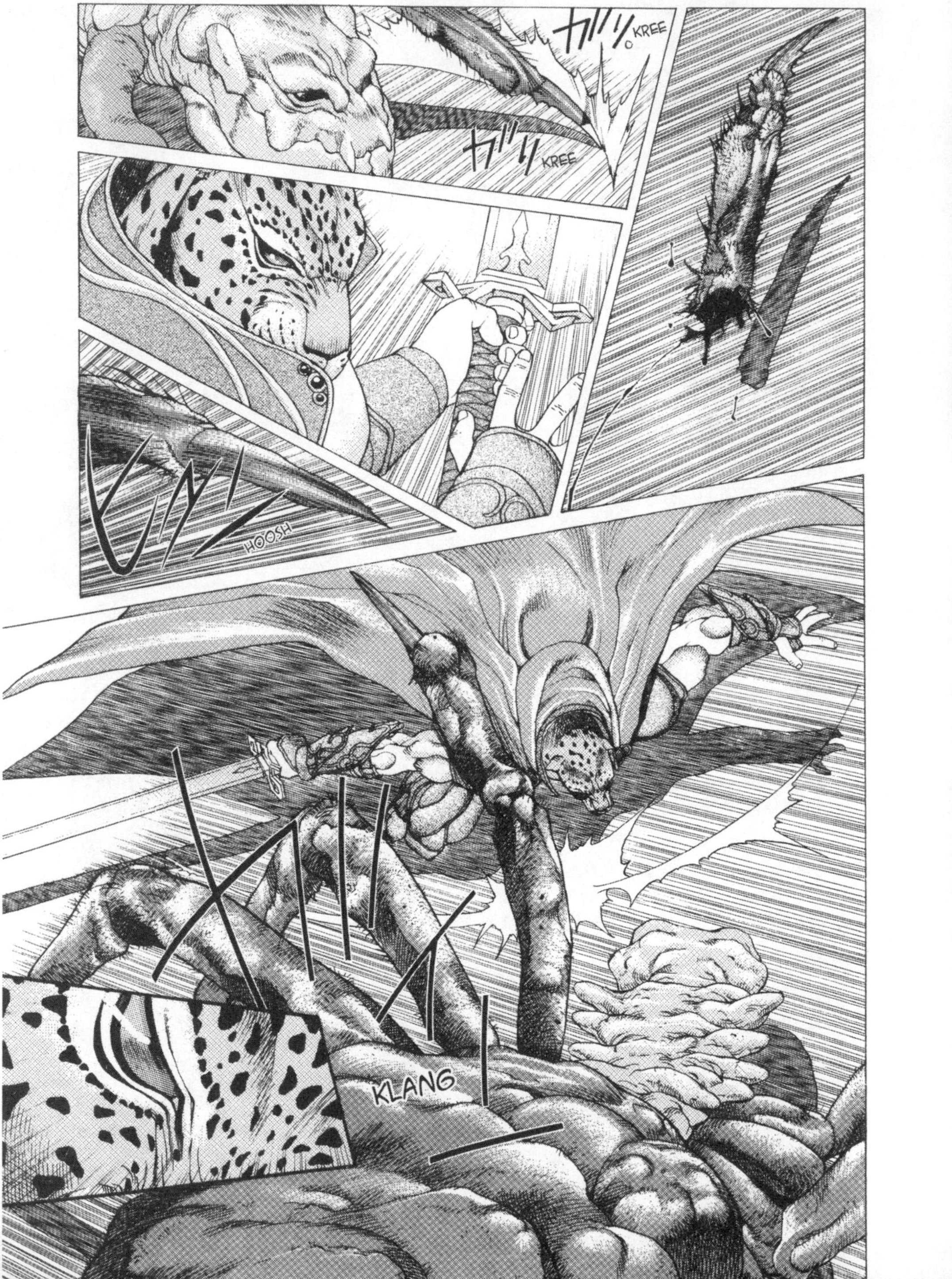

ガリッ。KREE
ガリリ KREE
HOOSH
KLANG

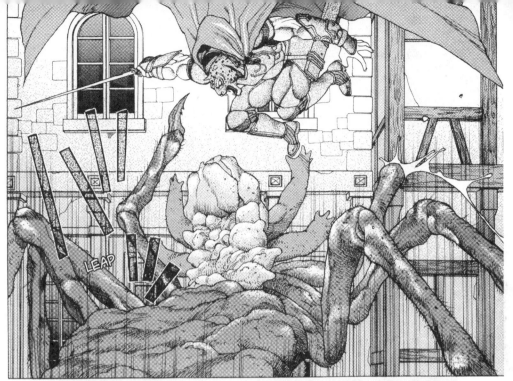

LEAP

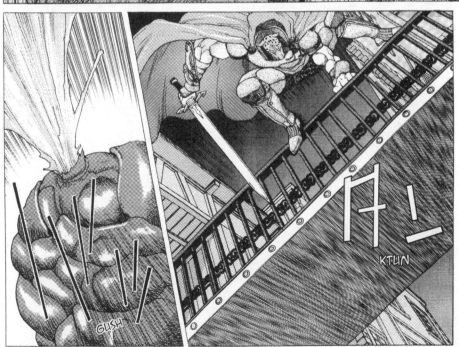

GUSH

KTUN

48

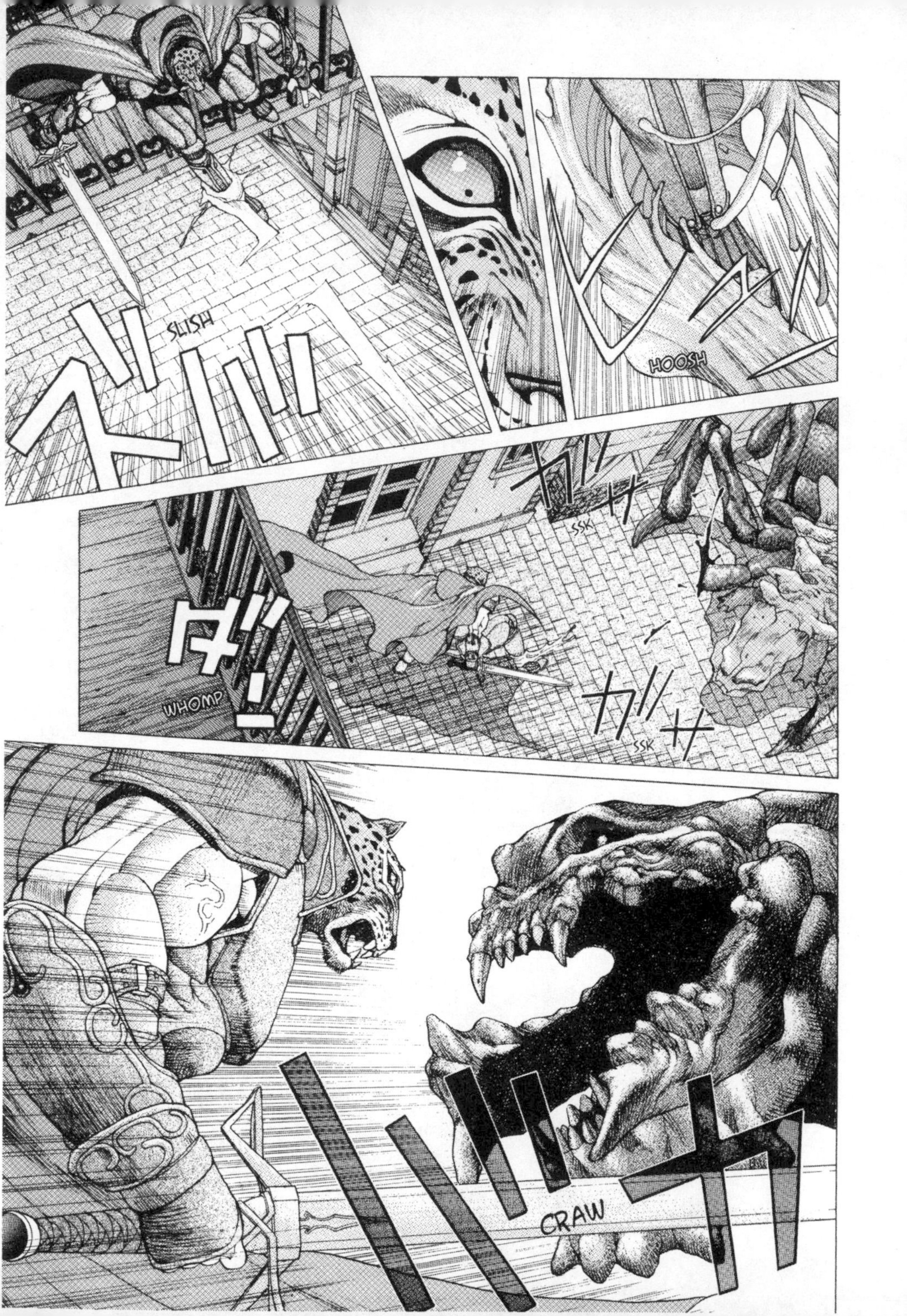
HOOSH
SLISH
SSK
SSK
WHOMP
CRAW

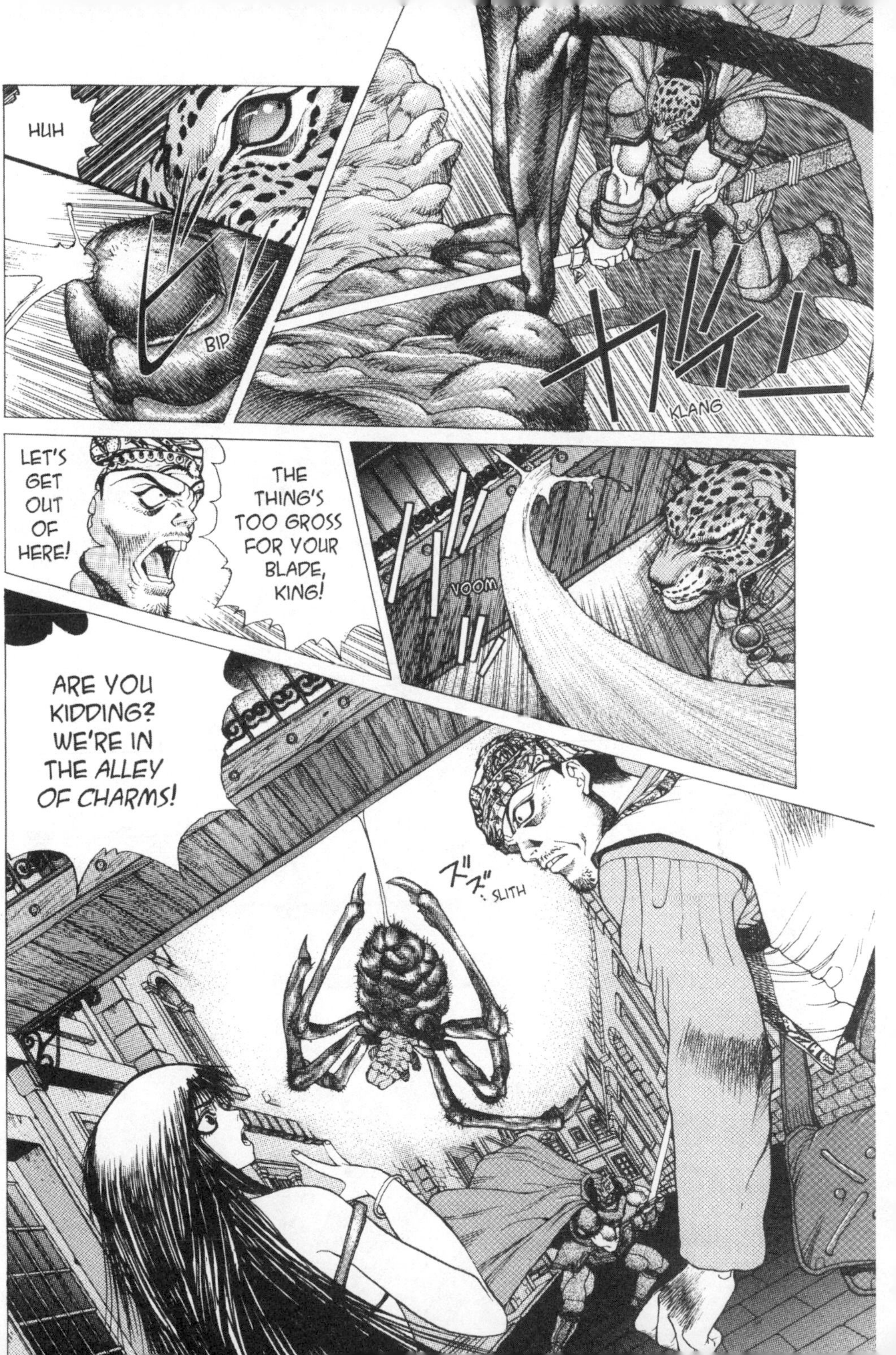
KLANG
HUH
BIP
VOOM
THE THING'S TOO GROSS FOR YOUR BLADE, KING!
LET'S GET OUT OF HERE!
ARE YOU KIDDING? WE'RE IN THE ALLEY OF CHARMS!
SLITH

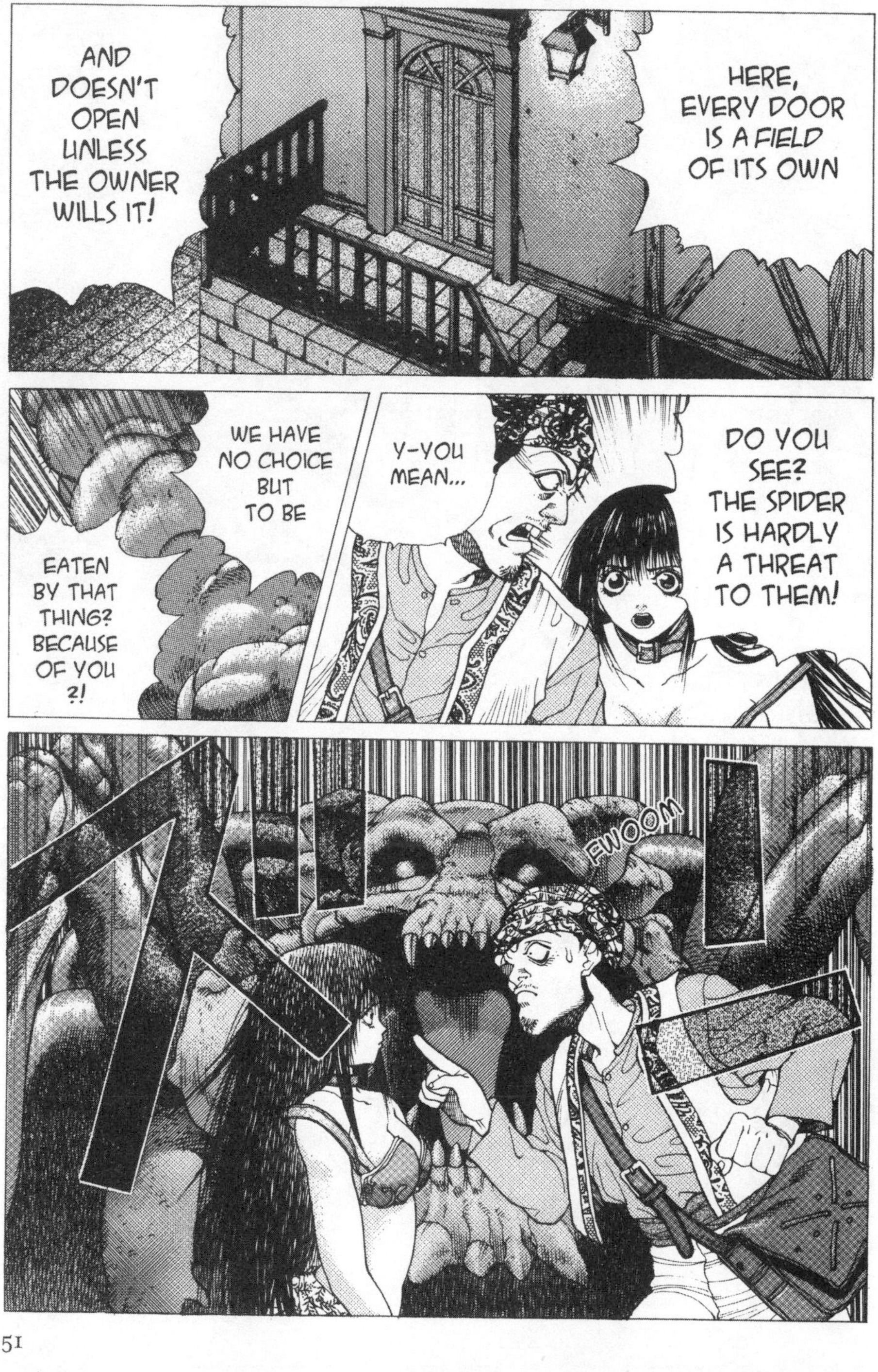
HERE, EVERY DOOR IS A FIELD OF ITS OWN
AND DOESN'T OPEN UNLESS THE OWNER WILLS IT!
DO YOU SEE? THE SPIDER IS HARDLY A THREAT TO THEM!
Y-YOU MEAN...
WE HAVE NO CHOICE BUT TO BE
EATEN BY THAT THING? BECAUSE OF YOU ?!
FWOOM

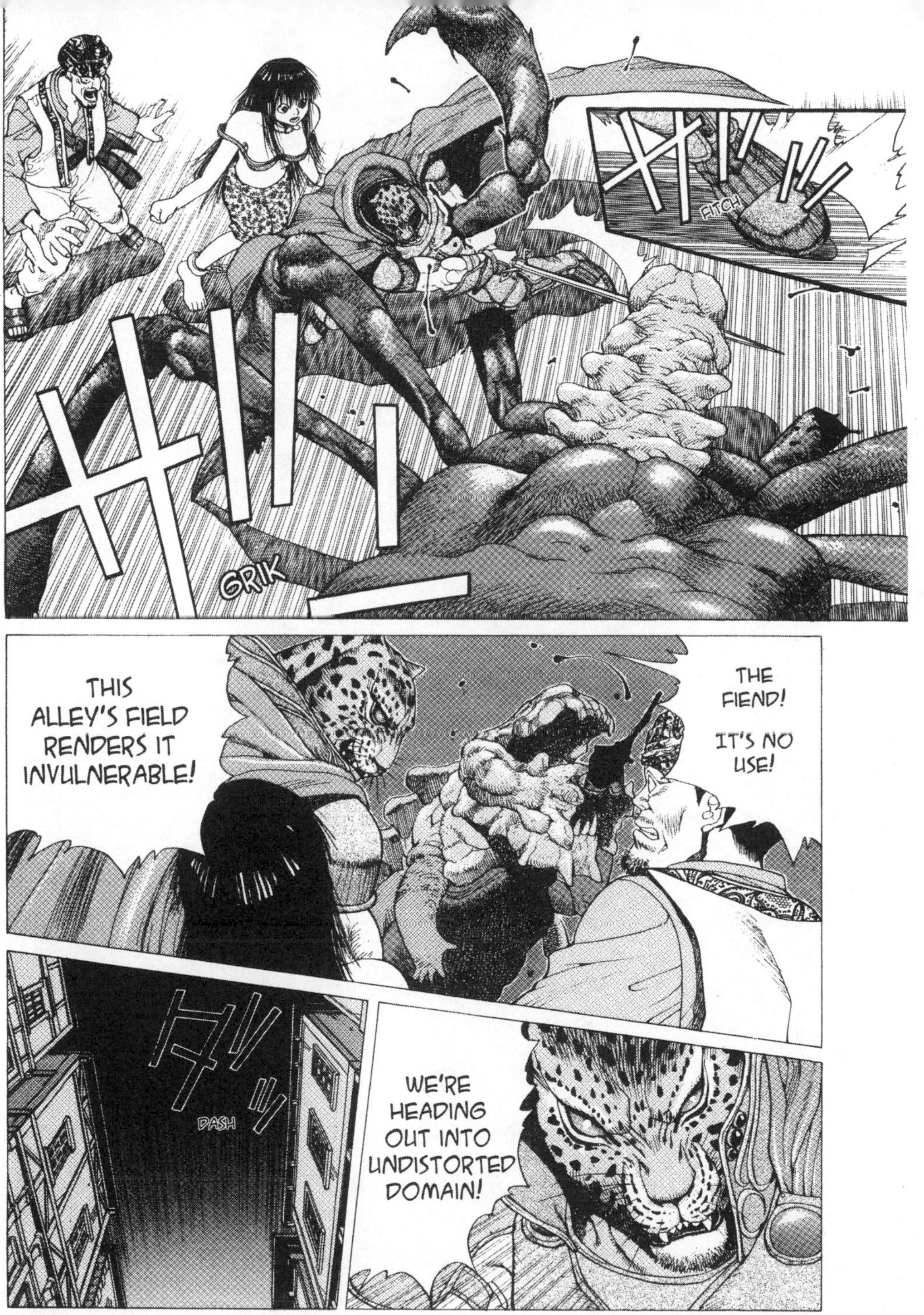
FITCH
GRIK
THE FIEND!
IT'S NO USE!
THIS ALLEY'S FIELD RENDERS IT INVULNERABLE!
WE'RE HEADING OUT INTO UNDISTORTED DOMAIN!
DASH

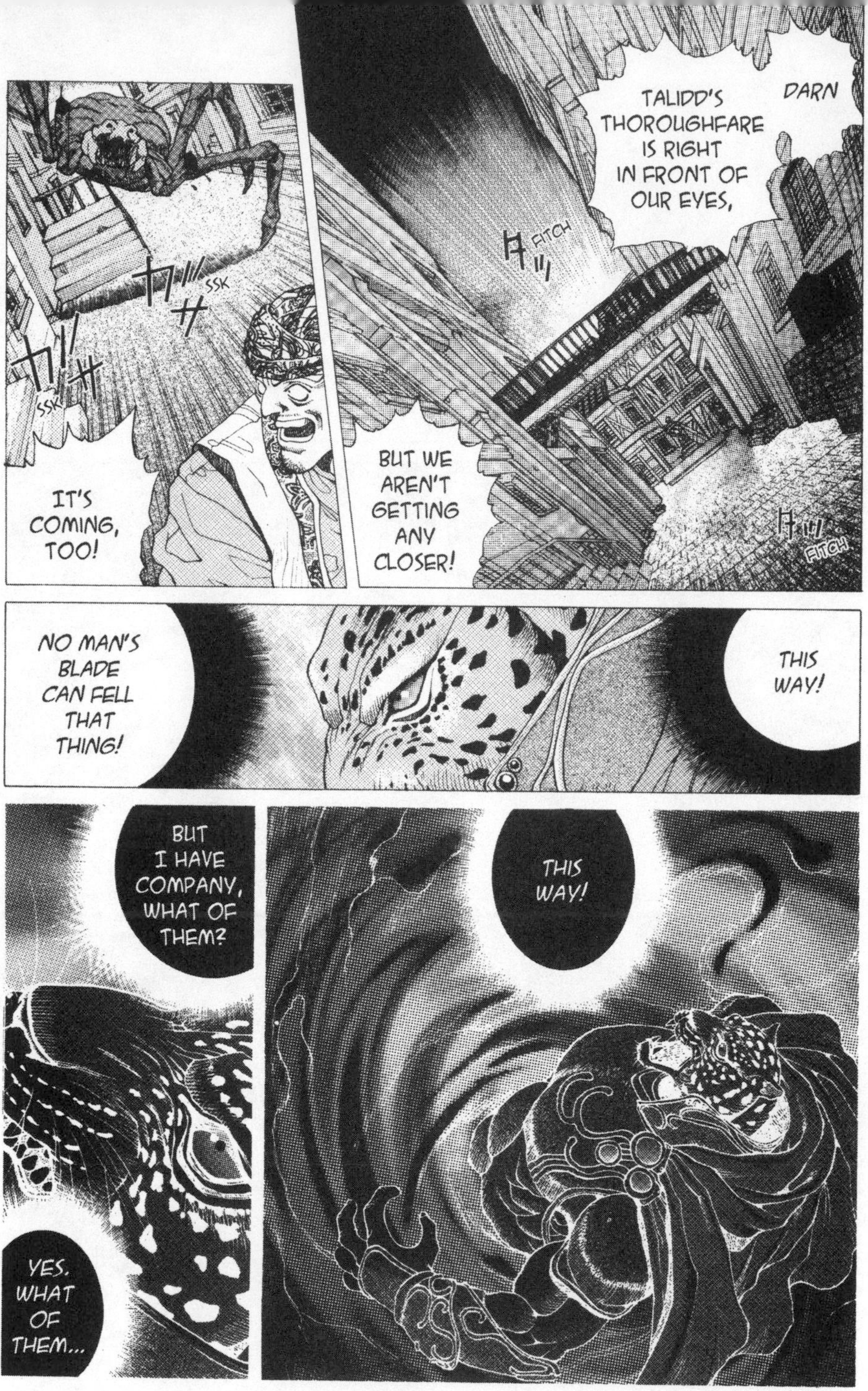
DARN
TALIDD'S THOROUGHFARE IS RIGHT IN FRONT OF OUR EYES,
FITCH
BUT WE AREN'T GETTING ANY CLOSER!
FITCH
SSK
SSK
IT'S COMING, TOO!
THIS WAY!
NO MAN'S BLADE CAN FELL THAT THING!
THIS WAY!
BUT I HAVE COMPANY, WHAT OF THEM?
YES. WHAT OF THEM...

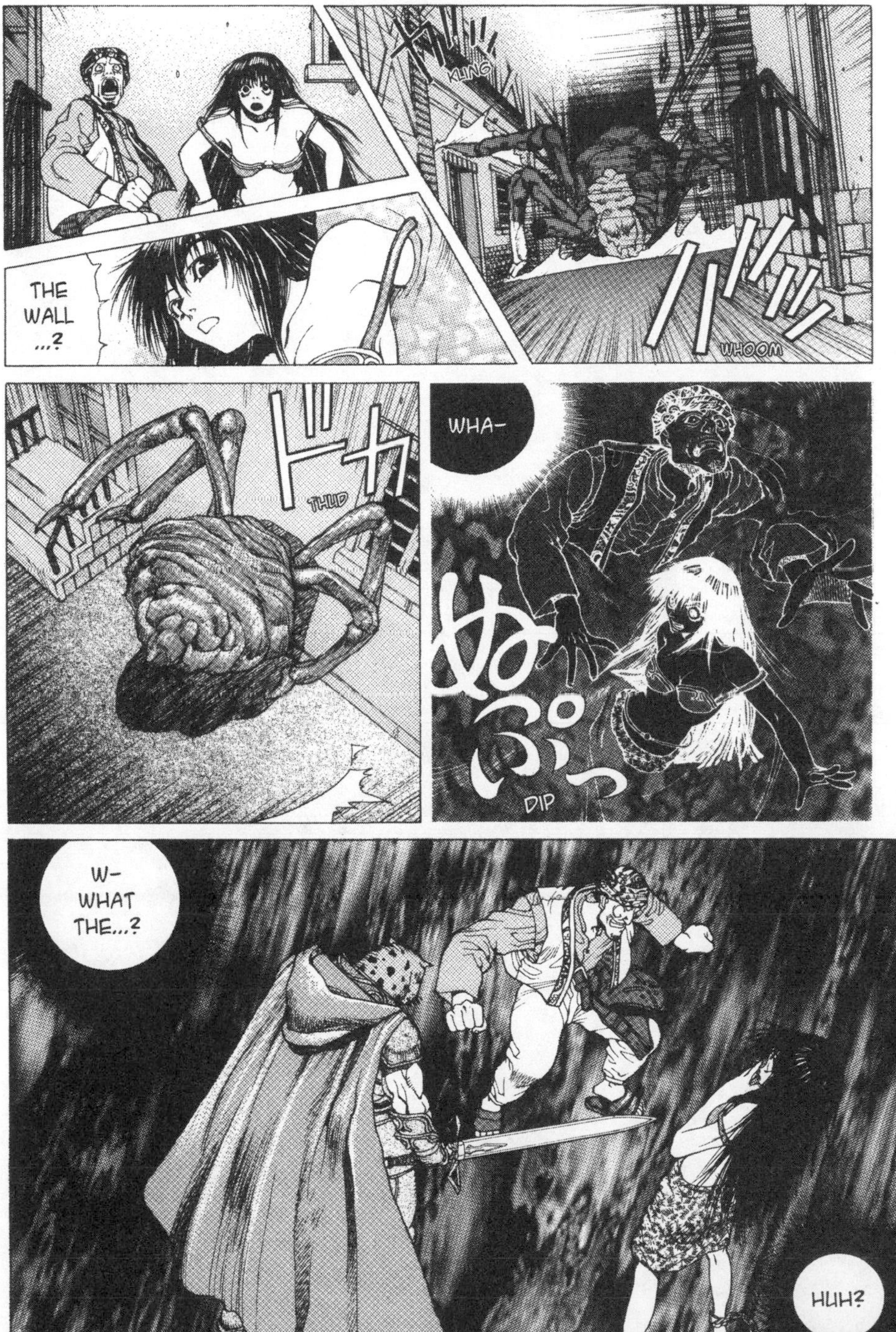
KLING
WHOOM
THE WALL ...?
WHA-
ぬぷっ
DIP
ドカ
THUD
W- WHAT THE...?
HUH?

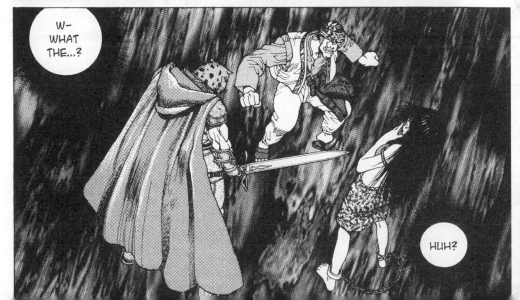

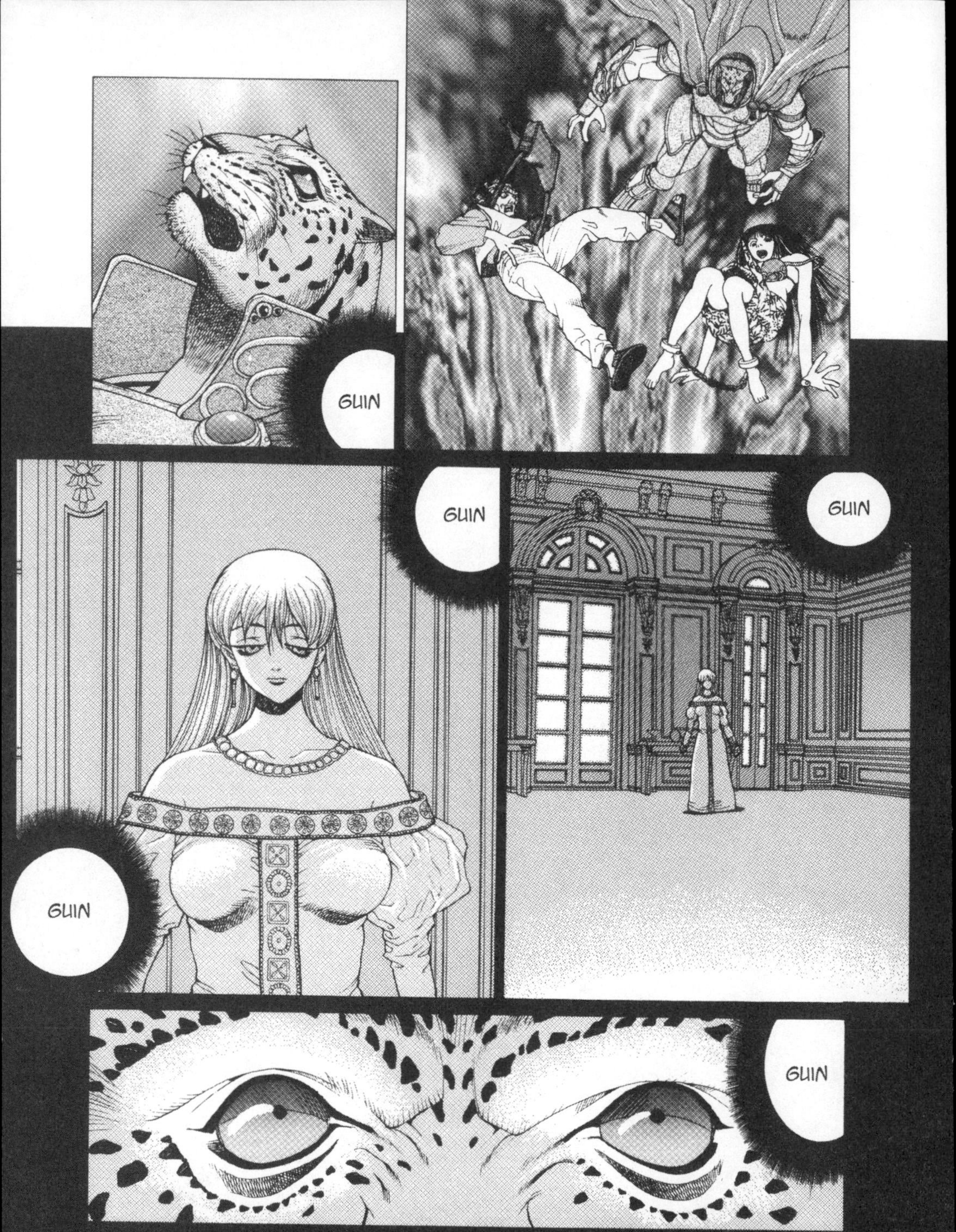
GUIN
GUIN
GUIN
GUIN
GUIN

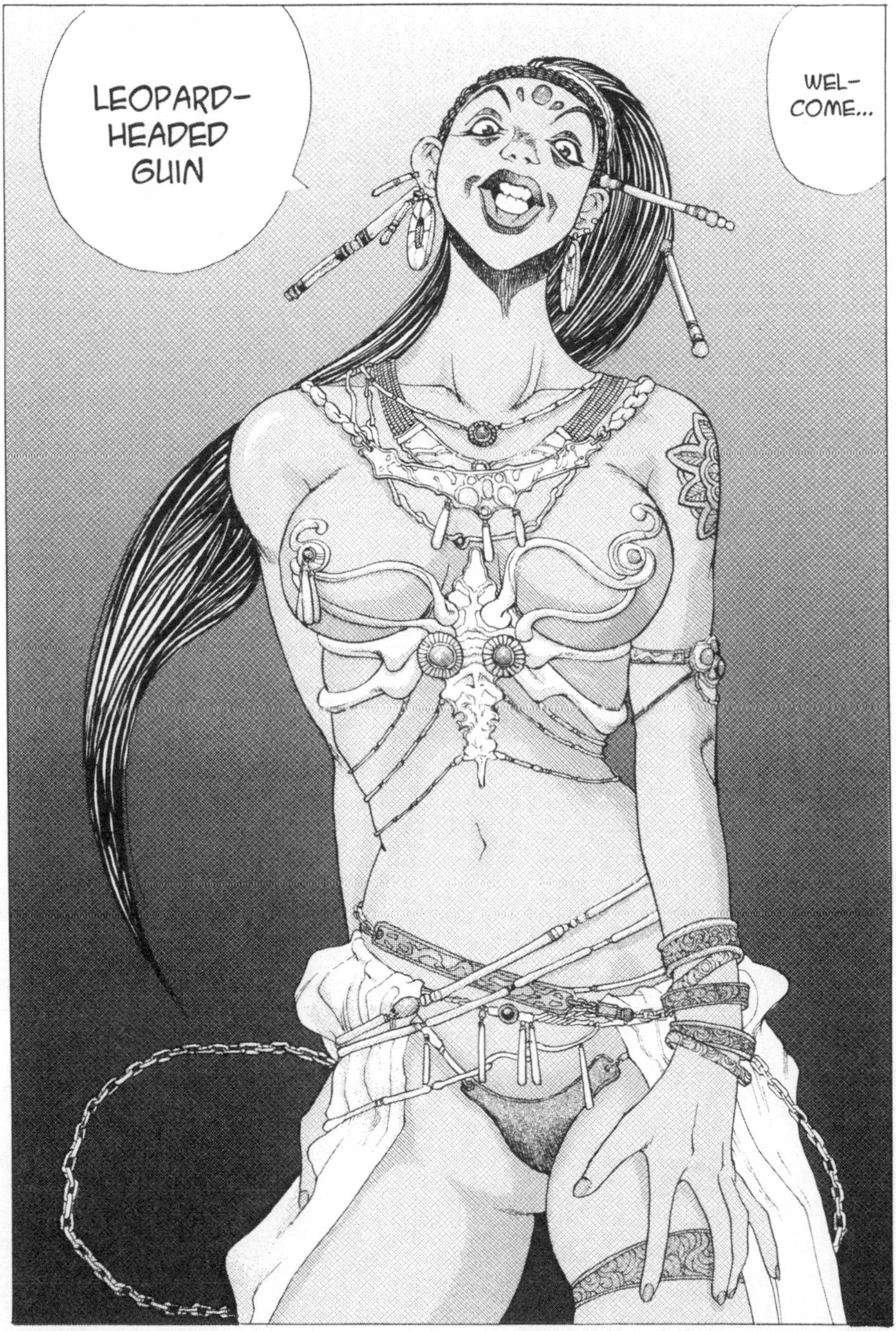
WEL-
COME...
LEOPARD-
HEADED
GUIN

CHAPTER 3

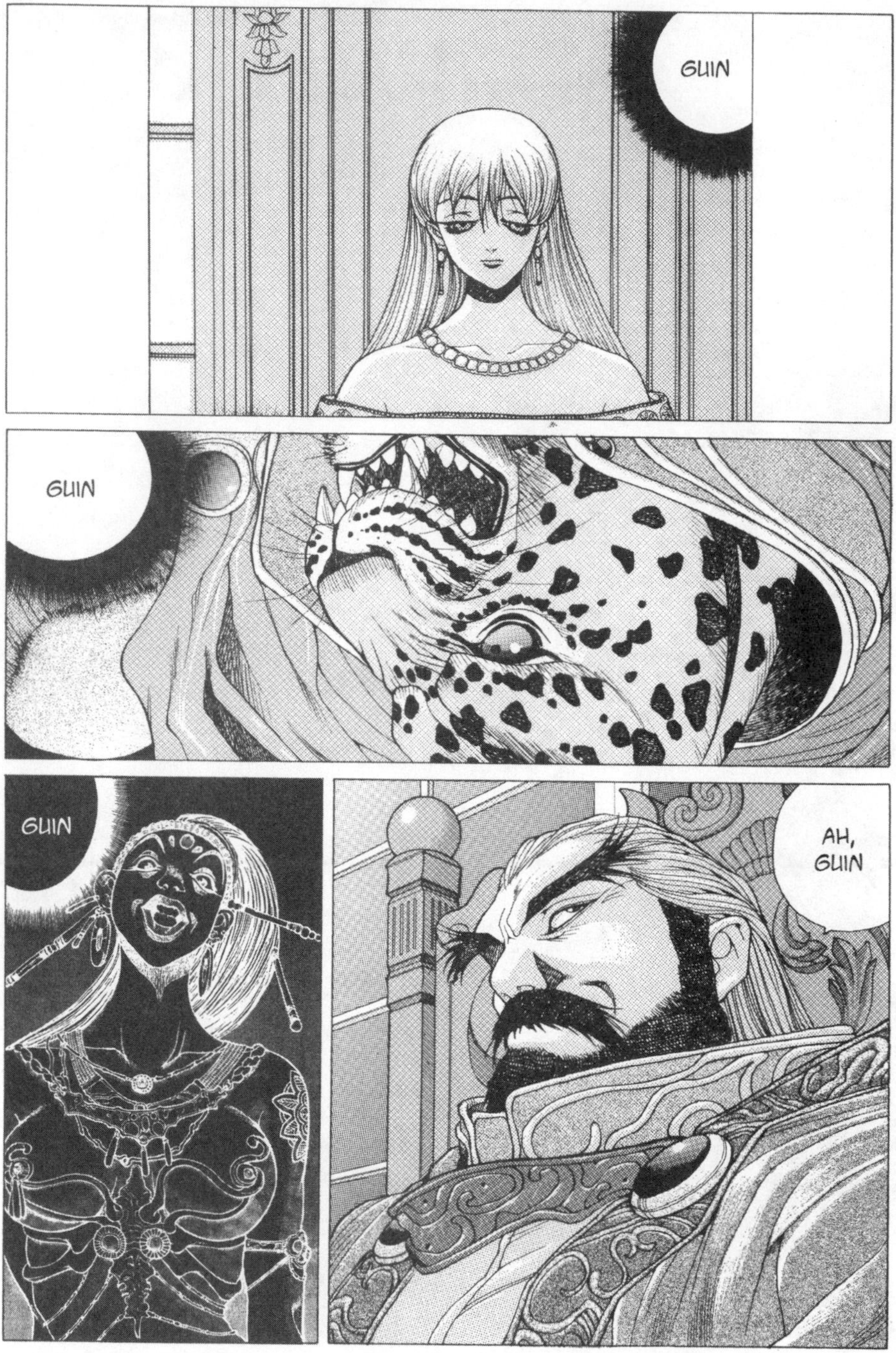
GUIN
GUIN
AH, GUIN
GUIN

Chapter 3

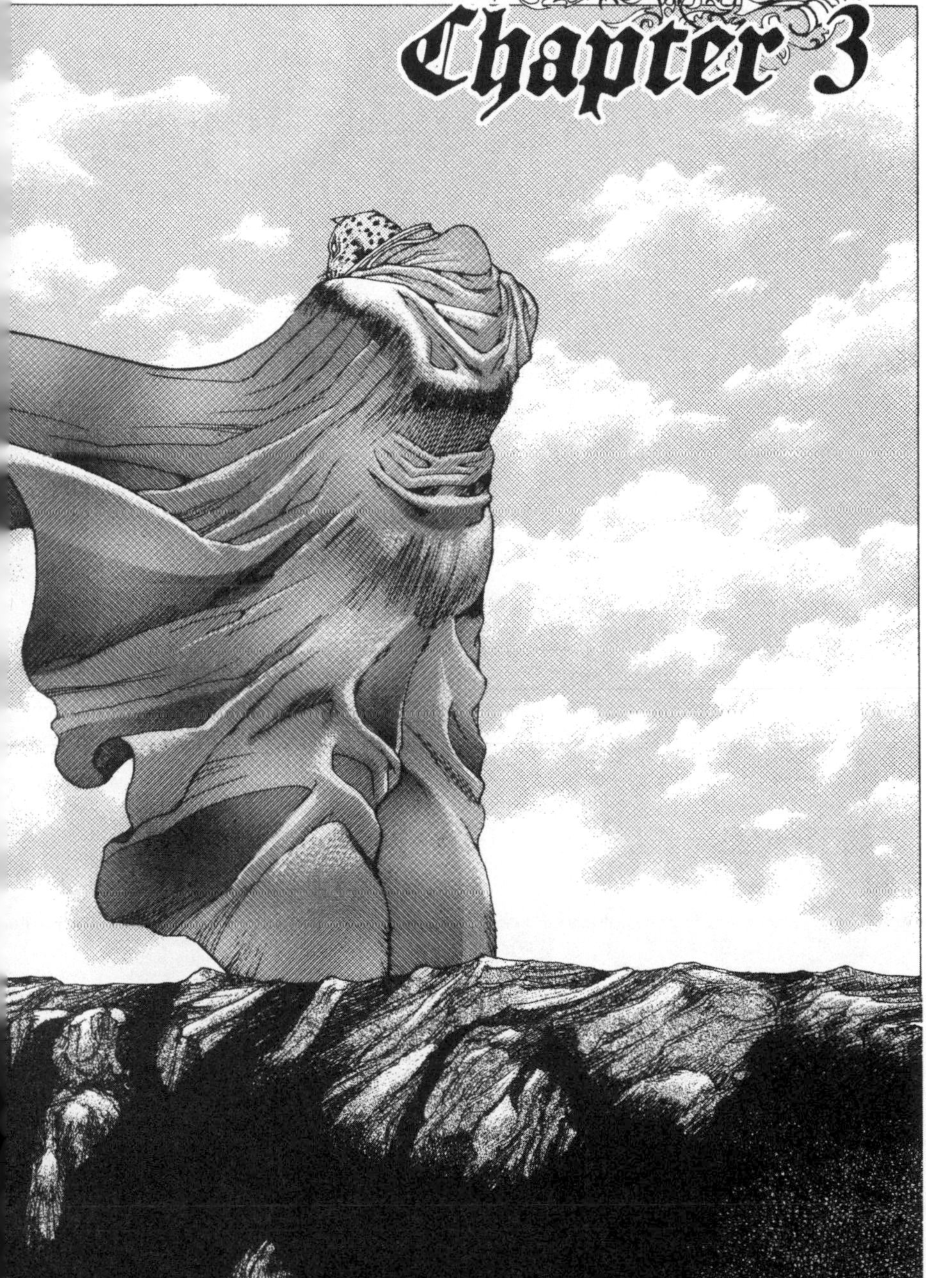

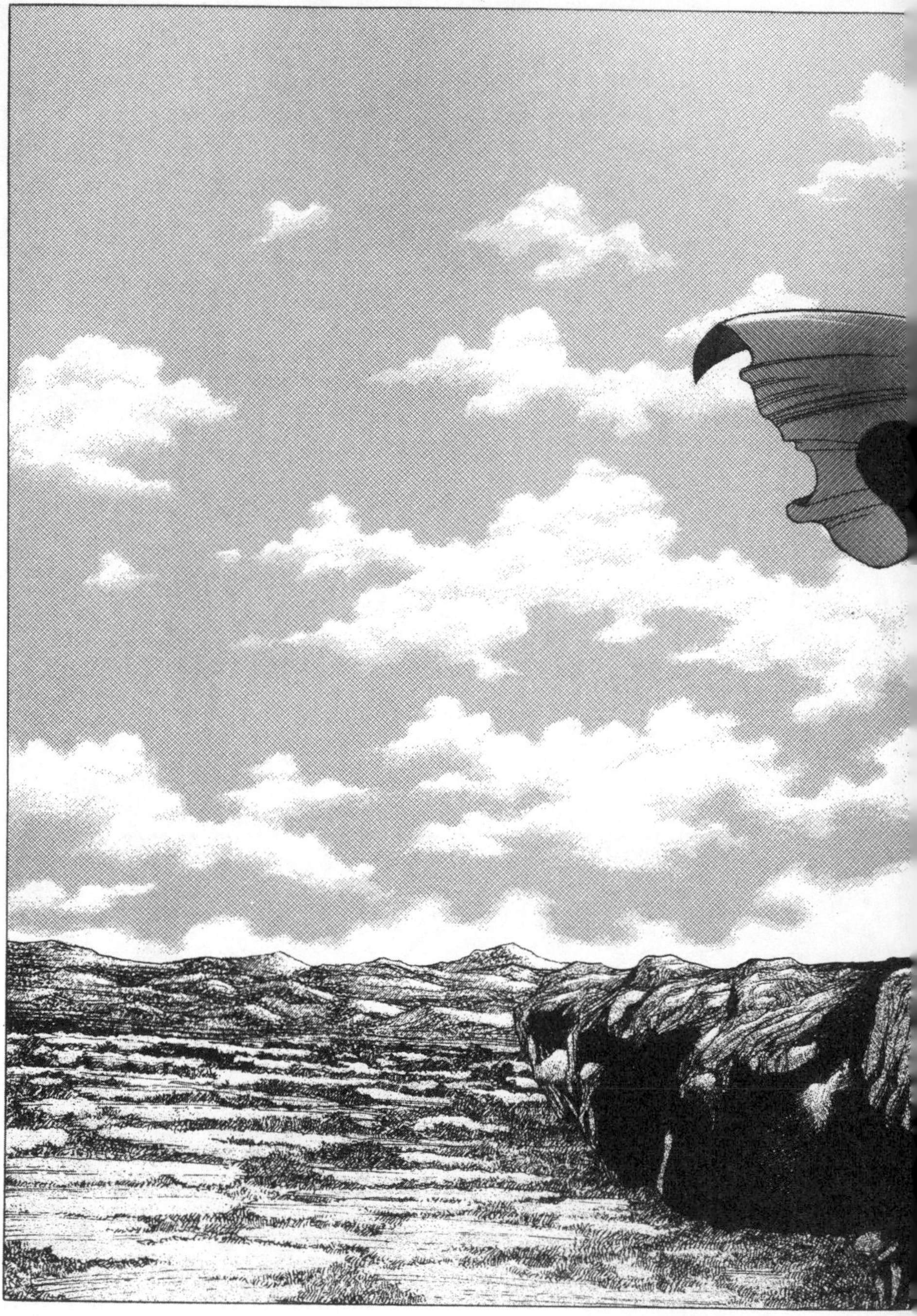

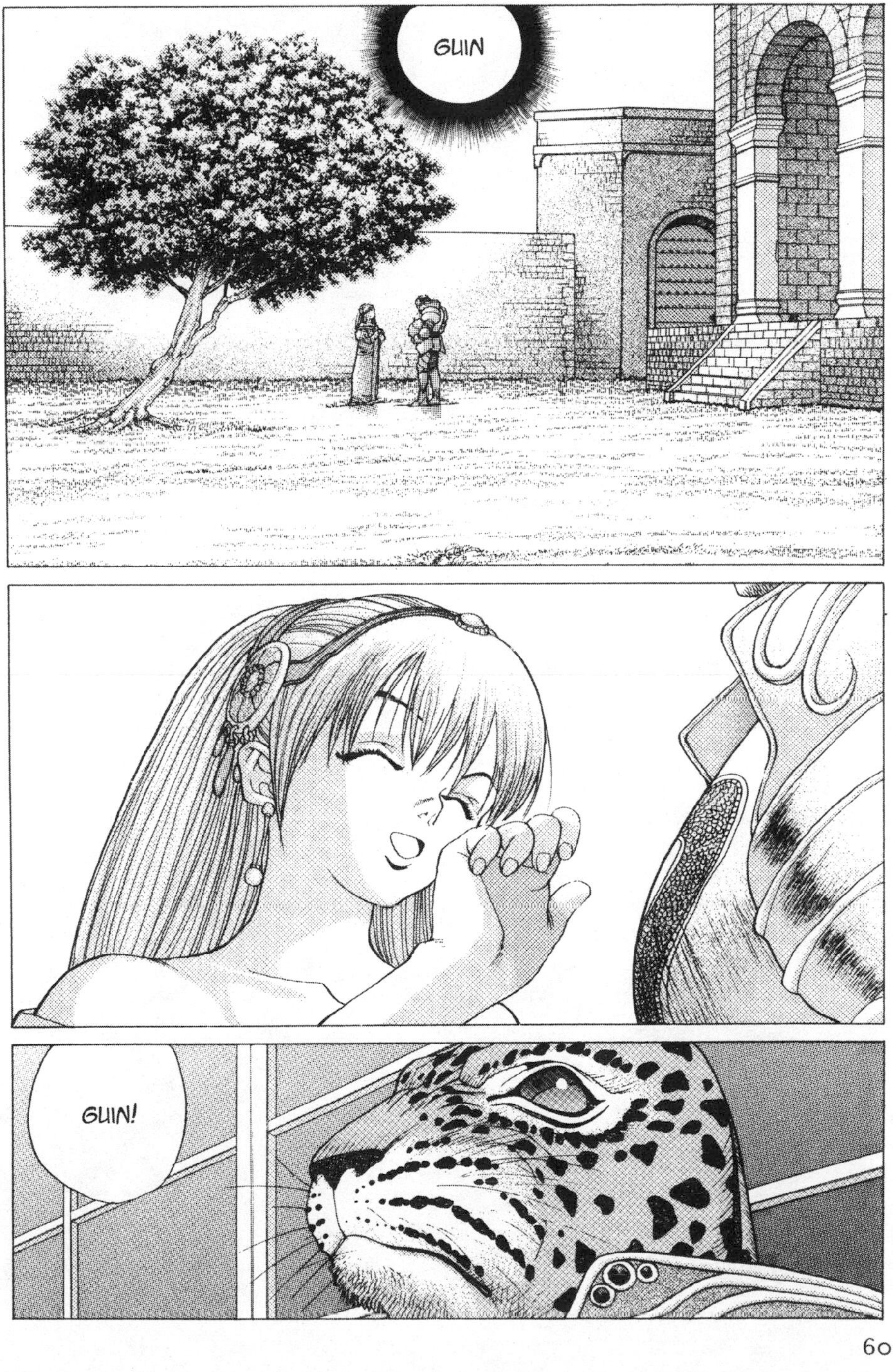
GUIN
GUIN!

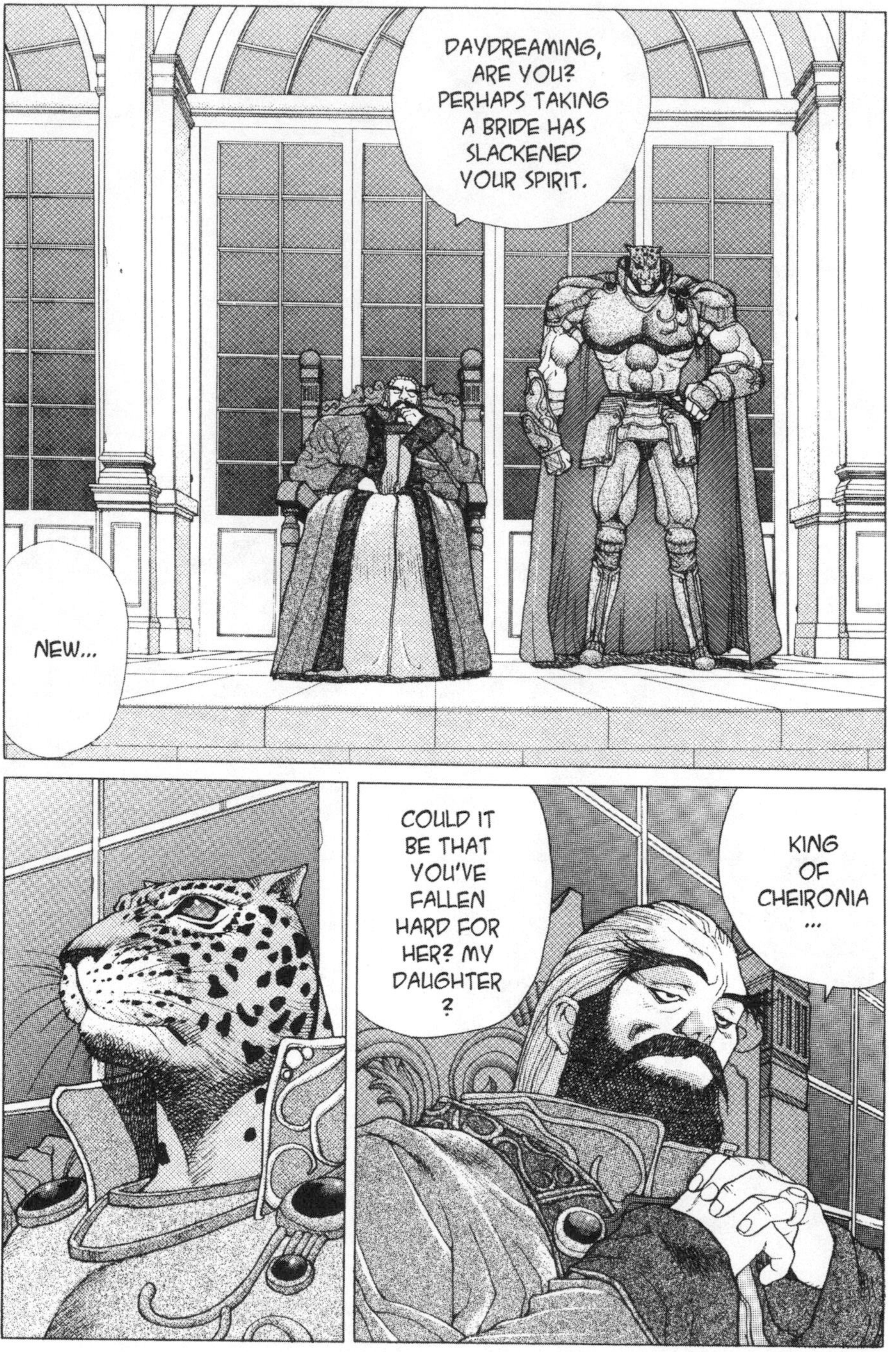
DAYDREAMING, ARE YOU? PERHAPS TAKING A BRIDE HAS SLACKENED YOUR SPIRIT.
NEW...
KING OF CHEIRONIA ...
COULD IT BE THAT YOU'VE FALLEN HARD FOR HER? MY DAUGHTER ?

AT ANY RATE, THE REALM WILL BE SECURE AS LONG AS YOU REIGN OVER IT.

SO I TRUST.

HMPH

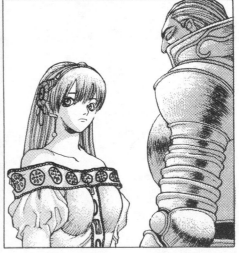

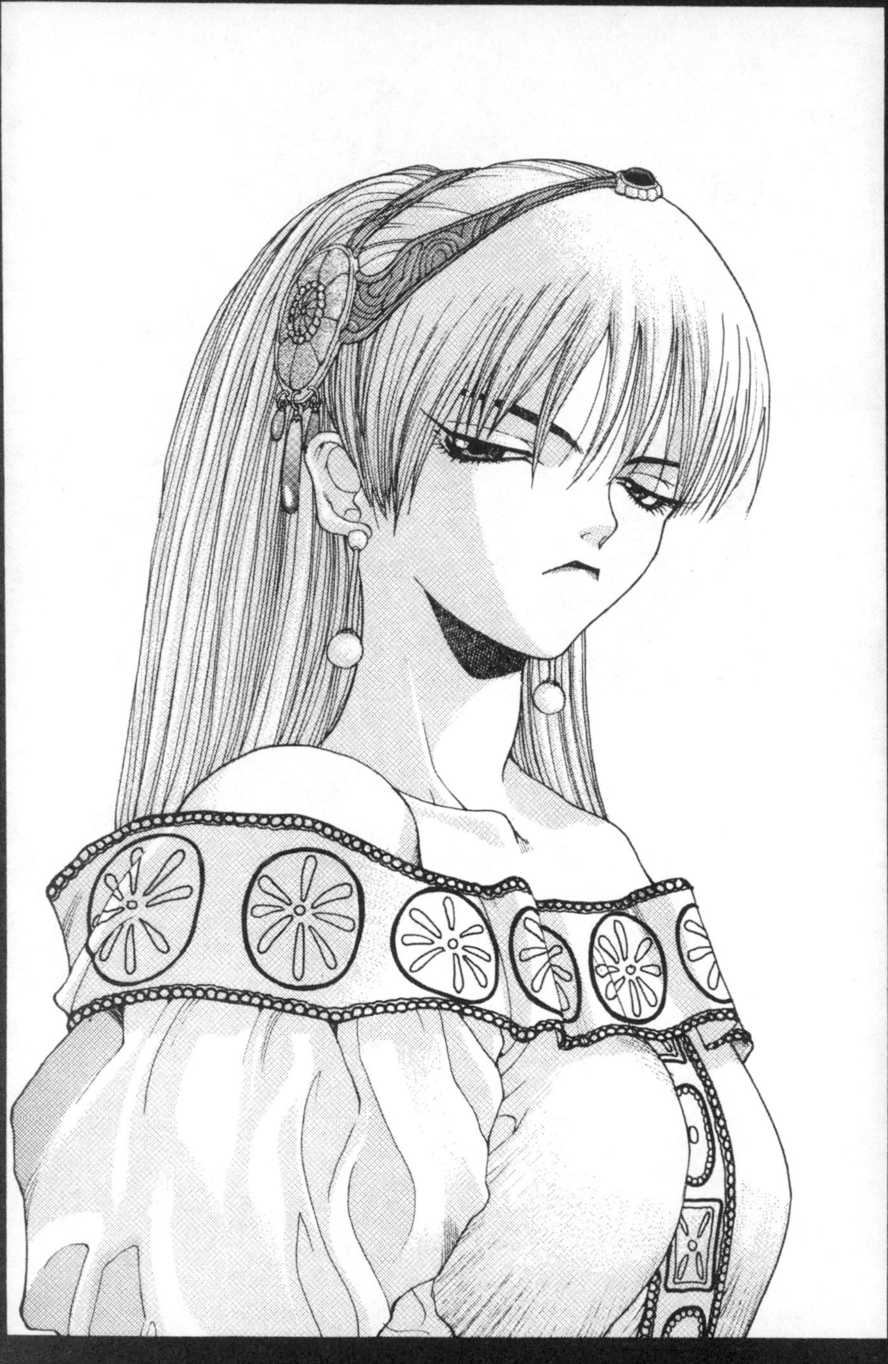

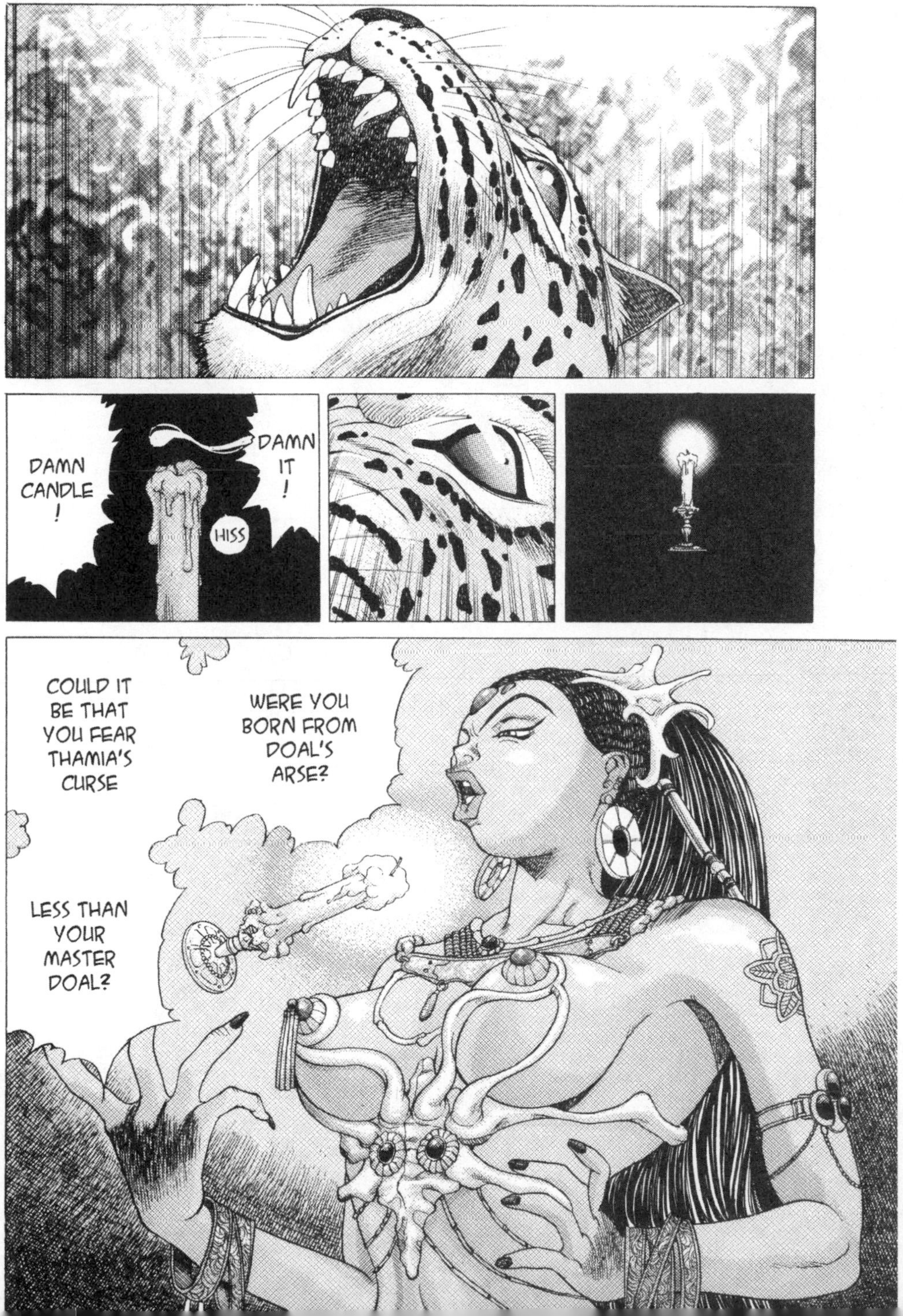
DAMN IT!
DAMN CANDLE!
HISS
WERE YOU BORN FROM DOAL'S ARSE?
COULD IT BE THAT YOU FEAR THAMIA'S CURSE
LESS THAN YOUR MASTER DOAL?

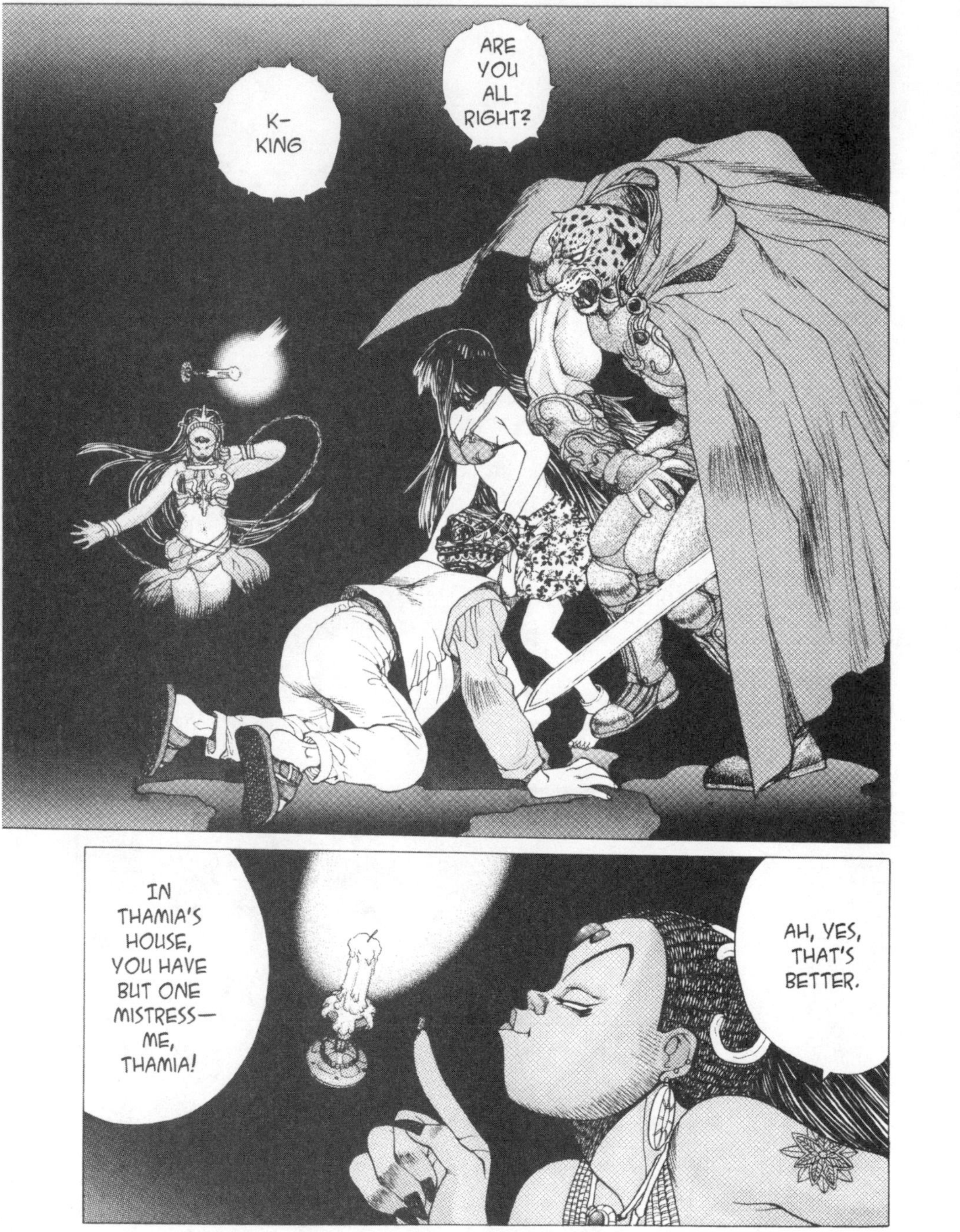
ARE YOU ALL RIGHT?
K- KING
AH, YES, THAT'S BETTER.
IN THAMIA'S HOUSE, YOU HAVE BUT ONE MISTRESS— ME, THAMIA!

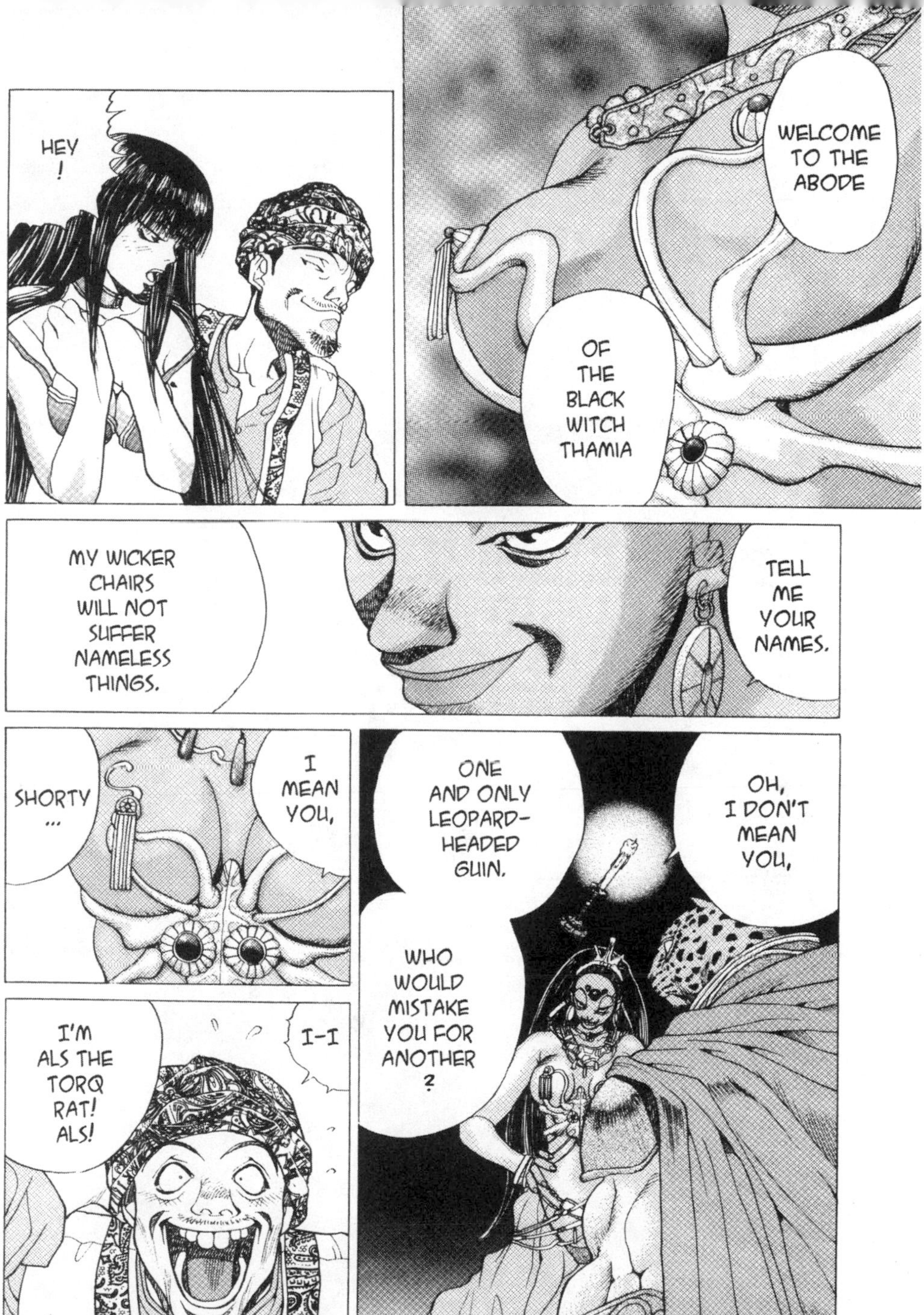
WELCOME TO THE ABODE
OF THE BLACK WITCH THAMIA
HEY !
TELL ME YOUR NAMES.
MY WICKER CHAIRS WILL NOT SUFFER NAMELESS THINGS.
OH, I DON'T MEAN YOU,
ONE AND ONLY LEOPARD-HEADED GUIN.
WHO WOULD MISTAKE YOU FOR ANOTHER ?
I MEAN YOU,
SHORTY ...
I-I
I'M ALS THE TORQ RAT! ALS!

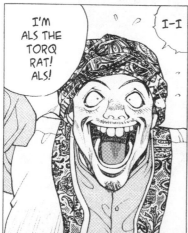

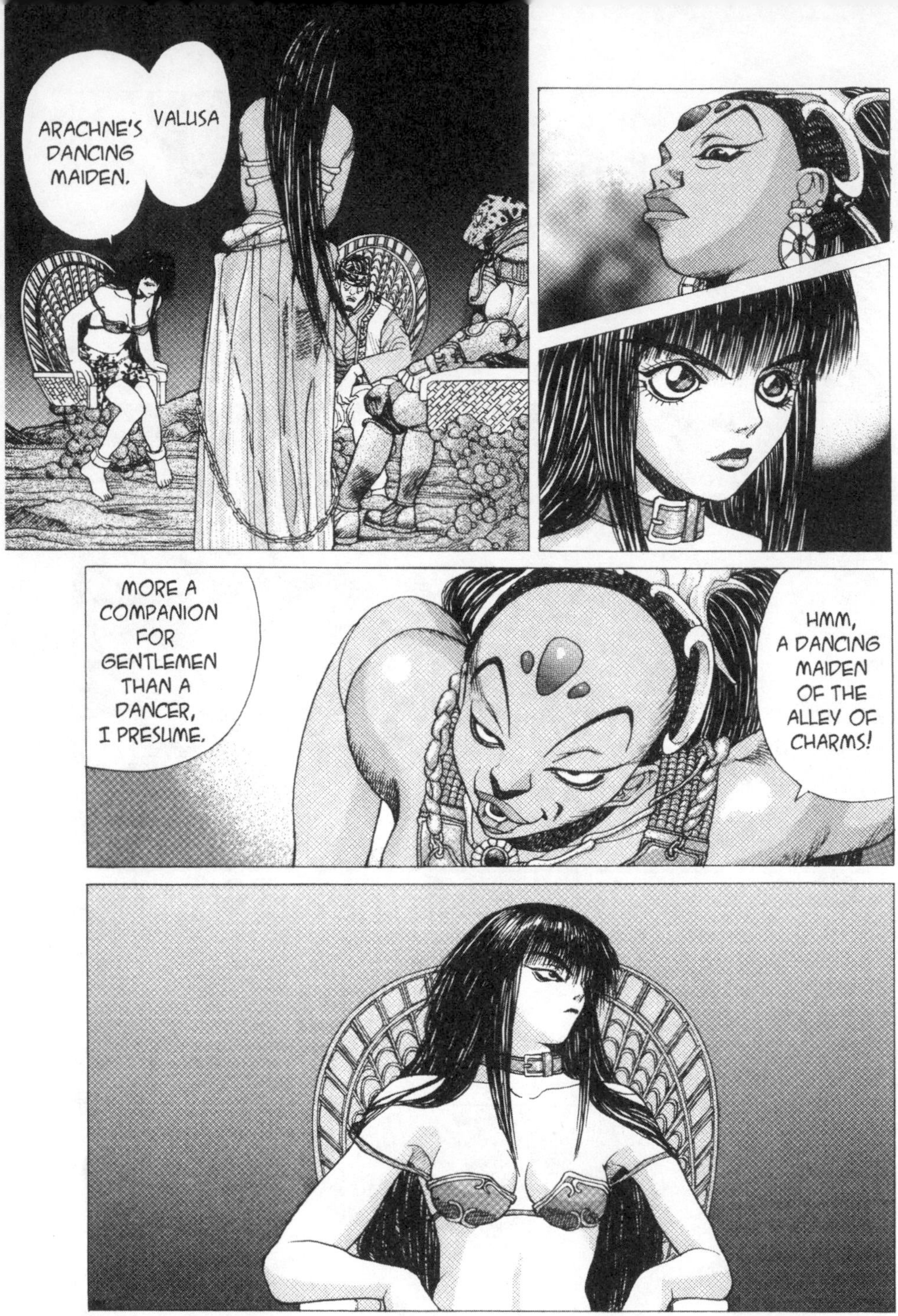
VALUSA
ARACHNE'S DANCING MAIDEN.
HMM, A DANCING MAIDEN OF THE ALLEY OF CHARMS!
MORE A COMPANION FOR GENTLEMEN THAN A DANCER, I PRESUME.

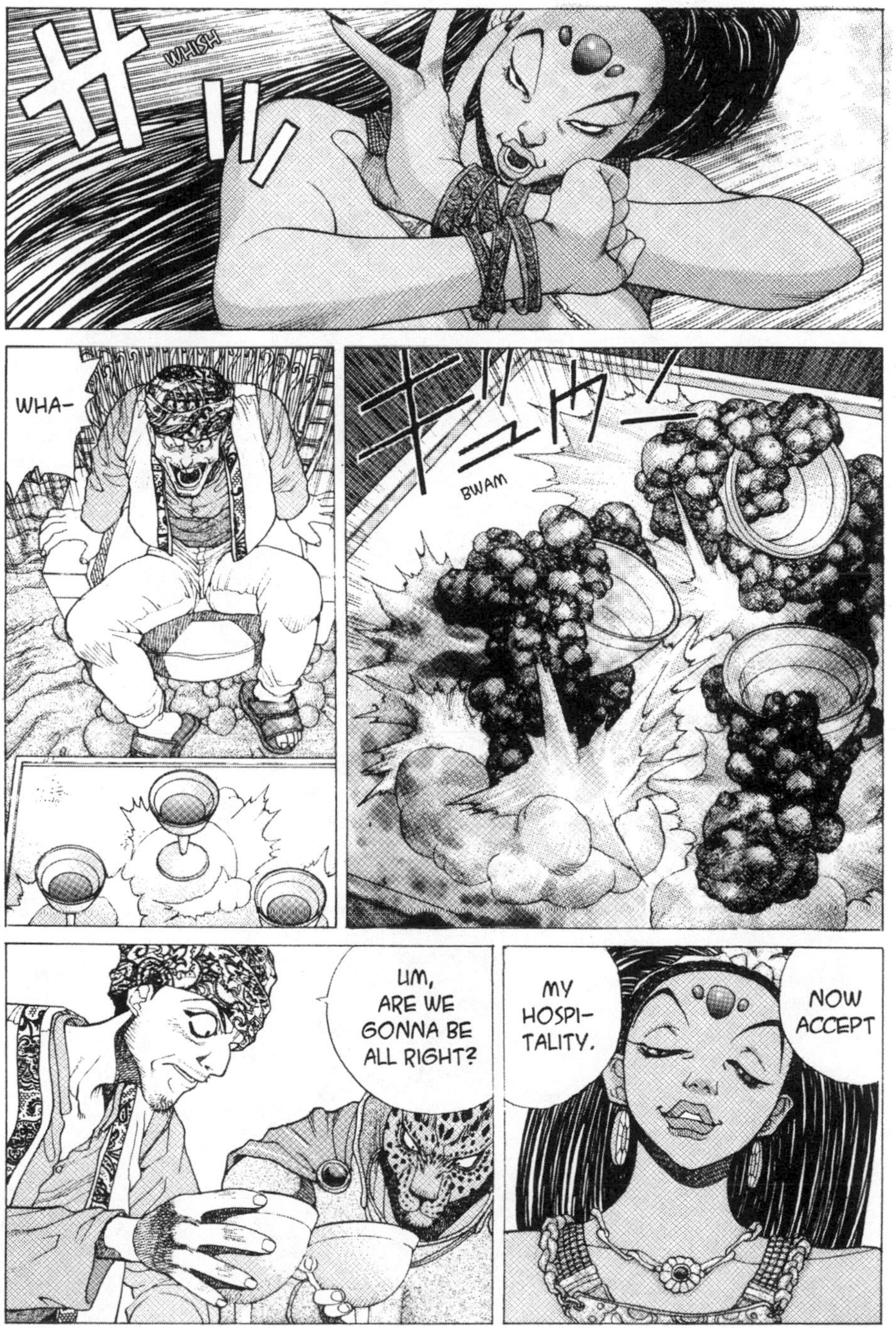
WHISH
BWAM
WHA-
NOW ACCEPT
MY HOSPI-TALITY.
UM, ARE WE GONNA BE ALL RIGHT?

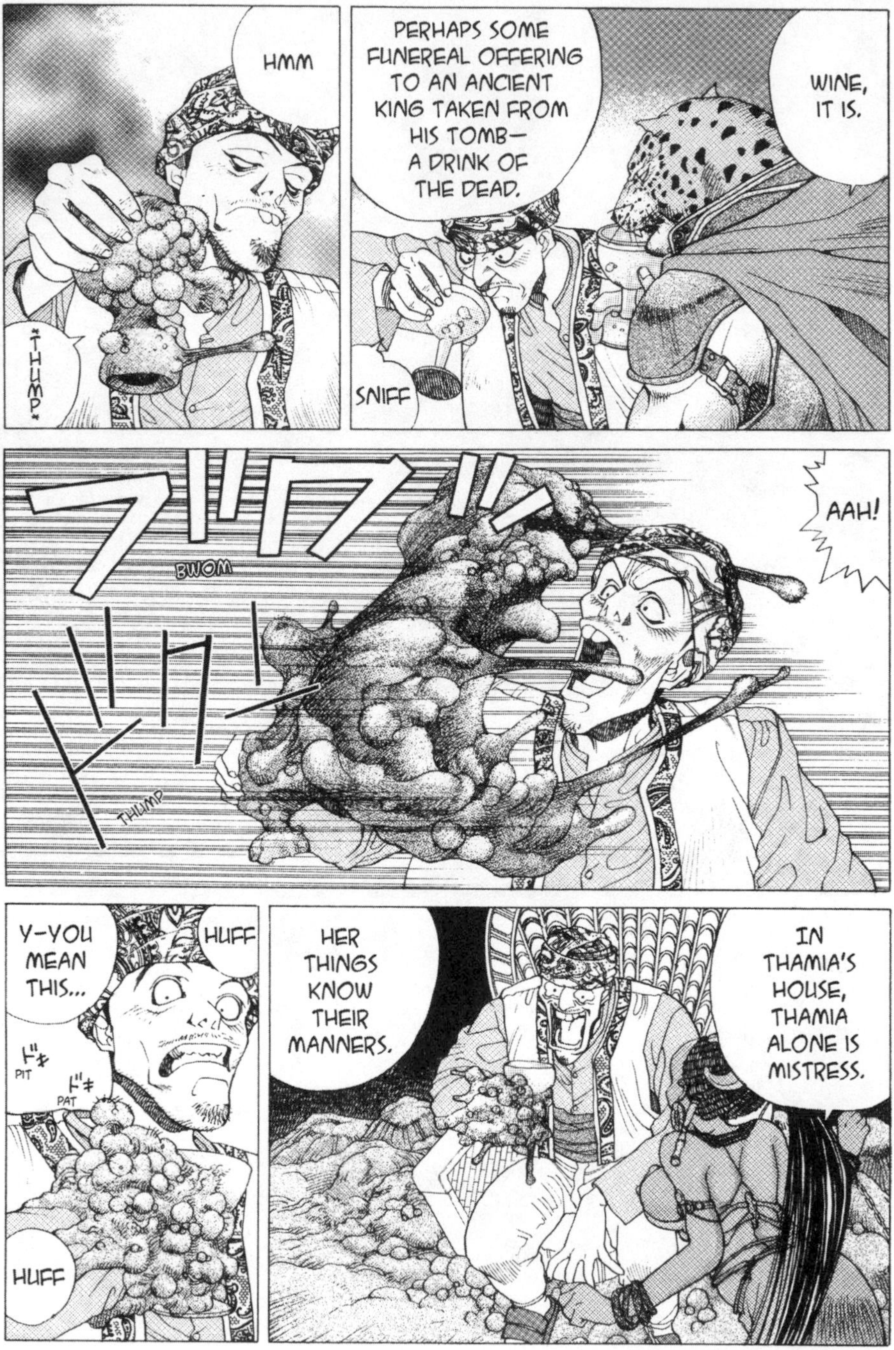
WINE, IT IS.
PERHAPS SOME FUNEREAL OFFERING TO AN ANCIENT KING TAKEN FROM HIS TOMB— A DRINK OF THE DEAD.
SNIFF
HMM
THUMP
AAH!
BWOM
THUMP
IN THAMIA'S HOUSE, THAMIA ALONE IS MISTRESS.
HER THINGS KNOW THEIR MANNERS.
HUFF
Y-YOU MEAN THIS...
ドキ
PIT
ドキ
PAT
HUFF

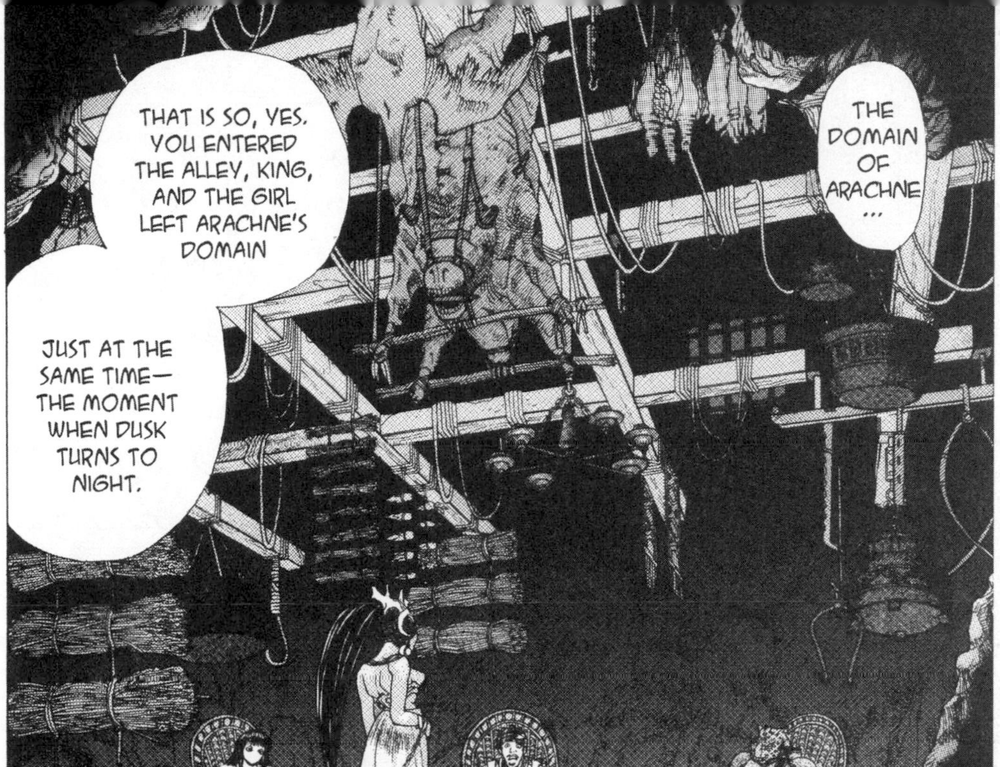
THE DOMAIN OF ARACHNE...
THAT IS SO, YES. YOU ENTERED THE ALLEY, KING, AND THE GIRL LEFT ARACHNE'S DOMAIN
JUST AT THE SAME TIME— THE MOMENT WHEN DUSK TURNS TO NIGHT.

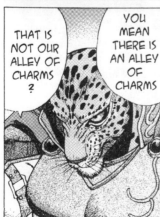

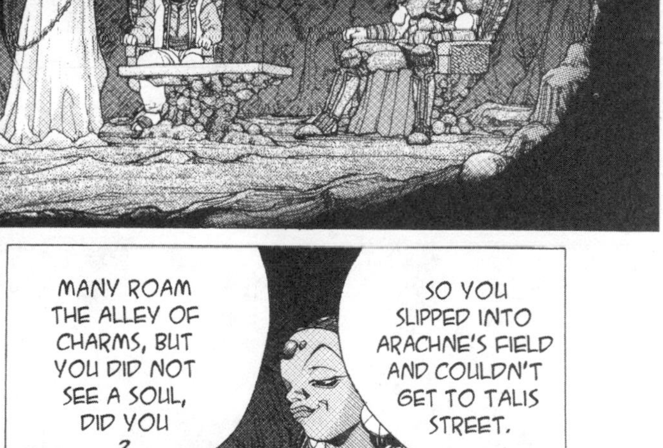
SO YOU SLIPPED INTO ARACHNE'S FIELD AND COULDN'T GET TO TALIS STREET.
MANY ROAM THE ALLEY OF CHARMS, BUT YOU DID NOT SEE A SOUL, DID YOU?

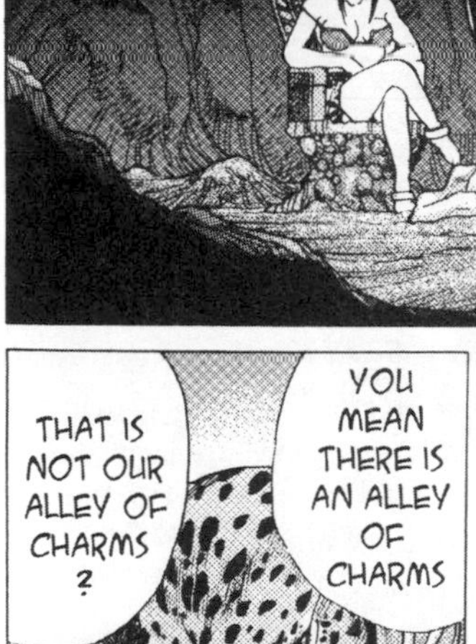
YOU MEAN THERE IS AN ALLEY OF CHARMS
THAT IS NOT OUR ALLEY OF CHARMS?

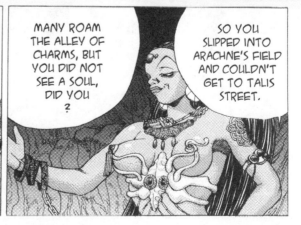

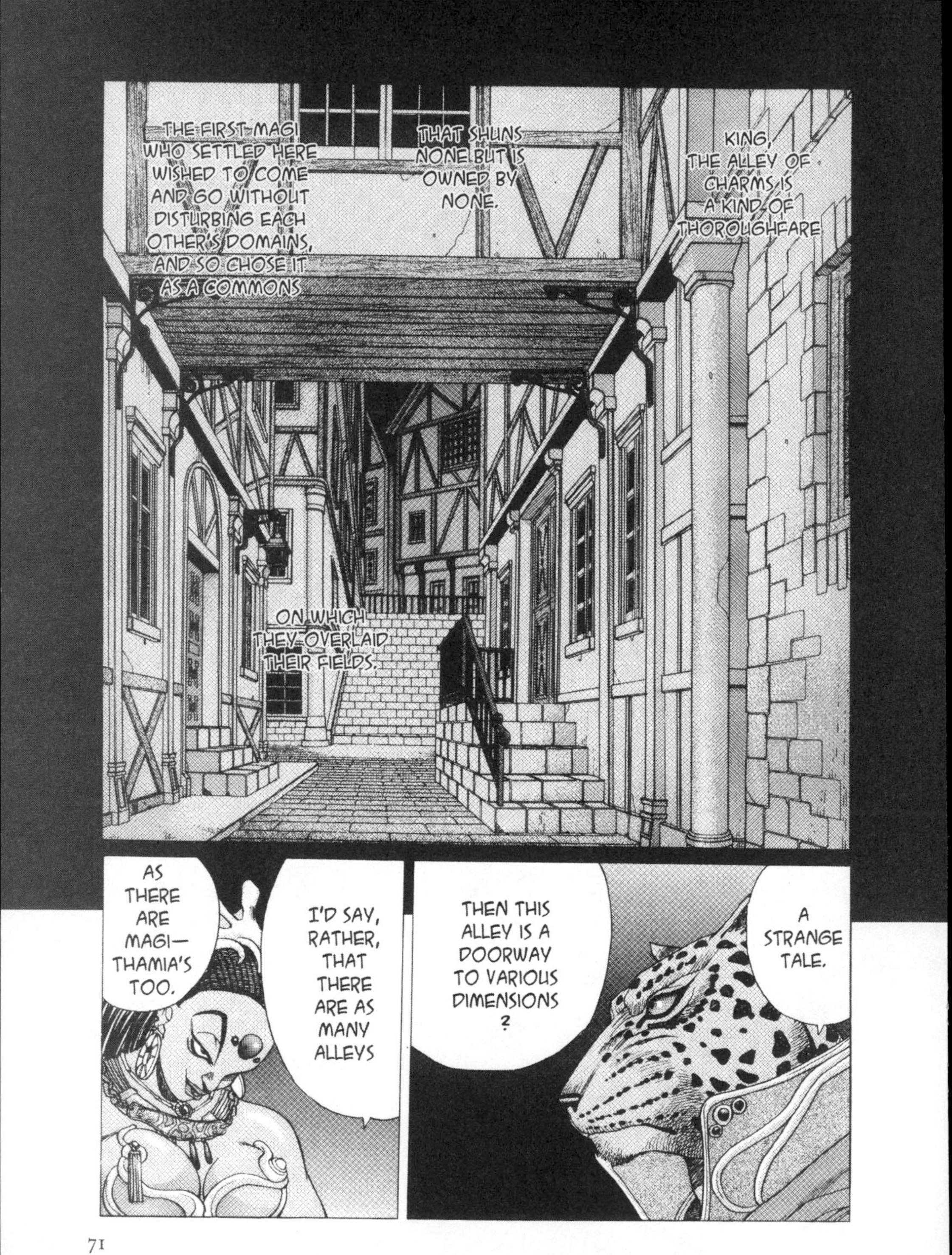
KING, THE ALLEY OF CHARMS IS A KIND OF THOROUGHFARE
THAT SHUNS NONE BUT IS OWNED BY NONE.
THE FIRST MAGI WHO SETTLED HERE WISHED TO COME AND GO WITHOUT DISTURBING EACH OTHER'S DOMAINS, AND SO CHOSE IT AS A COMMONS
ON WHICH THEY OVERLAID THEIR FIELDS.
A STRANGE TALE.
THEN THIS ALLEY IS A DOORWAY TO VARIOUS DIMENSIONS?
I'D SAY, RATHER, THAT THERE ARE AS MANY ALLEYS
AS THERE ARE MAGI— THAMIA'S TOO.

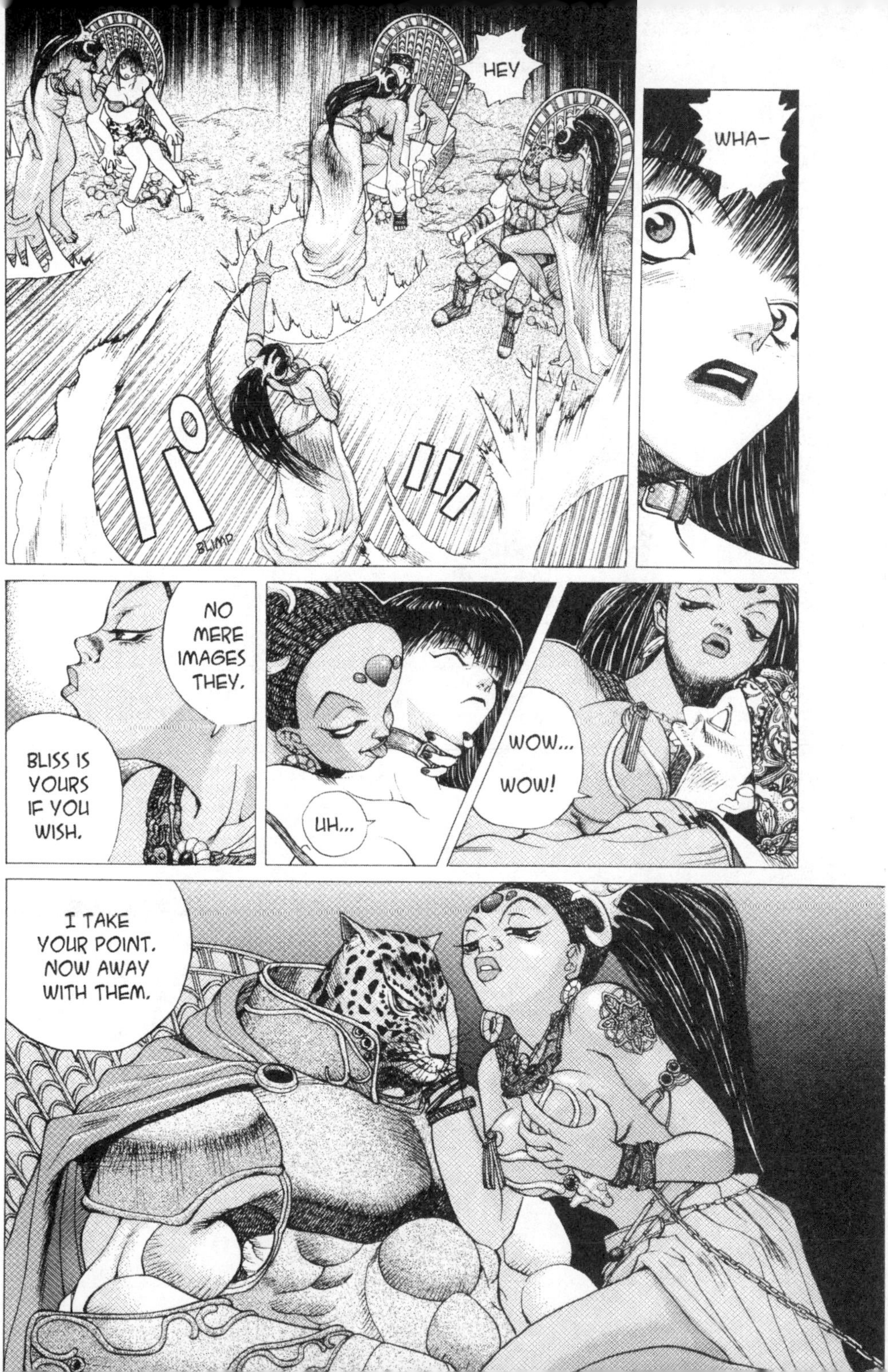
WHA-
HEY
BLIMP
WOW... WOW!
UH...
NO MERE IMAGES THEY.
BLISS IS YOURS IF YOU WISH.
I TAKE YOUR POINT. NOW AWAY WITH THEM.

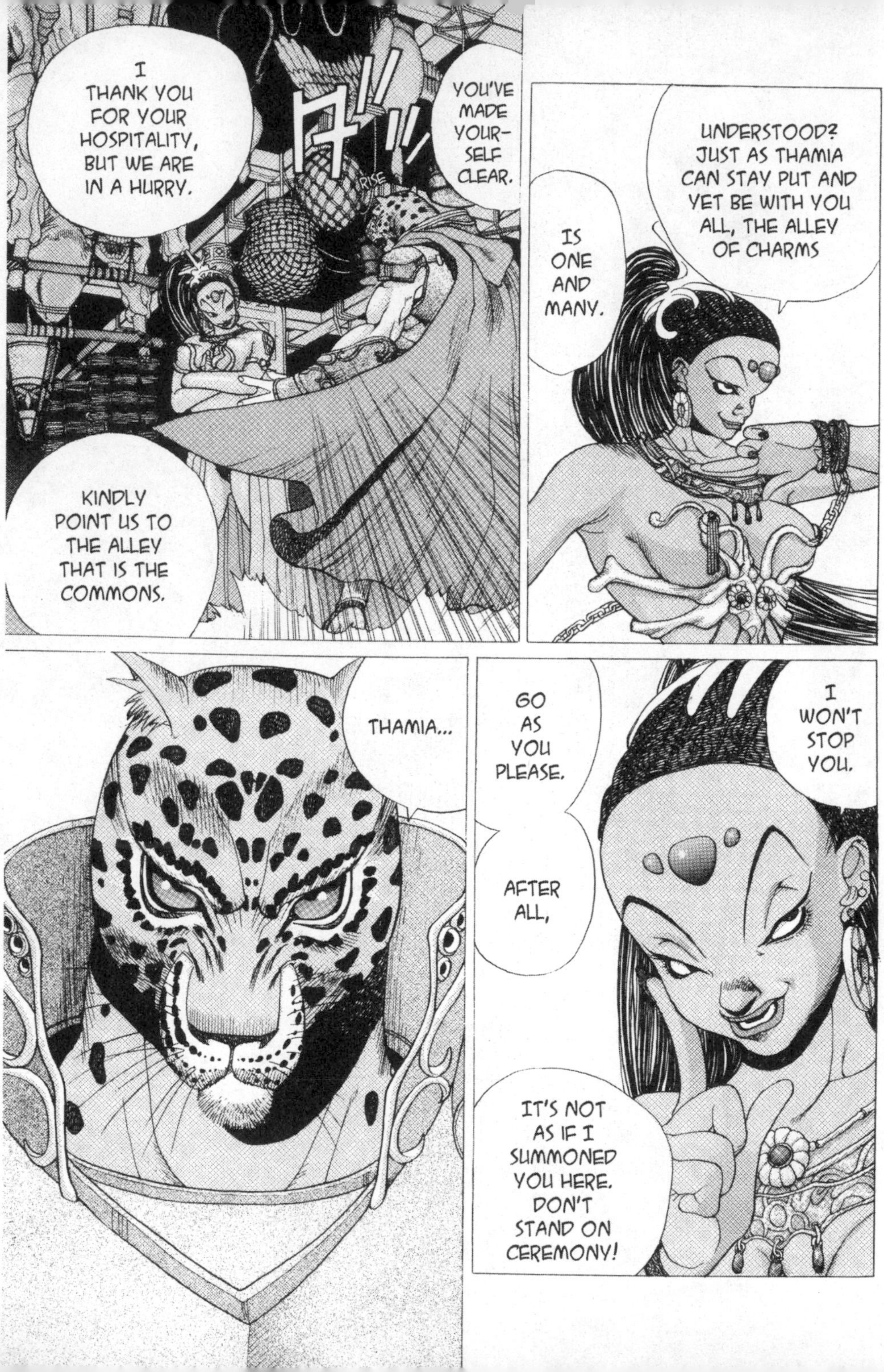
UNDERSTOOD? JUST AS THAMIA CAN STAY PUT AND YET BE WITH YOU ALL, THE ALLEY OF CHARMS
IS ONE AND MANY.
YOU'VE MADE YOUR-SELF CLEAR.
I THANK YOU FOR YOUR HOSPITALITY, BUT WE ARE IN A HURRY.
RISE
KINDLY POINT US TO THE ALLEY THAT IS THE COMMONS.
I WON'T STOP YOU.
GO AS YOU PLEASE.
AFTER ALL,
IT'S NOT AS IF I SUMMONED YOU HERE. DON'T STAND ON CEREMONY!
THAMIA...

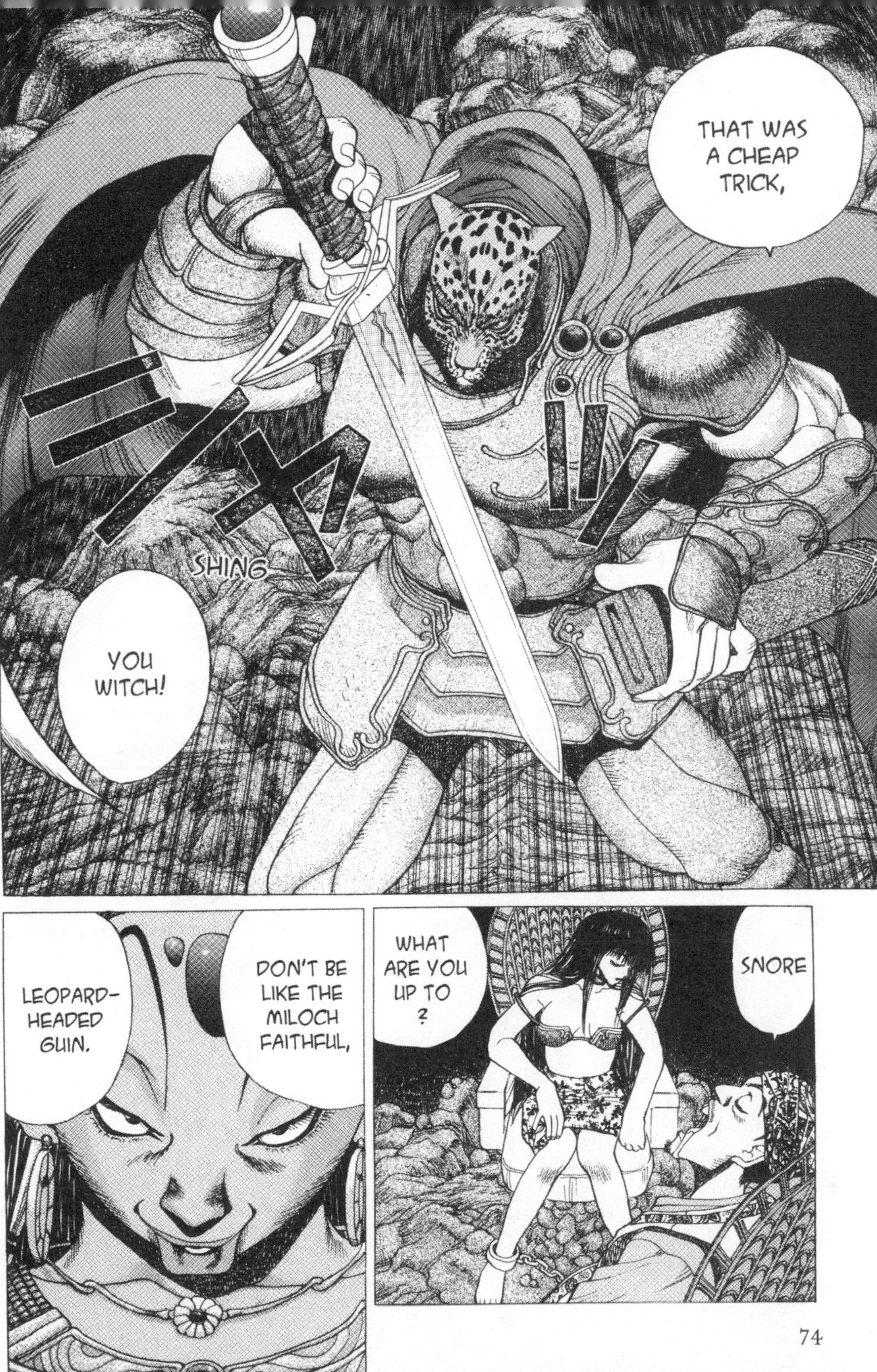
THAT WAS A CHEAP TRICK,
SHING
YOU WITCH!
SNORE
WHAT ARE YOU UP TO ?
DON'T BE LIKE THE MILOCH FAITHFUL,
LEOPARD-HEADED GUIN.

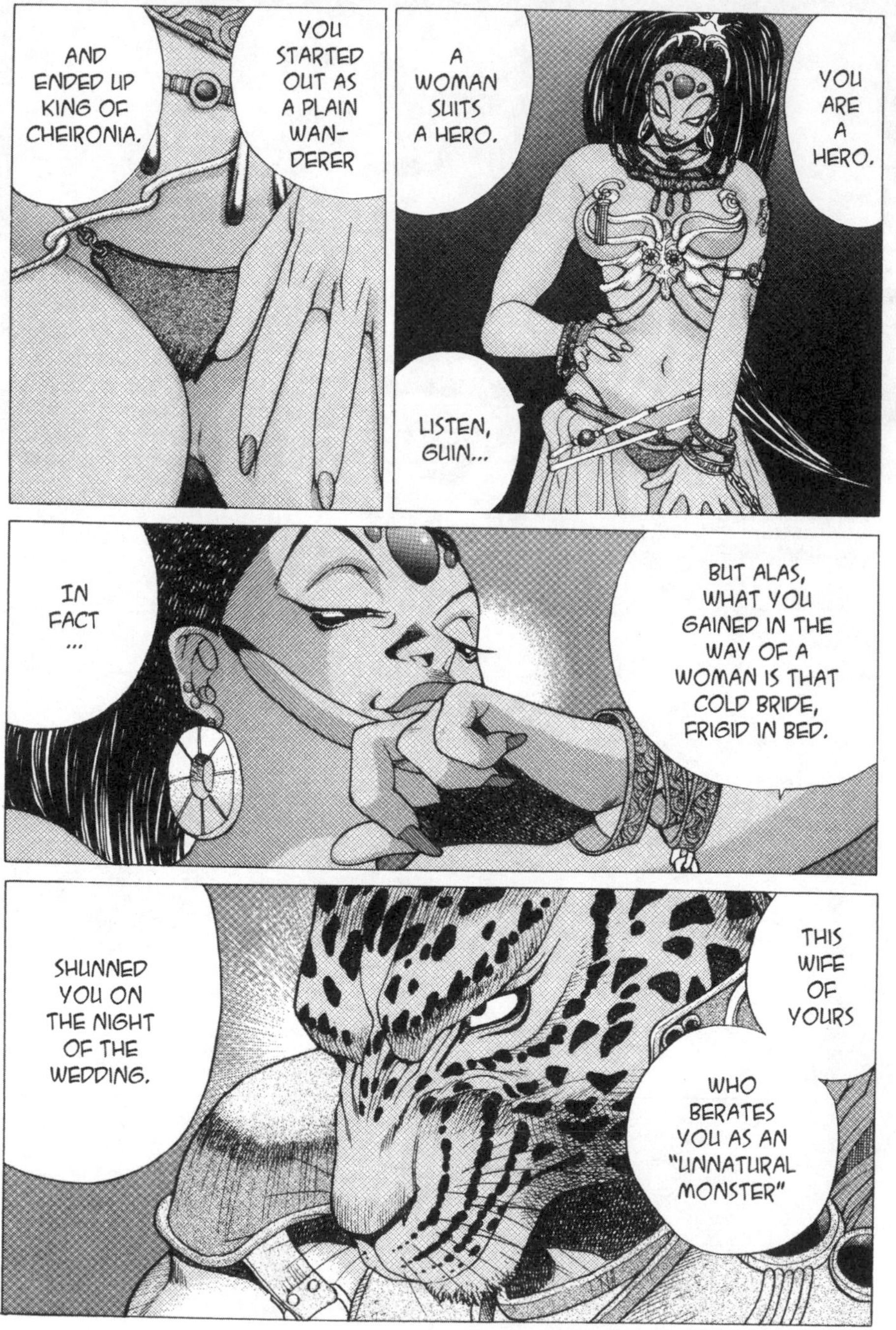
YOU ARE A HERO.
A WOMAN SUITS A HERO.
LISTEN, GUIN...
YOU STARTED OUT AS A PLAIN WAN-DERER
AND ENDED UP KING OF CHEIRONIA.
BUT ALAS, WHAT YOU GAINED IN THE WAY OF A WOMAN IS THAT COLD BRIDE, FRIGID IN BED.
IN FACT ...
THIS WIFE OF YOURS
WHO BERATES YOU AS AN "UNNATURAL MONSTER"
SHUNNED YOU ON THE NIGHT OF THE WEDDING.

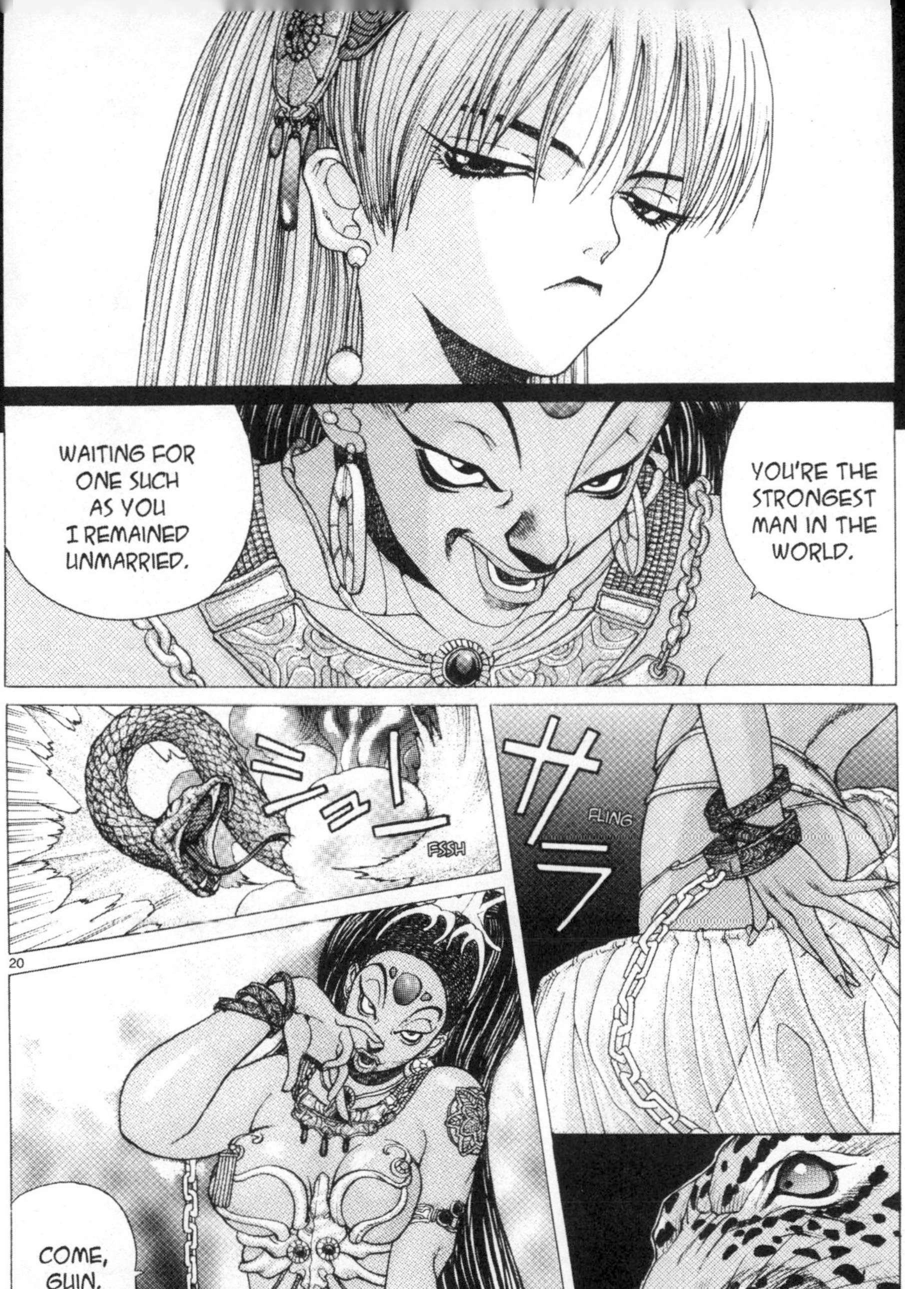

YOU'RE THE STRONGEST MAN IN THE WORLD.
WAITING FOR ONE SUCH AS YOU I REMAINED UNMARRIED.
サラ
FLING
シュー
FSSH
COME, GUIN.

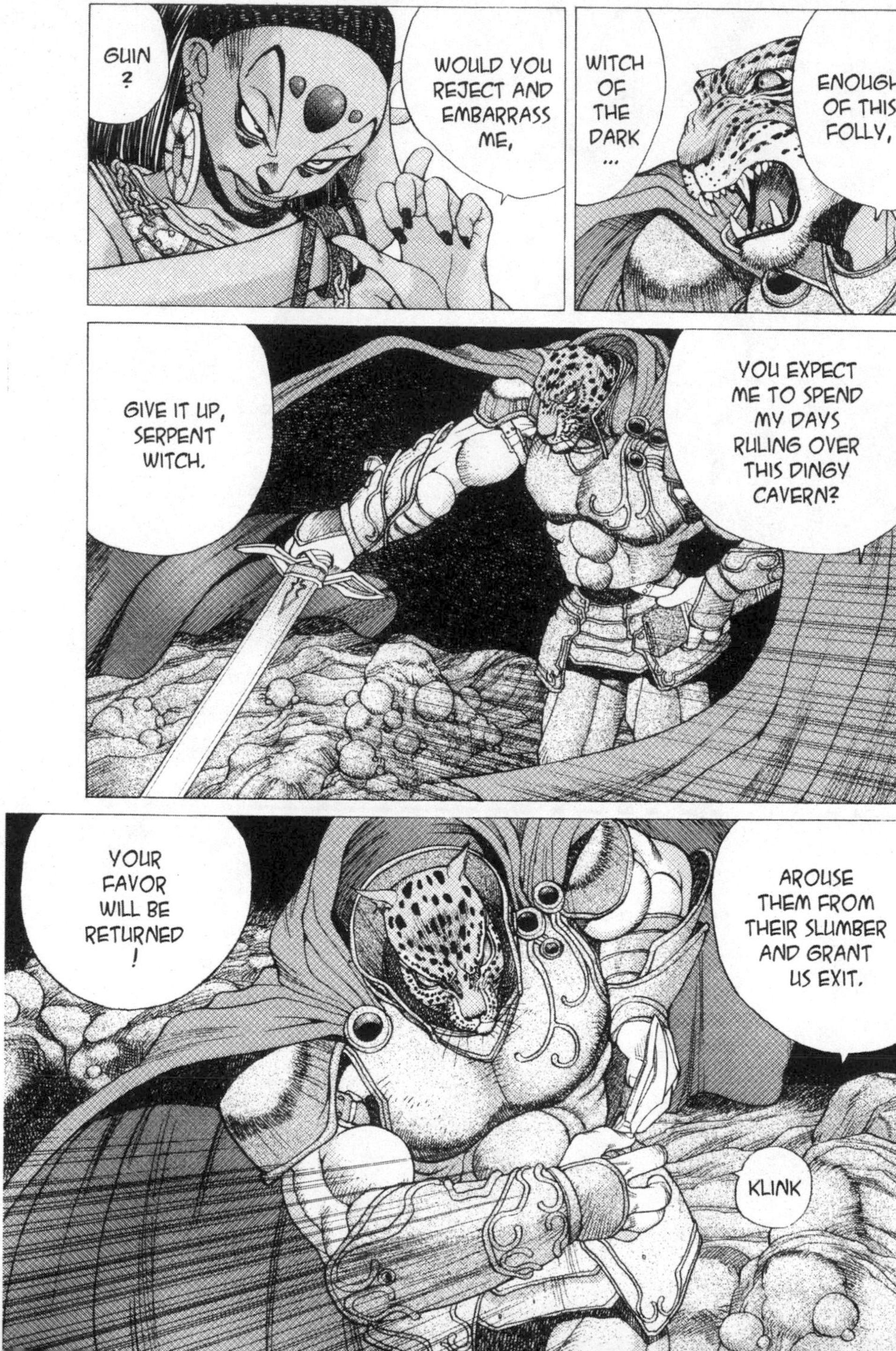
ENOUGH OF THIS FOLLY,
WITCH OF THE DARK ...
WOULD YOU REJECT AND EMBARRASS ME,
GUIN ?
YOU EXPECT ME TO SPEND MY DAYS RULING OVER THIS DINGY CAVERN?
GIVE IT UP, SERPENT WITCH.
AROUSE THEM FROM THEIR SLUMBER AND GRANT US EXIT.
YOUR FAVOR WILL BE RETURNED !
KLINK

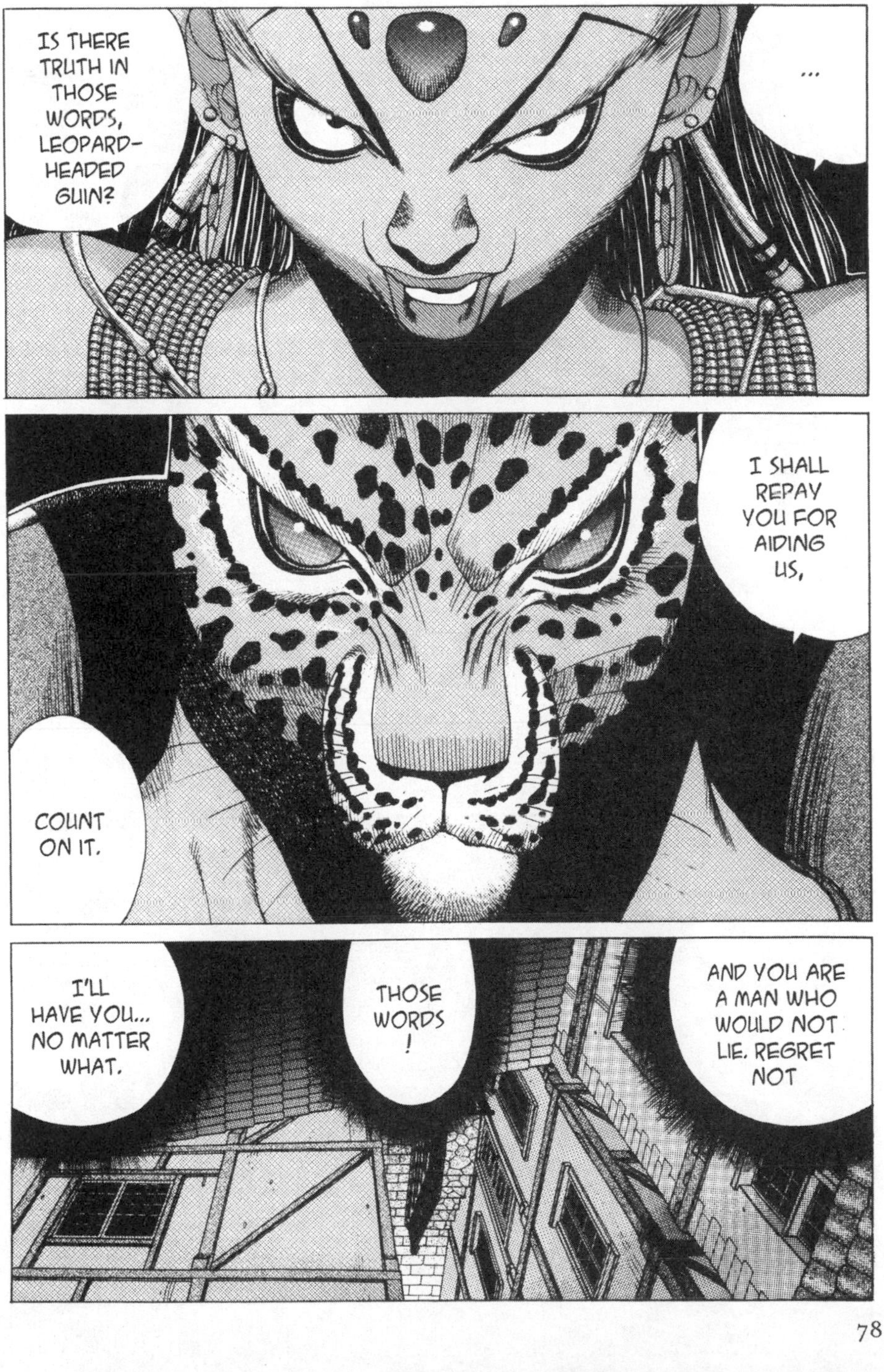
...
IS THERE TRUTH IN THOSE WORDS, LEOPARD-HEADED GUIN?
I SHALL REPAY YOU FOR AIDING US,
COUNT ON IT.
AND YOU ARE A MAN WHO WOULD NOT LIE. REGRET NOT
THOSE WORDS !
I'LL HAVE YOU... NO MATTER WHAT.

THE MAN YOU'RE LOOKING FOR...

WHEE

BOOM

THE DOAL-PURSUED YELISHA'S HOUSE IS FIVE DOORS AHEAD!

DOAL NEVER QUITS HIS PURSUIT FOR YELISHA.

TAKE CARE ...

YELISHA?

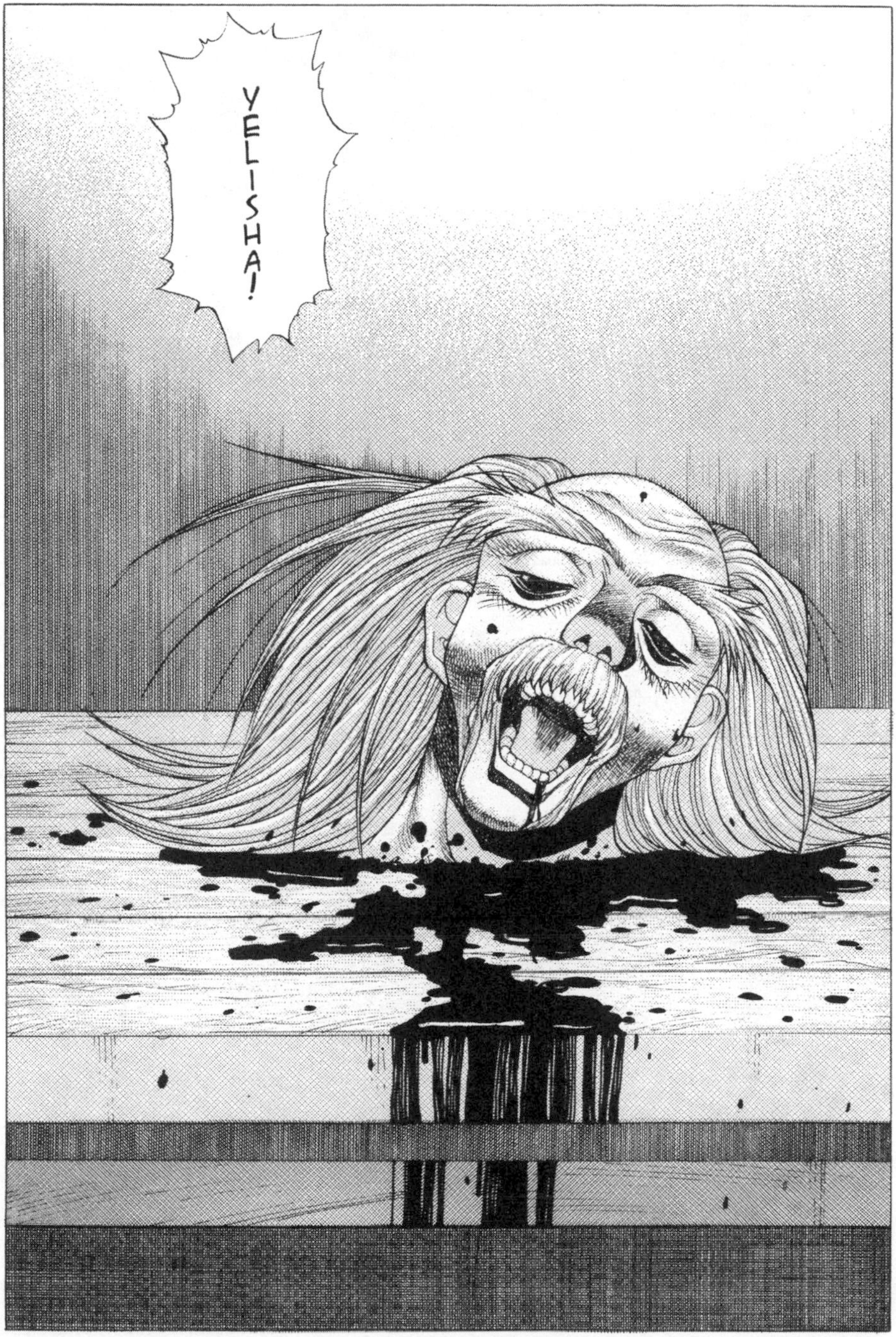
YELISHA!

CHAPTER 4

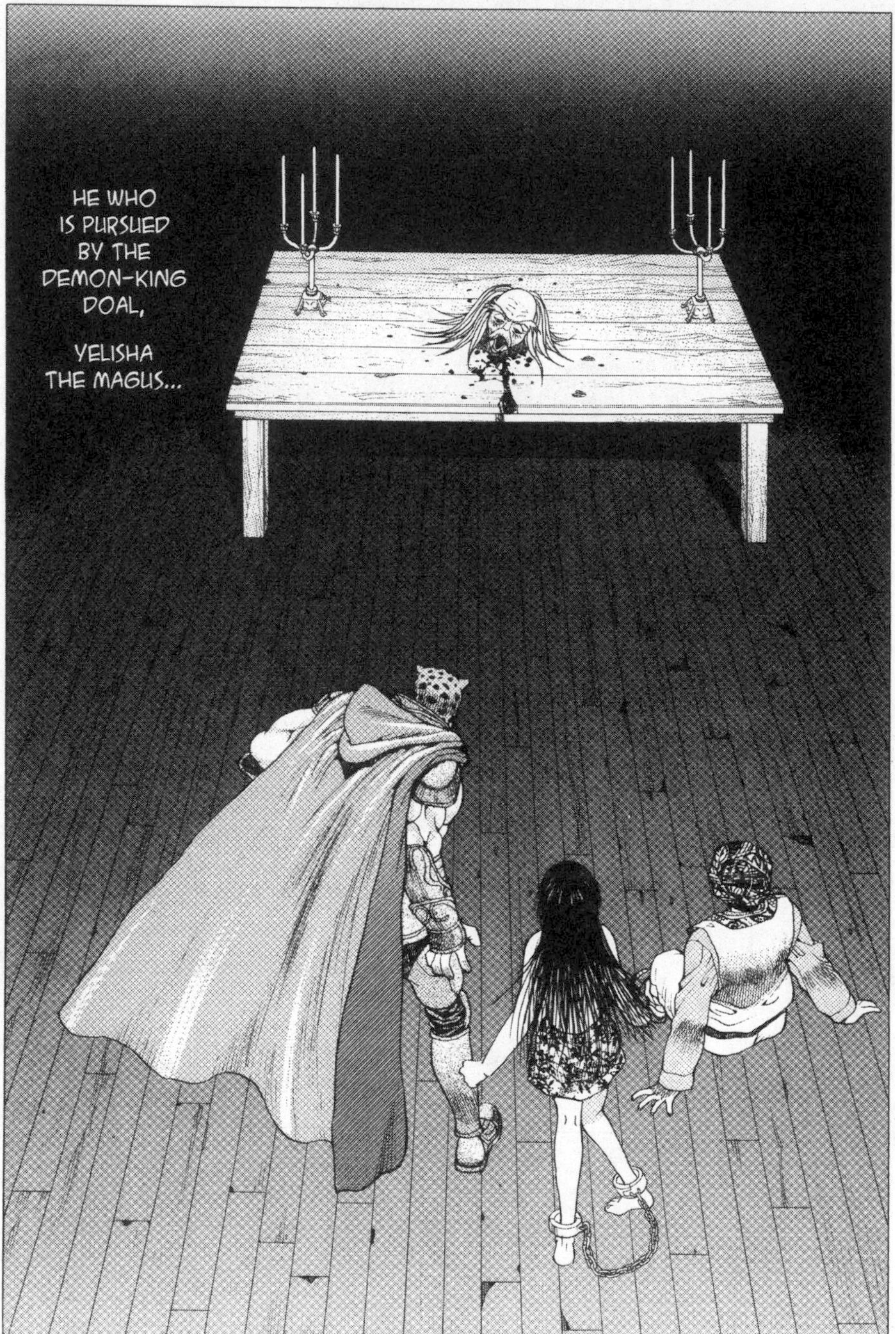
HE WHO IS PURSUED BY THE DEMON-KING DOAL,
YELISHA THE MAGUS...

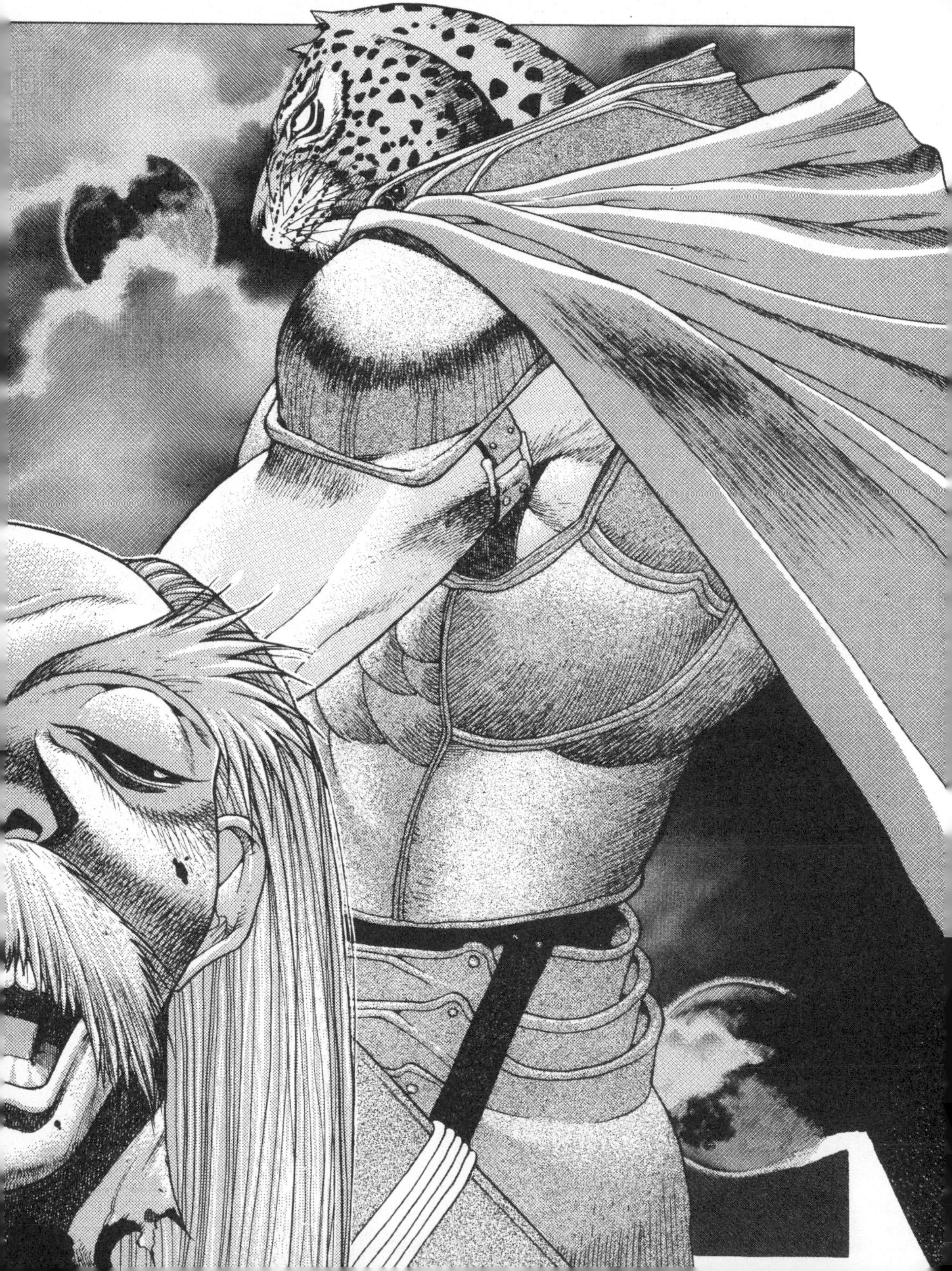

Chapter 4

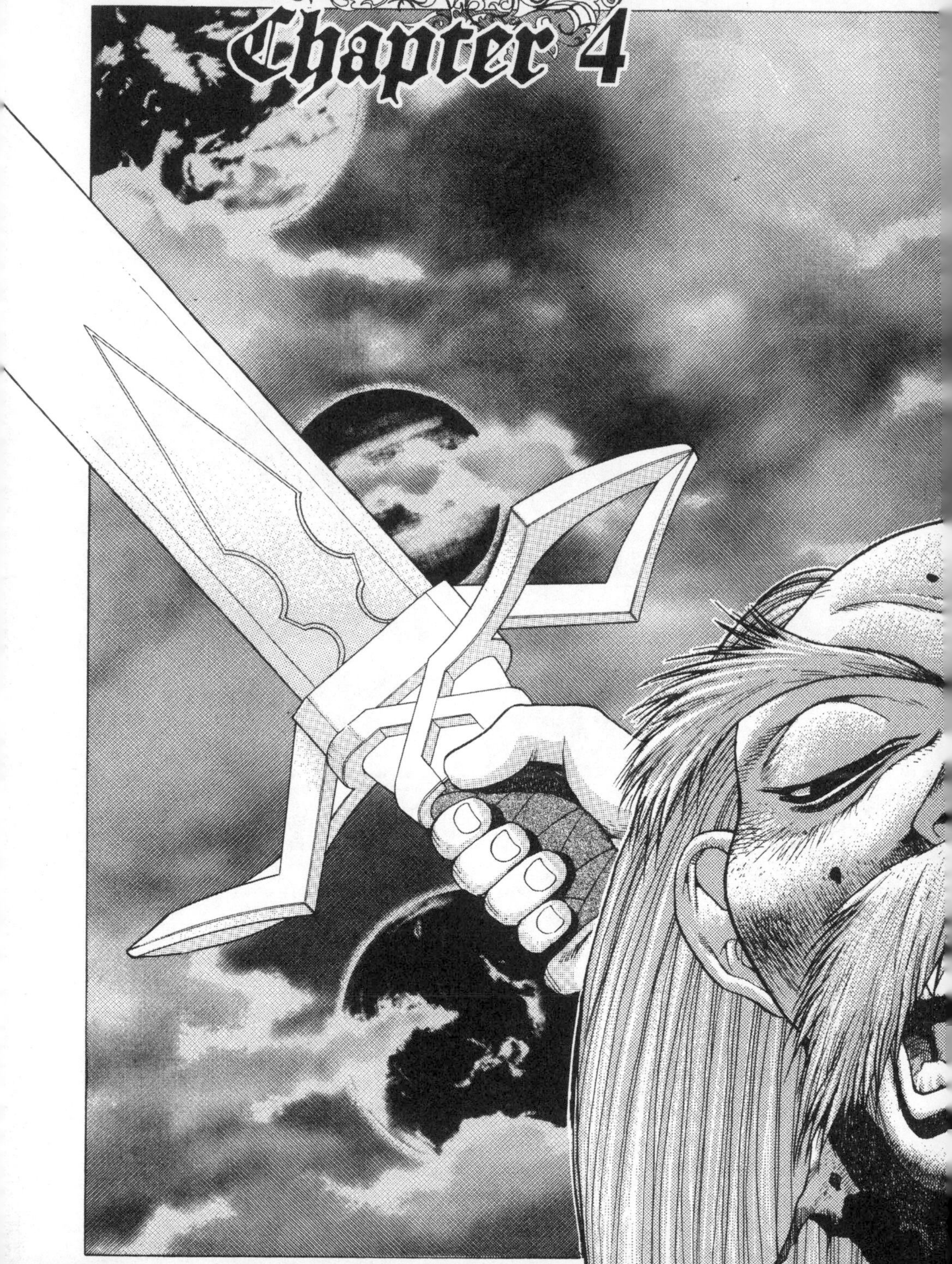

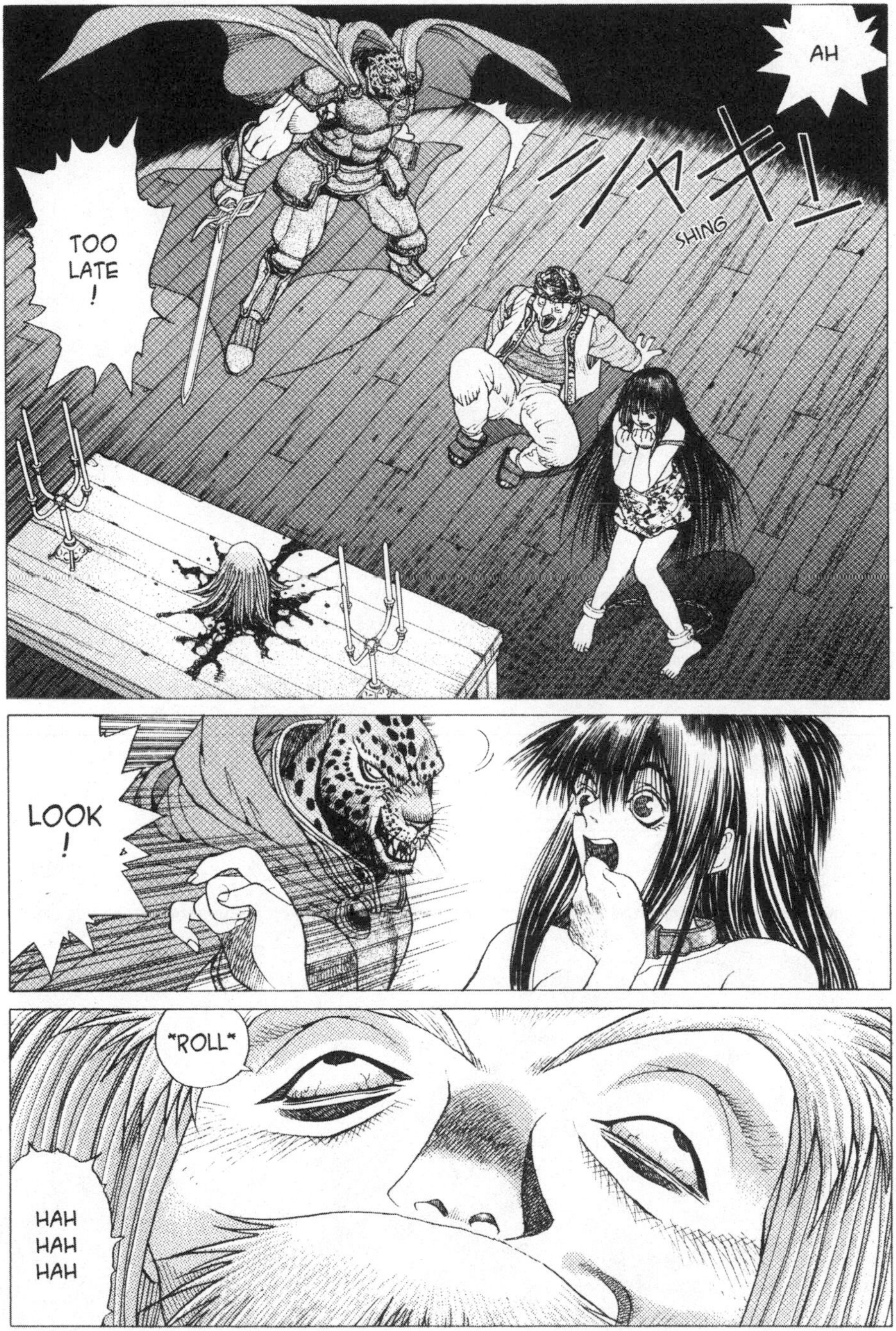
AH
シャキン
SHING
TOO LATE !
LOOK !
ROLL
HAH HAH HAH

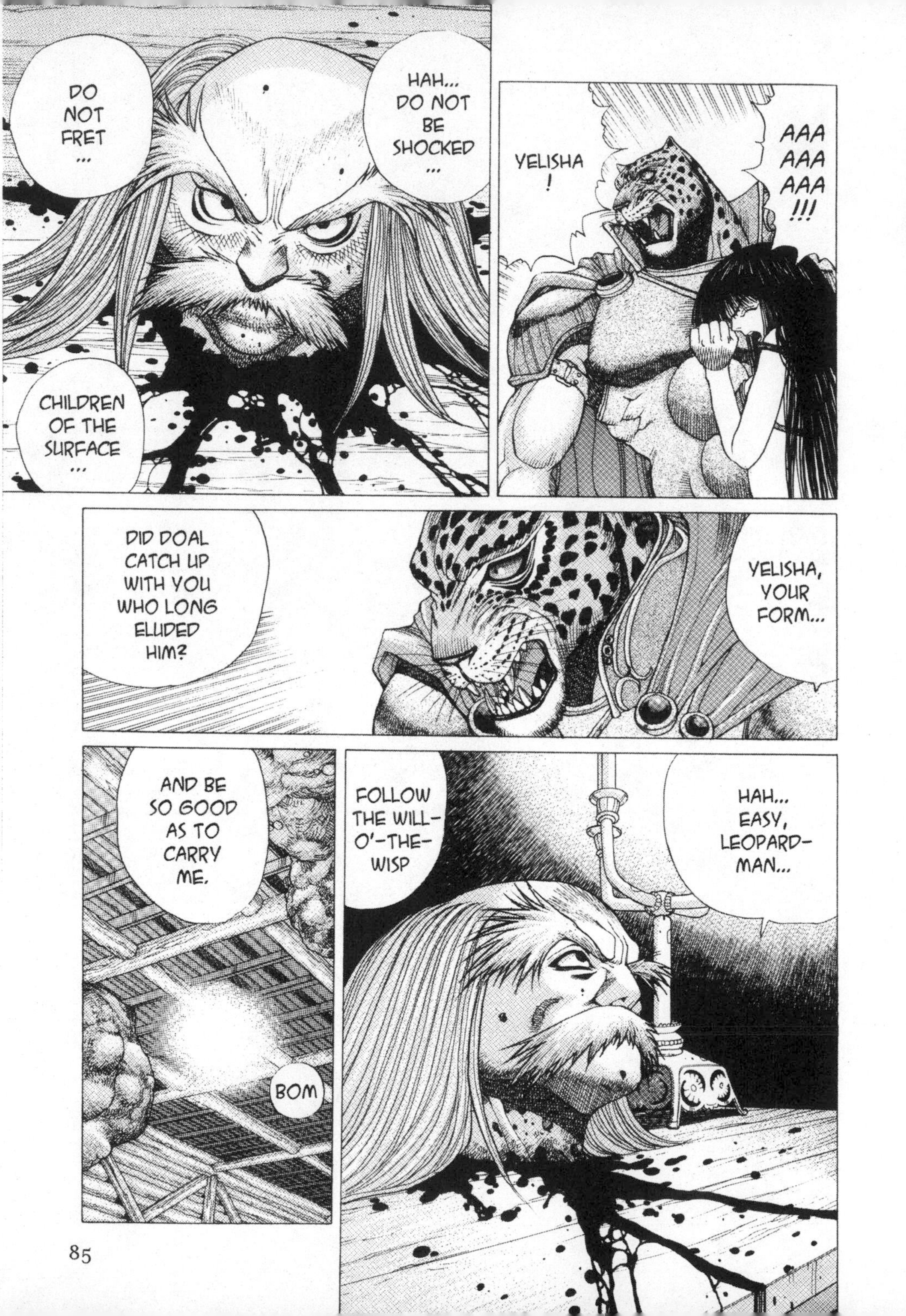
AAA AAA AAA !!!
YELISHA !
HAH... DO NOT BE SHOCKED ...
DO NOT FRET ...
CHILDREN OF THE SURFACE ...
YELISHA, YOUR FORM...
DID DOAL CATCH UP WITH YOU WHO LONG ELUDED HIM?
HAH... EASY, LEOPARD-MAN...
FOLLOW THE WILL-O'-THE-WISP
AND BE SO GOOD AS TO CARRY ME.
BOM

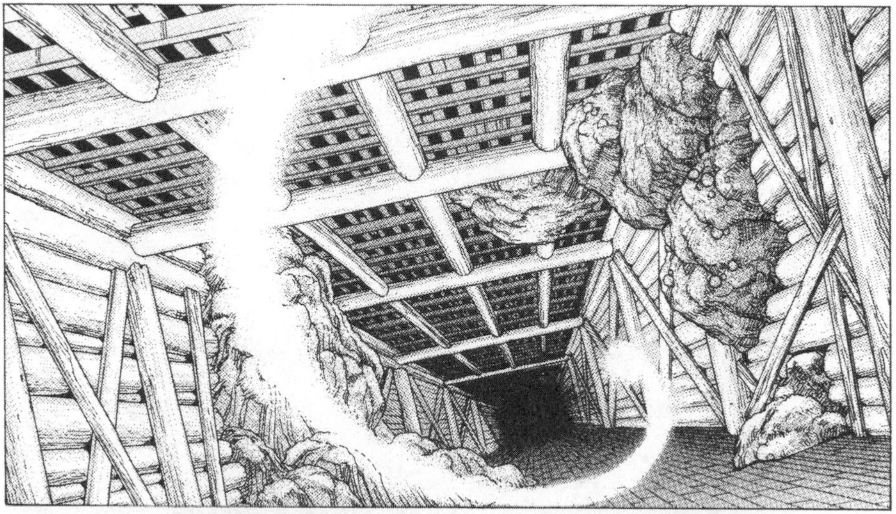

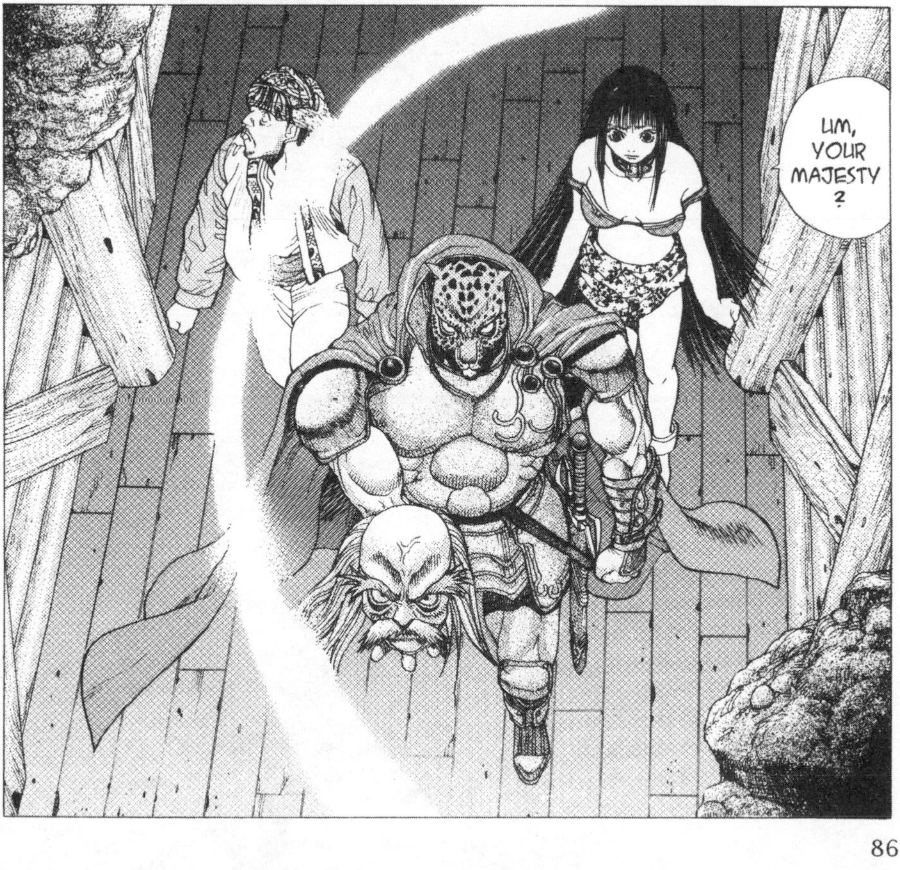
UM, YOUR MAJESTY ?

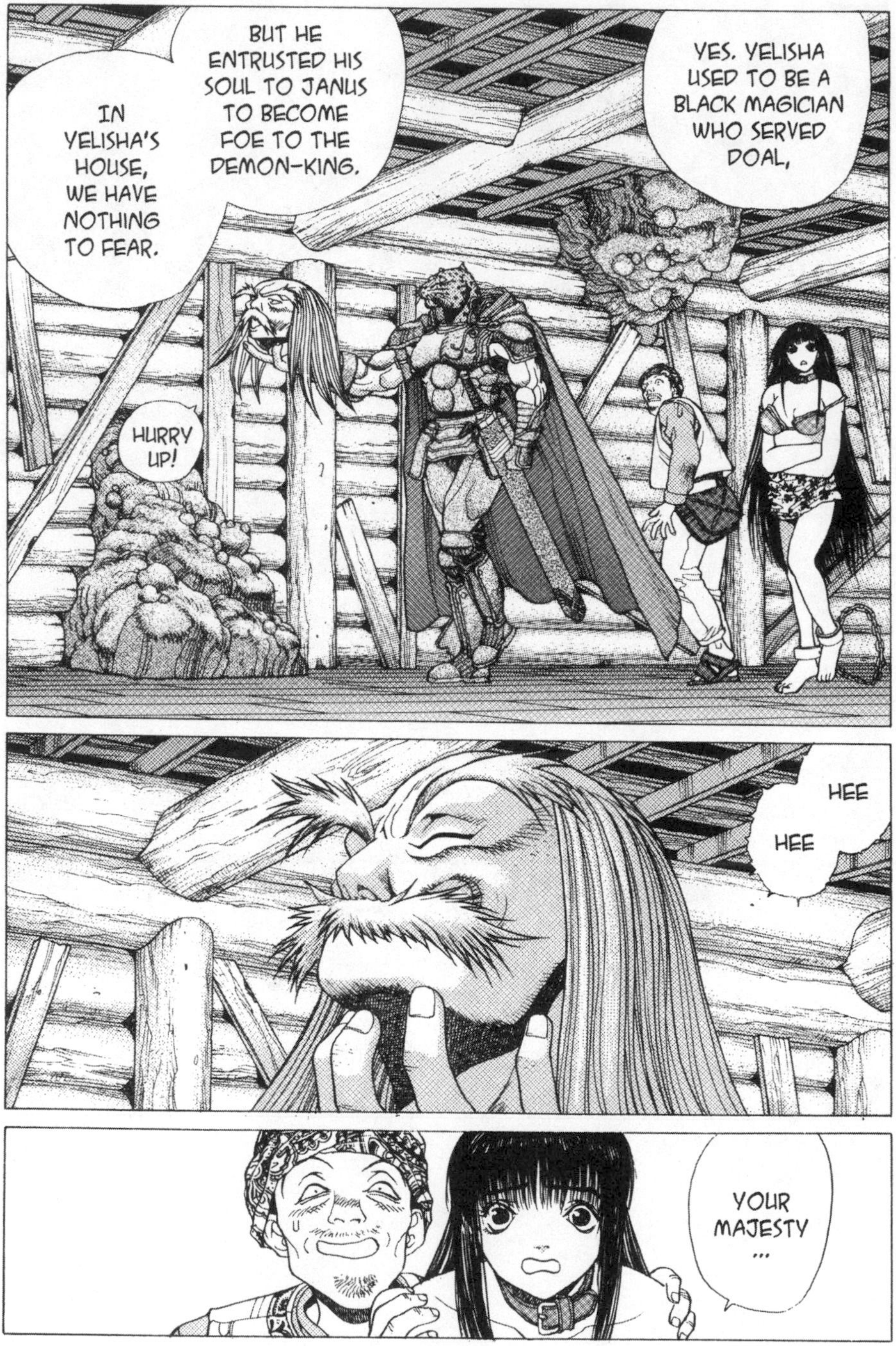
YES. YELISHA USED TO BE A BLACK MAGICIAN WHO SERVED DOAL,
BUT HE ENTRUSTED HIS SOUL TO JANUS TO BECOME FOE TO THE DEMON-KING.
IN YELISHA'S HOUSE, WE HAVE NOTHING TO FEAR.
HURRY UP!
HEE HEE
YOUR MAJESTY ...

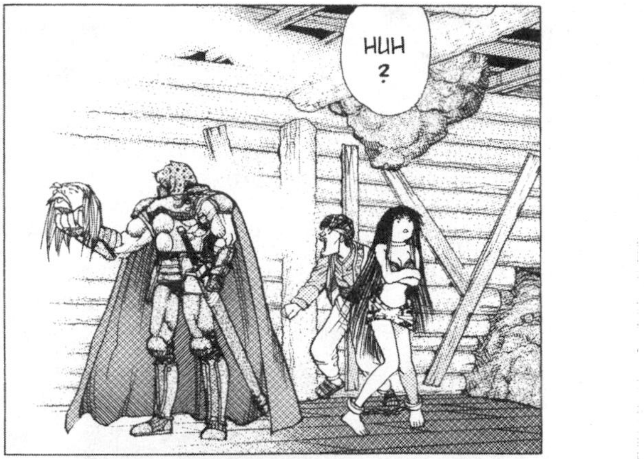
HUH?
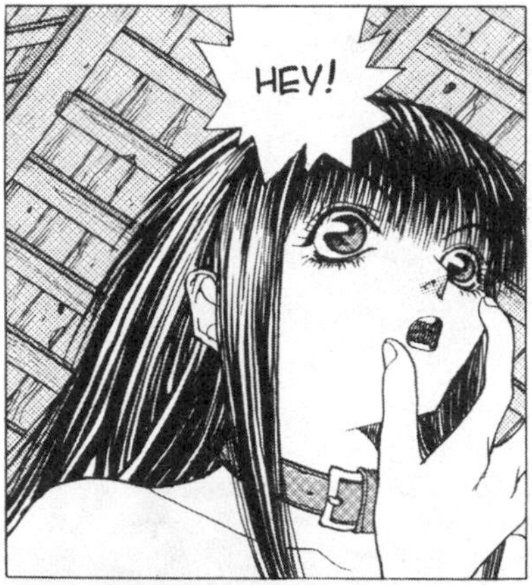
HEY!
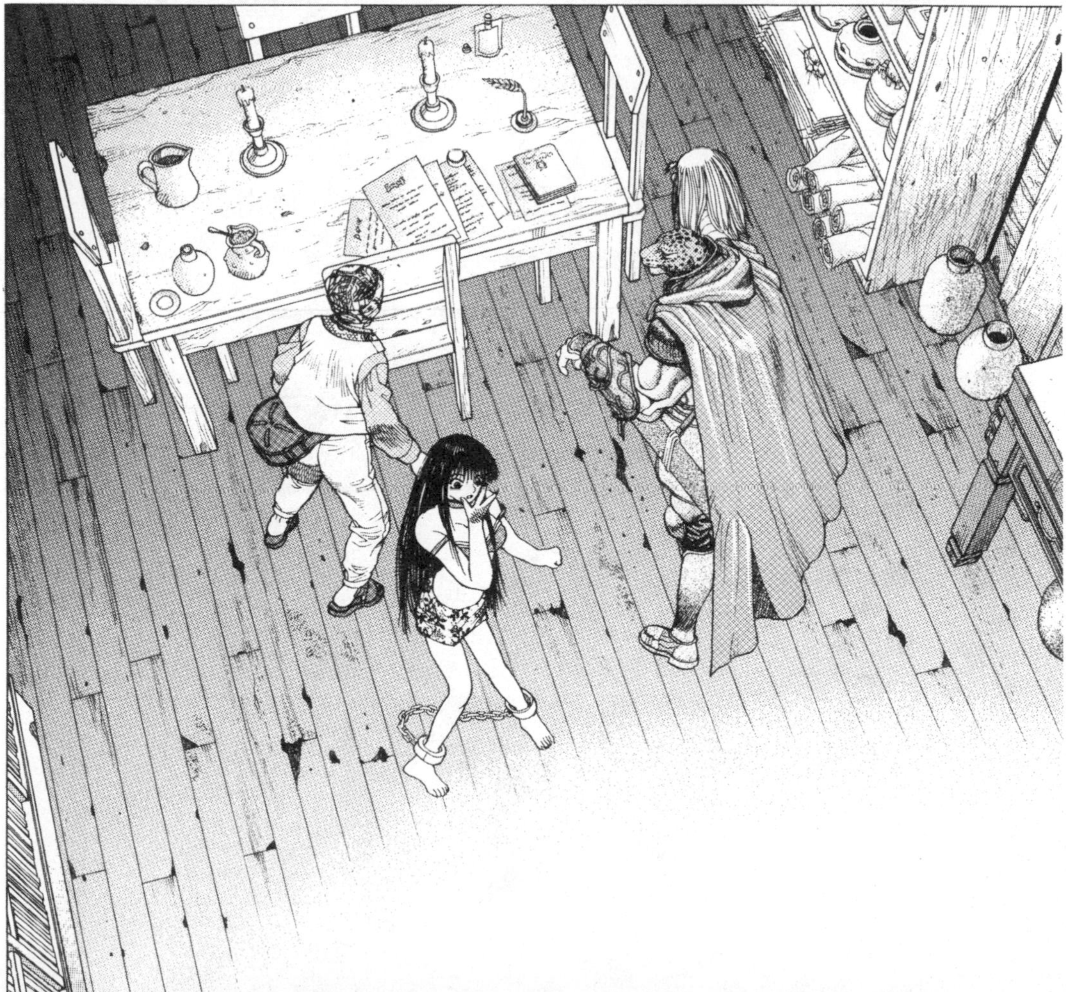

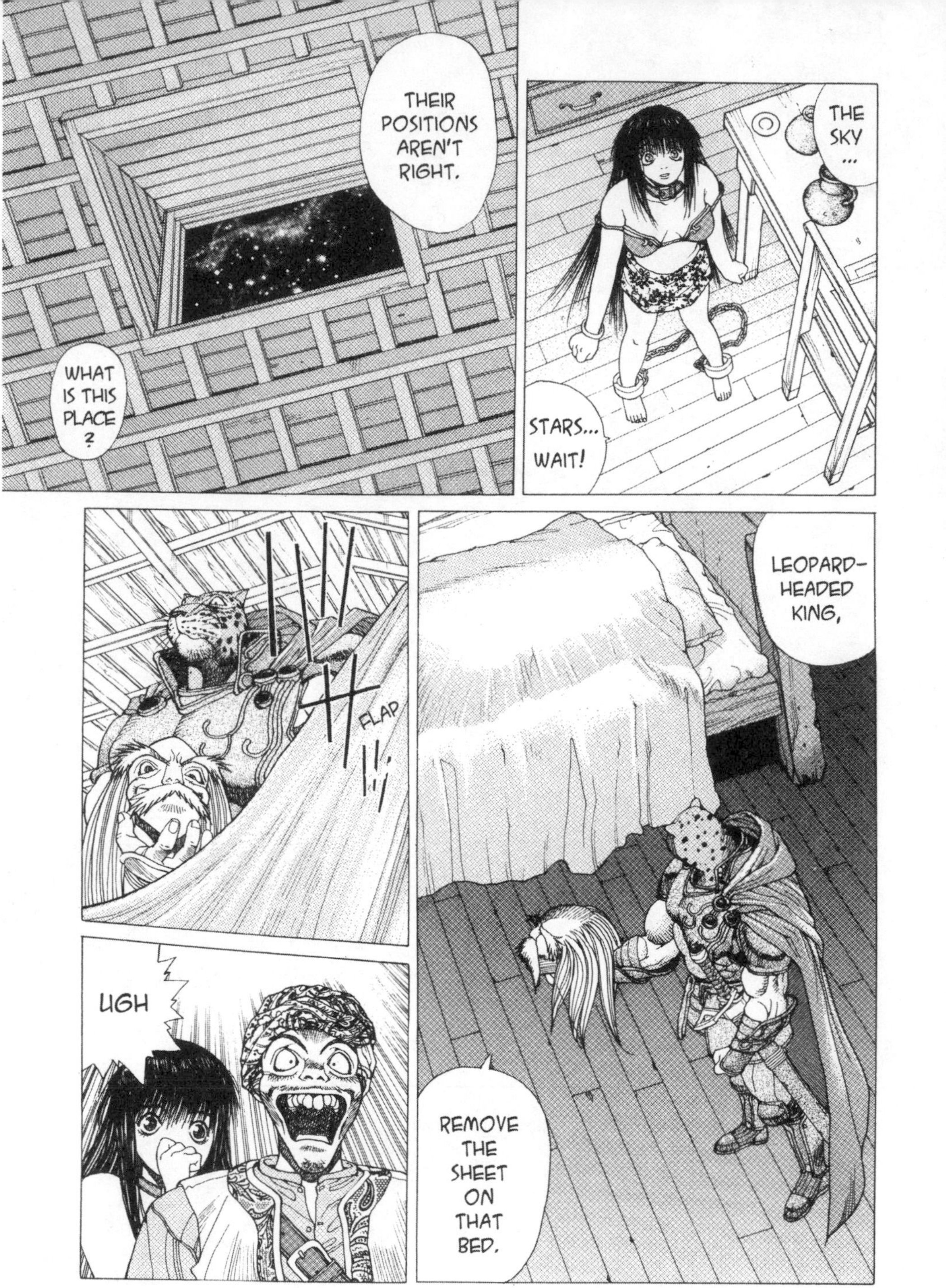
THE SKY ...
STARS... WAIT!
THEIR POSITIONS AREN'T RIGHT.
WHAT IS THIS PLACE ?
LEOPARD-HEADED KING,
REMOVE THE SHEET ON THAT BED.
FLAP
UGH

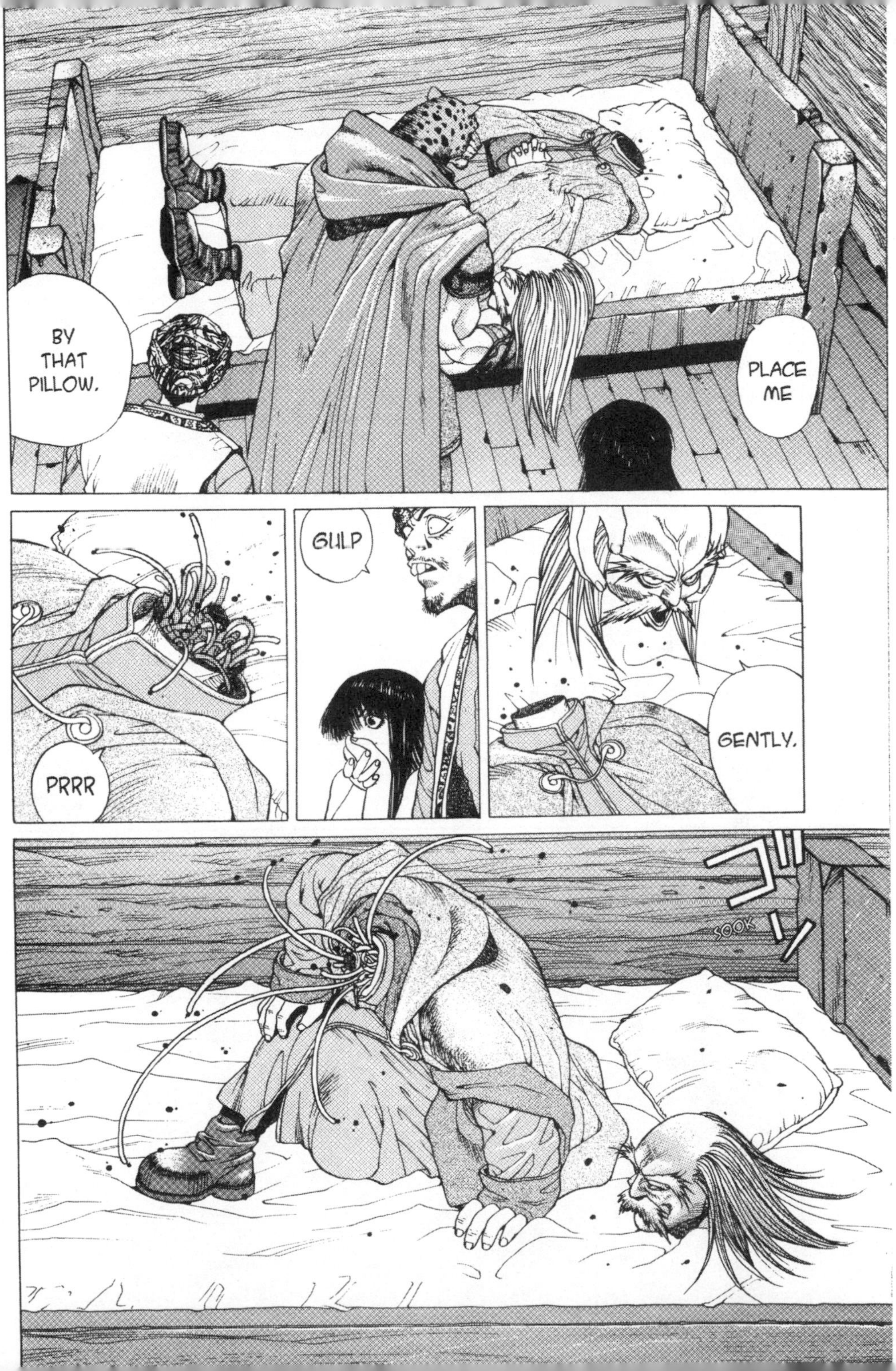
PLACE ME
BY THAT PILLOW.
GENTLY.
GULP
PRRR
SOOK

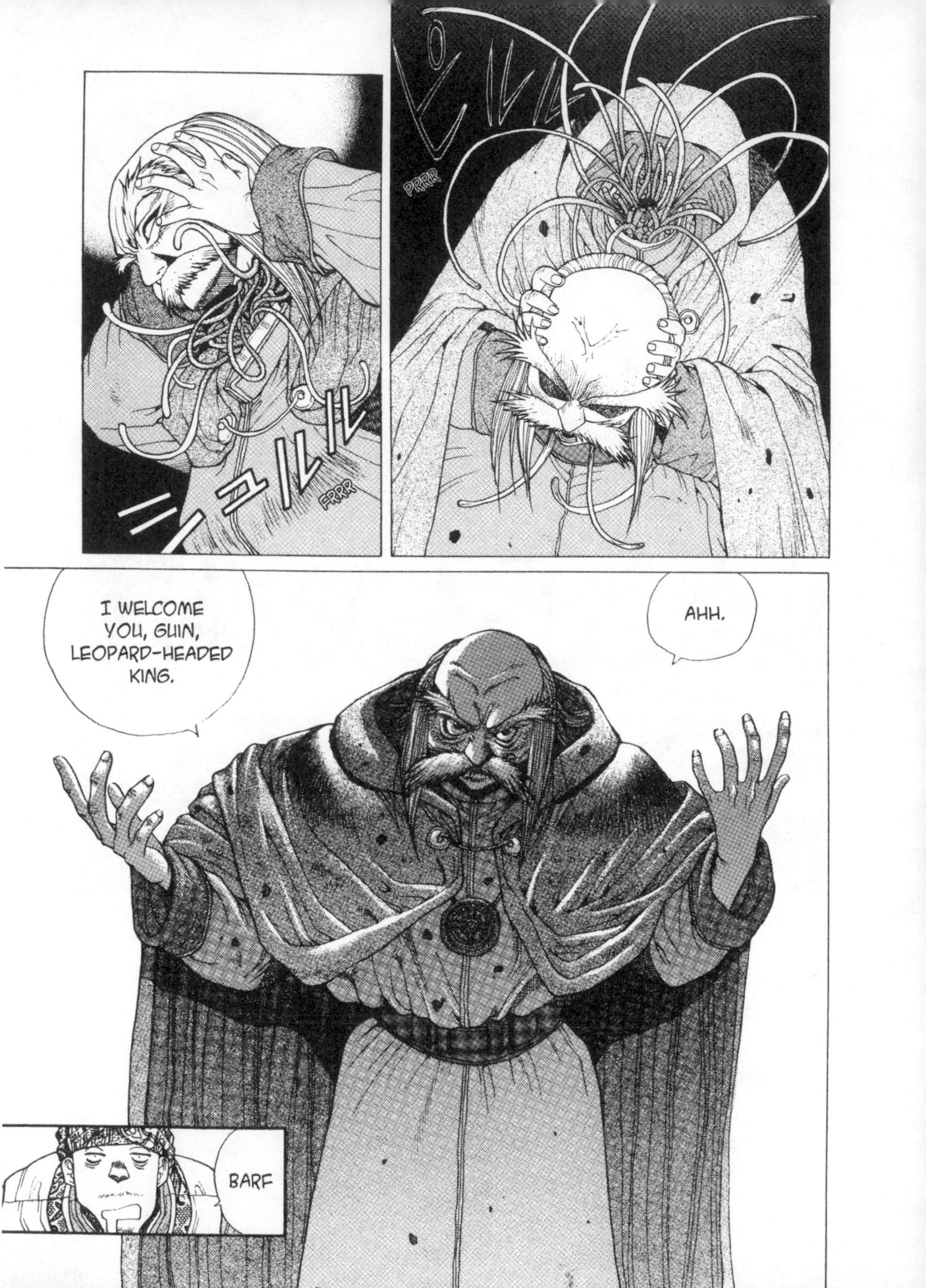
PRRR
FRRR
AHH.
I WELCOME YOU, GUIN, LEOPARD-HEADED KING.
BARF

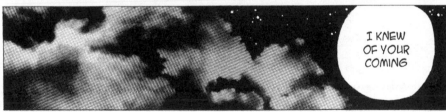

I KNEW
OF YOUR
COMING

FROM THE
POSITIONS
OF THE
HEAVENLY
BODIES.

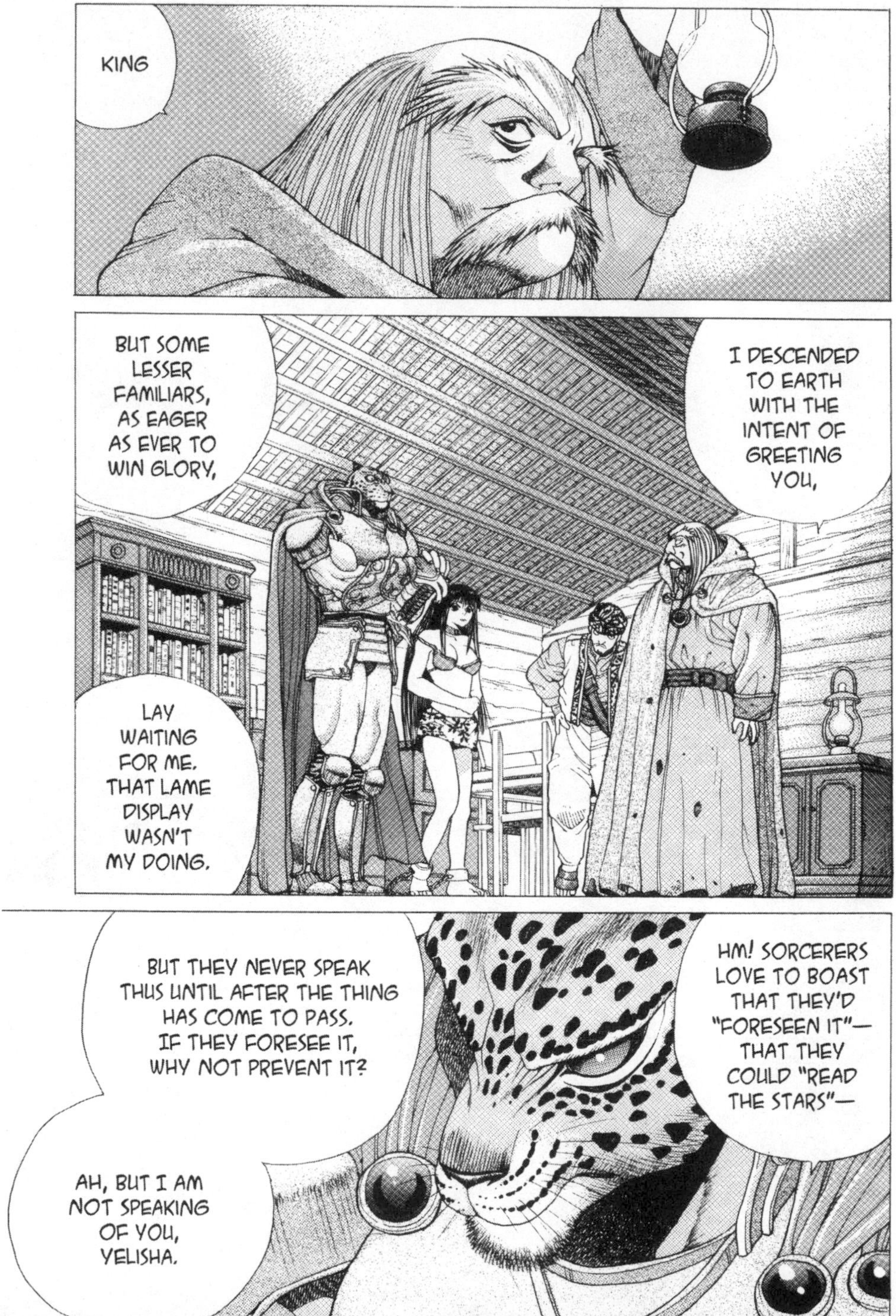
KING
I DESCENDED TO EARTH WITH THE INTENT OF GREETING YOU,
BUT SOME LESSER FAMILIARS, AS EAGER AS EVER TO WIN GLORY,
LAY WAITING FOR ME. THAT LAME DISPLAY WASN'T MY DOING.
HM! SORCERERS LOVE TO BOAST THAT THEY'D "FORESEEN IT"— THAT THEY COULD "READ THE STARS"—
BUT THEY NEVER SPEAK THUS UNTIL AFTER THE THING HAS COME TO PASS. IF THEY FORESEE IT, WHY NOT PREVENT IT?
AH, BUT I AM NOT SPEAKING OF YOU, YELISHA.

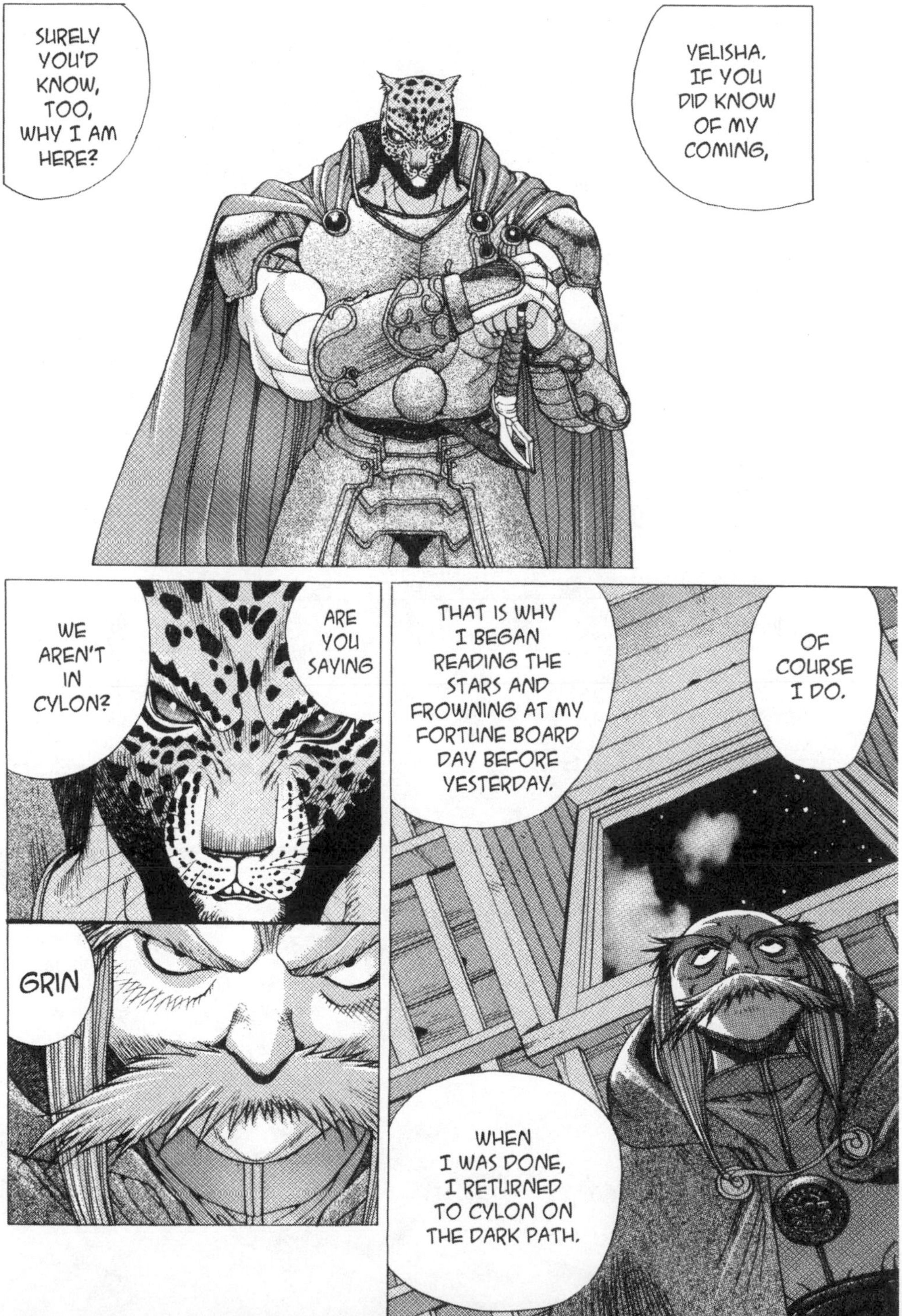
YELISHA. IF YOU DID KNOW OF MY COMING,
SURELY YOU'D KNOW, TOO, WHY I AM HERE?
OF COURSE I DO.
THAT IS WHY I BEGAN READING THE STARS AND FROWNING AT MY FORTUNE BOARD DAY BEFORE YESTERDAY.
WHEN I WAS DONE, I RETURNED TO CYLON ON THE DARK PATH.
ARE YOU SAYING
WE AREN'T IN CYLON?
GRIN

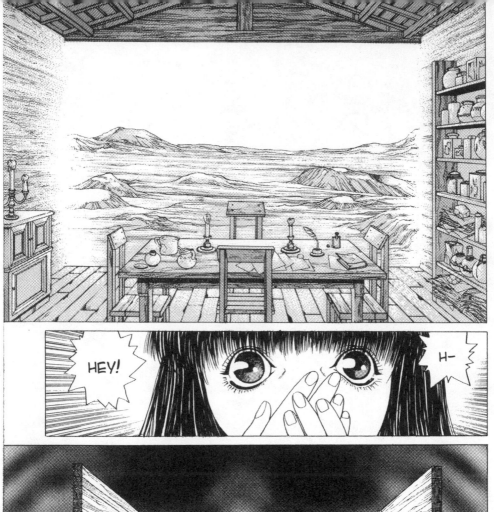

HEY!

H—

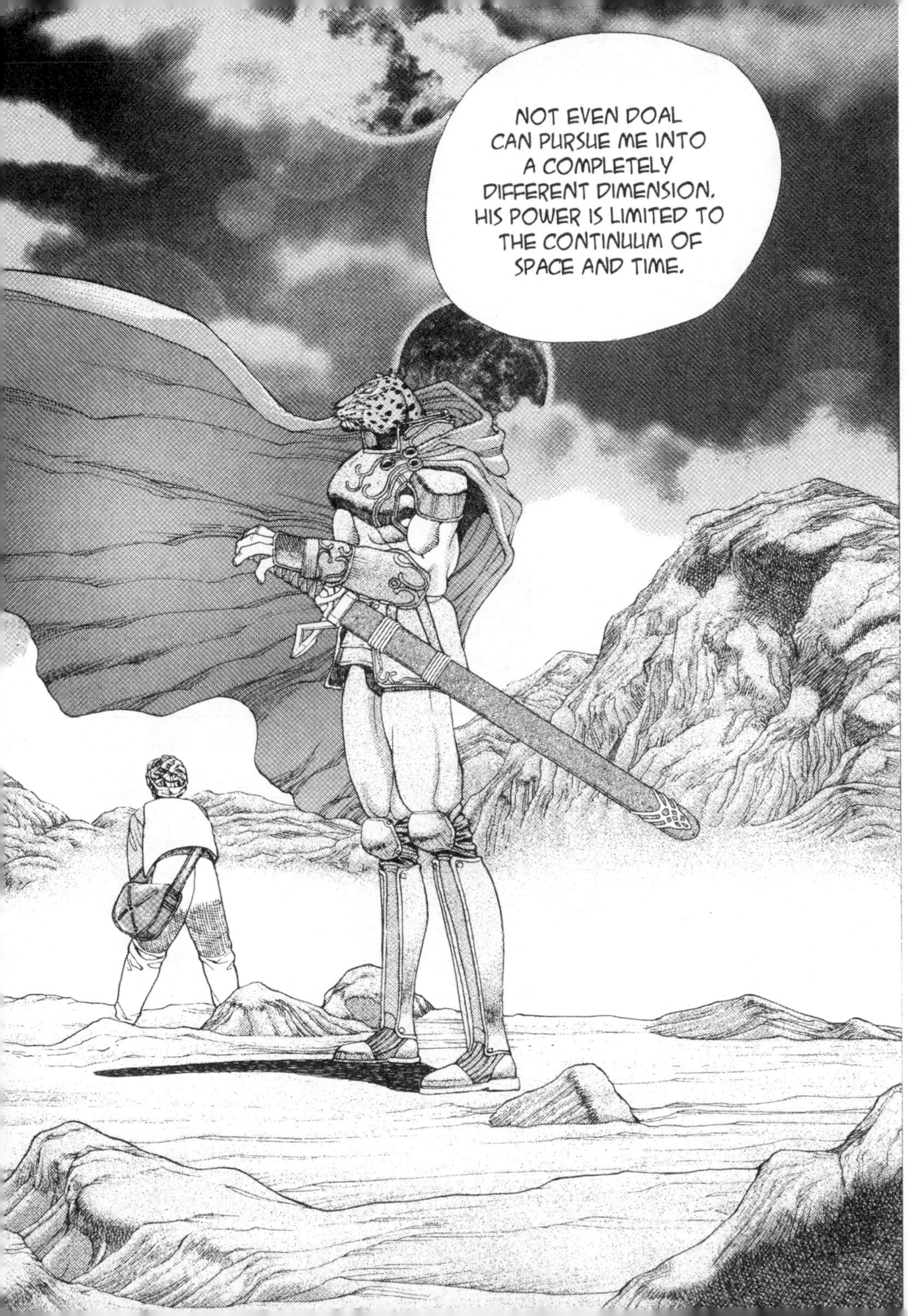
NOT EVEN DOAL CAN PURSUE ME INTO A COMPLETELY DIFFERENT DIMENSION. HIS POWER IS LIMITED TO THE CONTINUUM OF SPACE AND TIME.

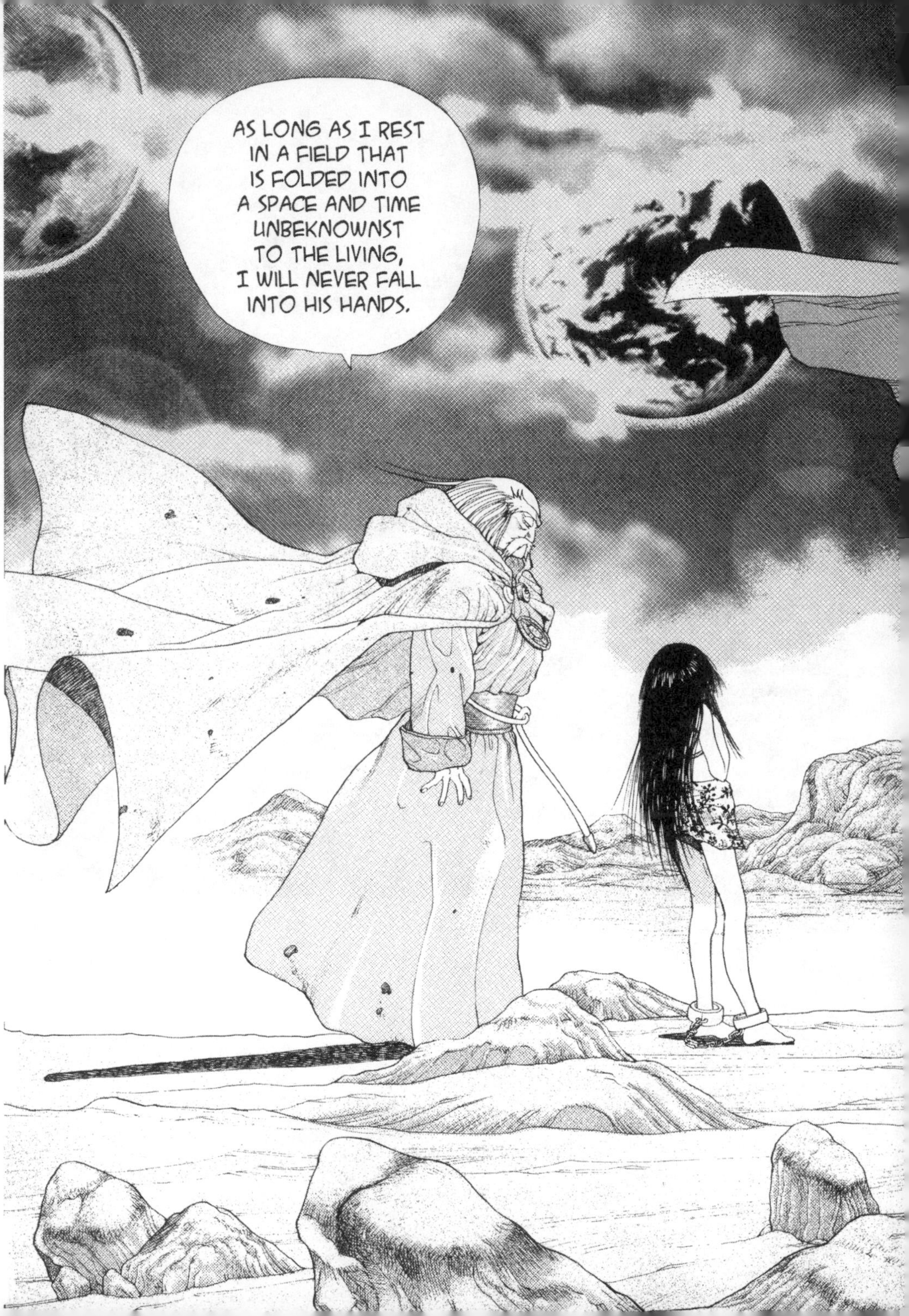
AS LONG AS I REST IN A FIELD THAT IS FOLDED INTO A SPACE AND TIME UNBEKNOWNST TO THE LIVING, I WILL NEVER FALL INTO HIS HANDS.

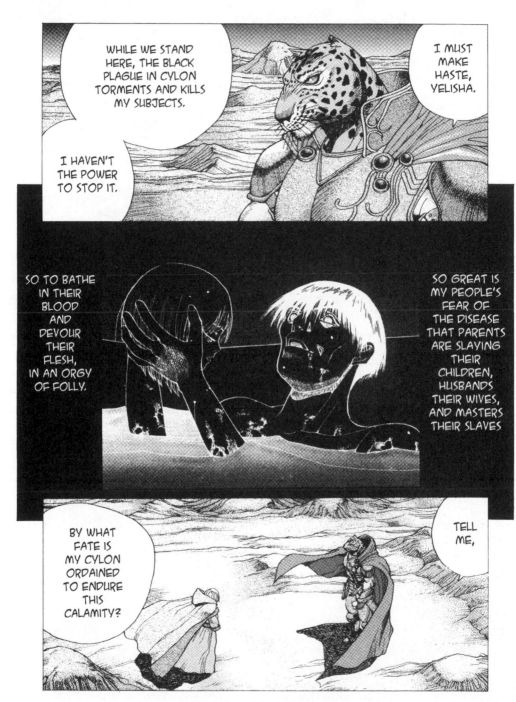

I MUST MAKE HASTE, YELISHA.
WHILE WE STAND HERE, THE BLACK PLAGUE IN CYLON TORMENTS AND KILLS MY SUBJECTS.
I HAVEN'T THE POWER TO STOP IT.
SO GREAT IS MY PEOPLE'S FEAR OF THE DISEASE THAT PARENTS ARE SLAYING THEIR CHILDREN, HUSBANDS THEIR WIVES, AND MASTERS THEIR SLAVES
SO TO BATHE IN THEIR BLOOD AND DEVOUR THEIR FLESH, IN AN ORGY OF FOLLY.
TELL ME,
BY WHAT FATE IS MY CYLON ORDAINED TO ENDURE THIS CALAMITY?

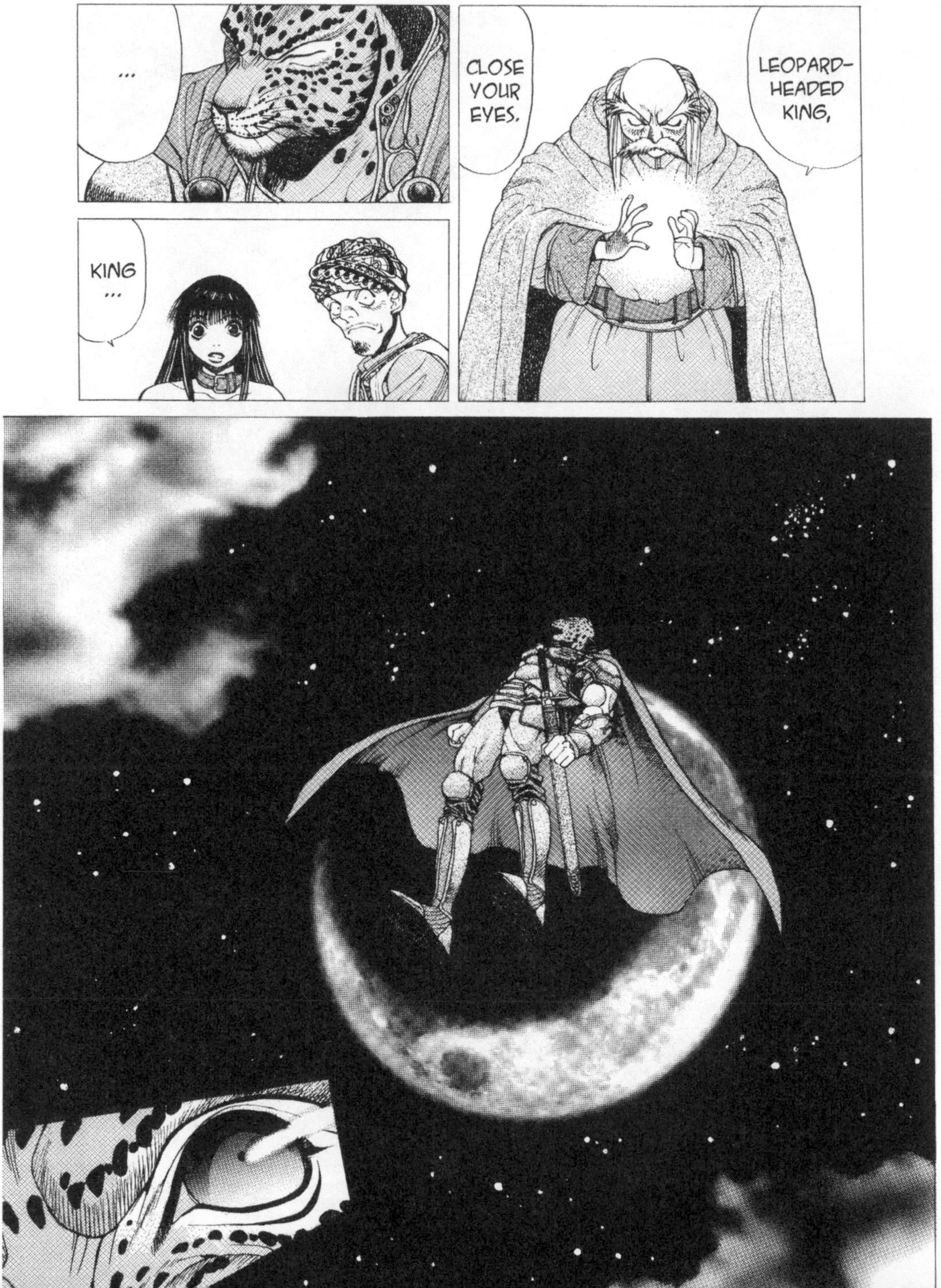
LEOPARD-HEADED KING,
CLOSE YOUR EYES.
...
KING ...

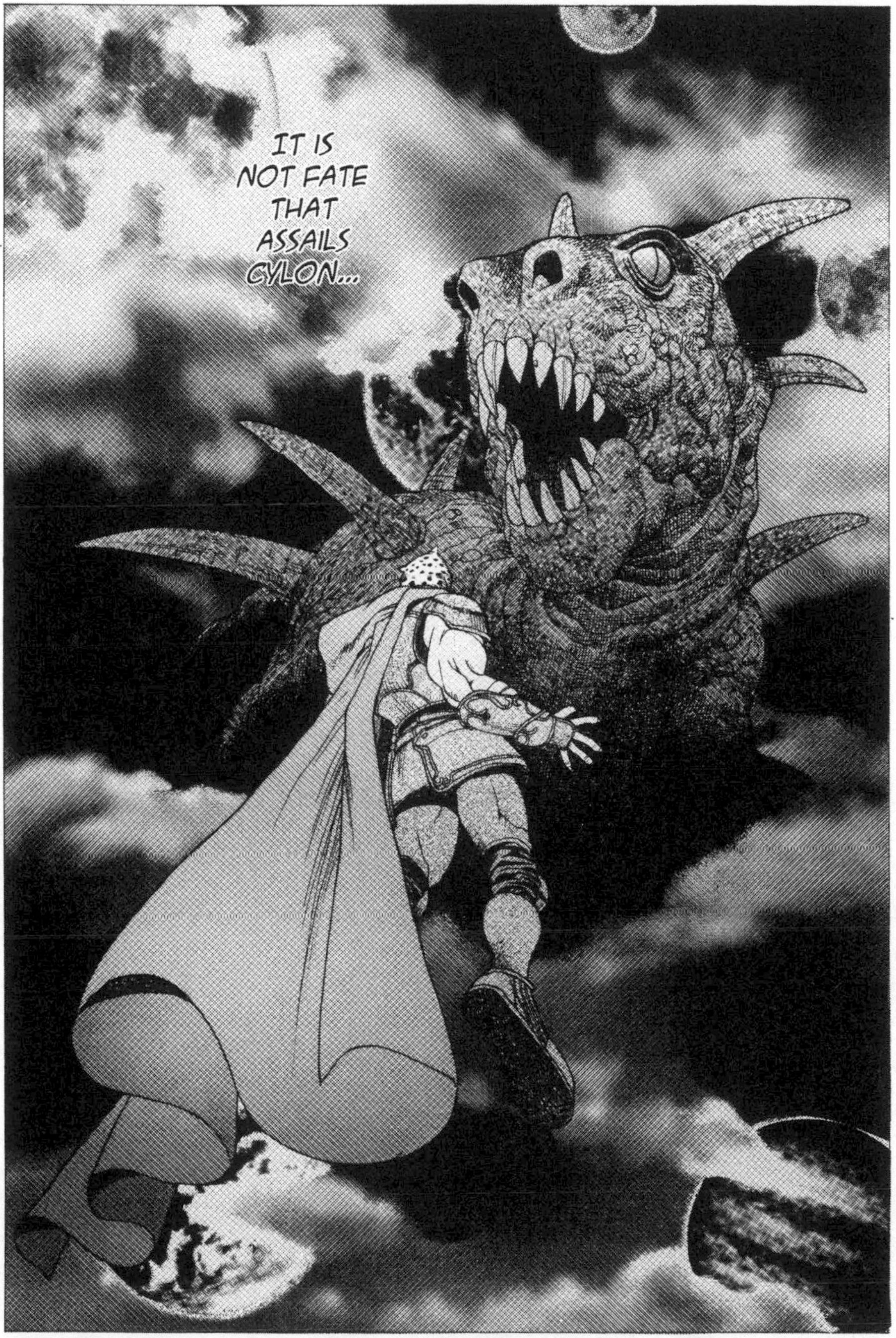
IT IS NOT FATE THAT ASSAILS CYLON...

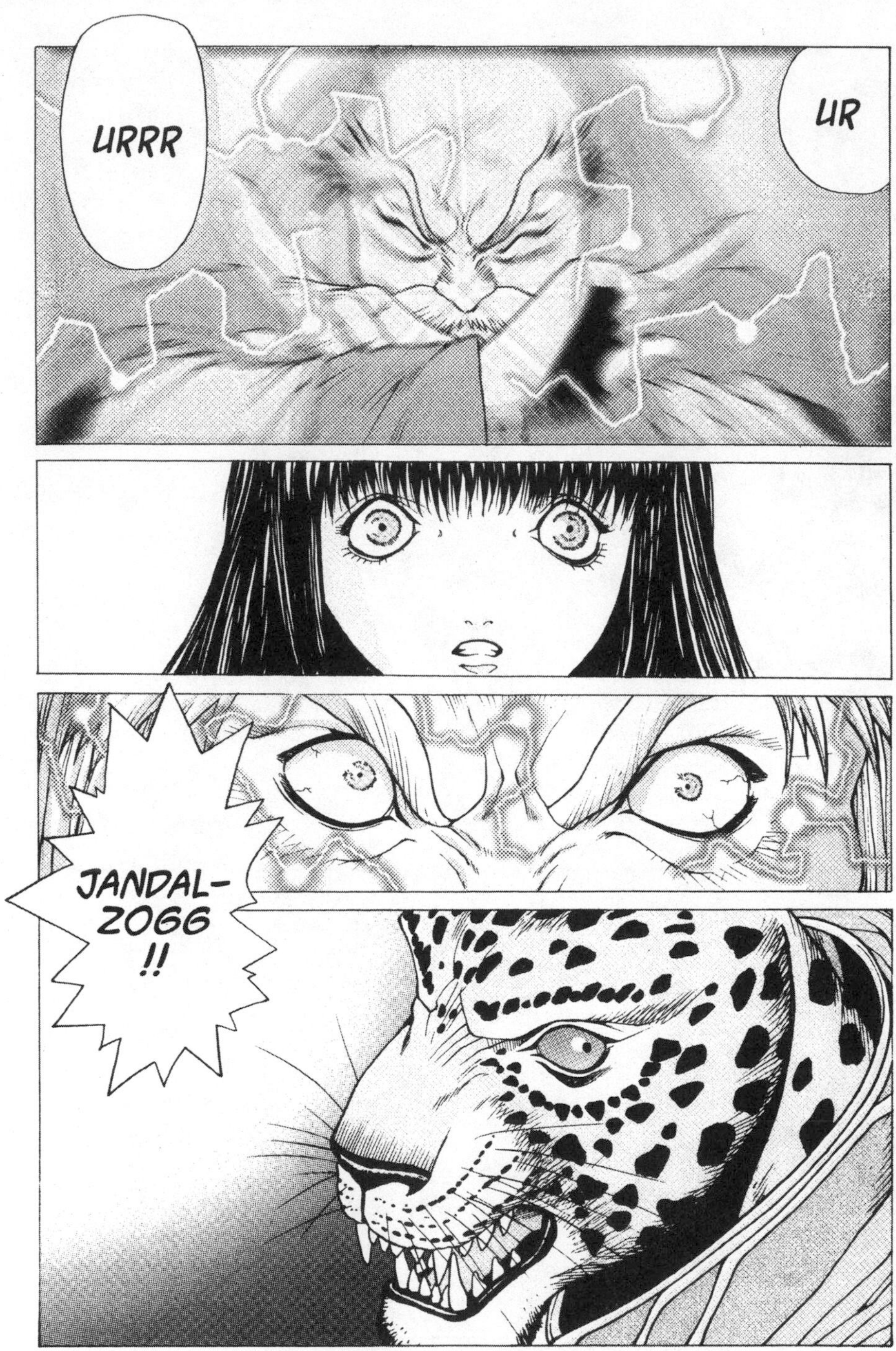
UR
URRR
JANDAL-
ZOGG
!!

CHAPTER 5

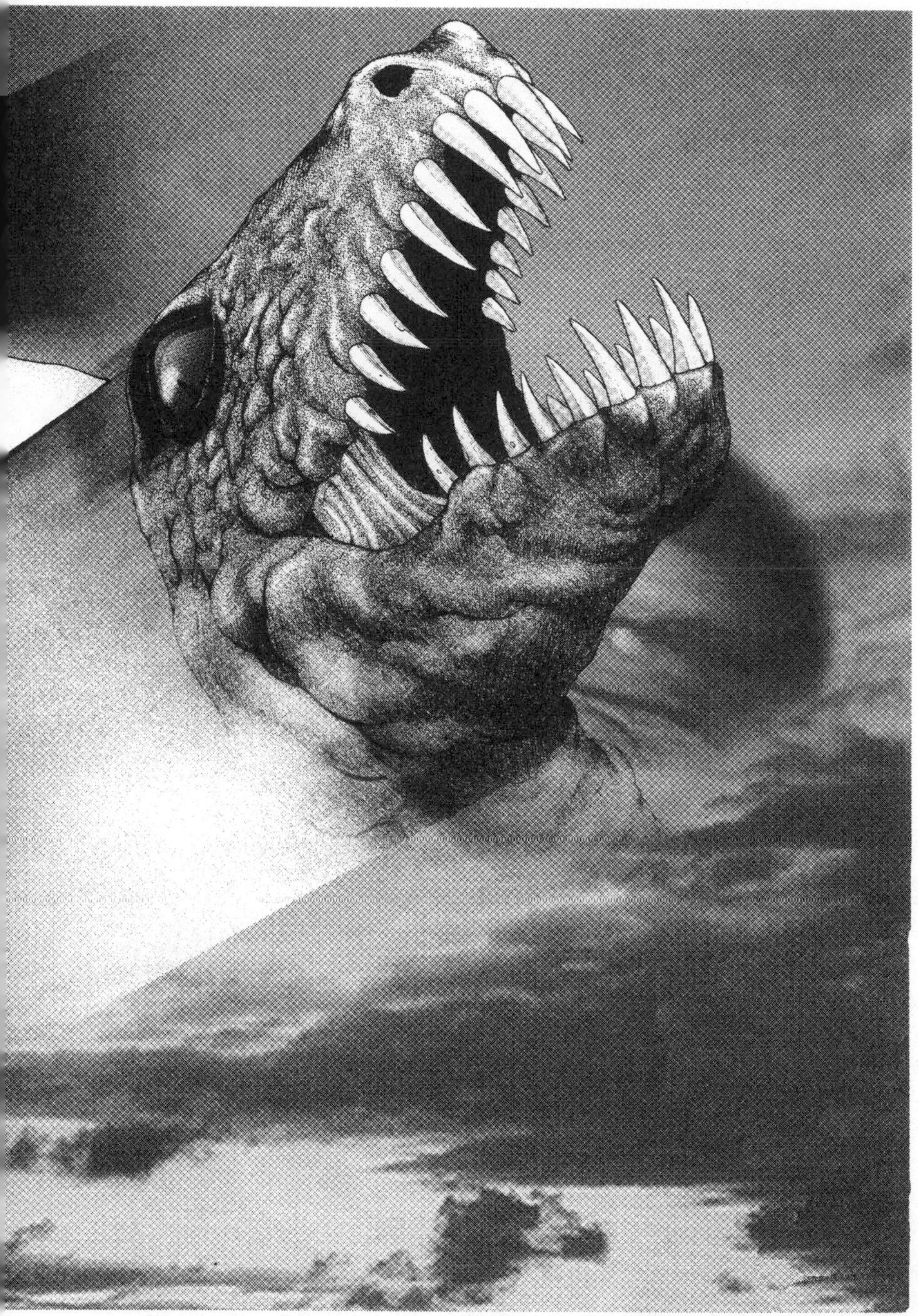

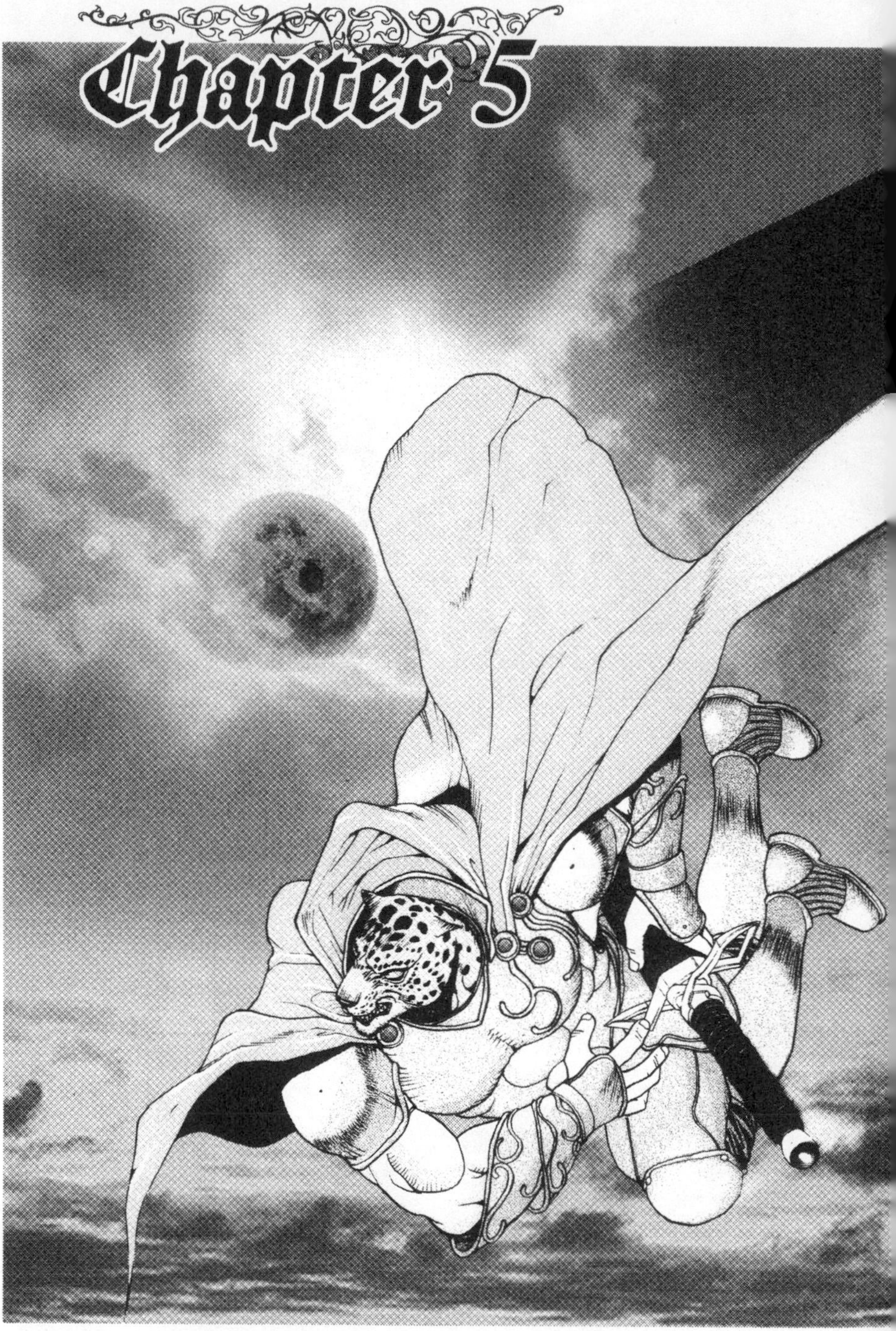
Chapter 5

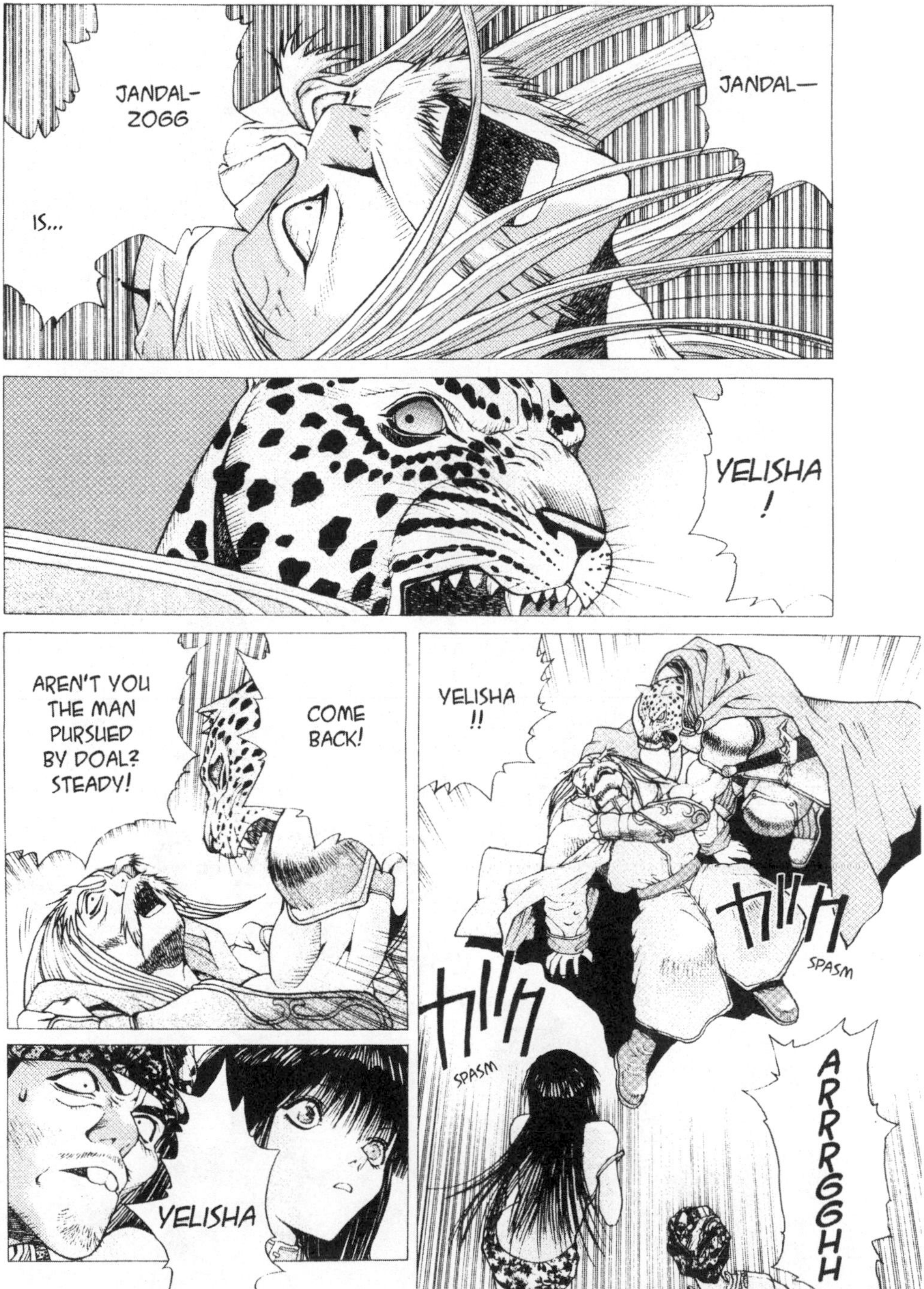
JANDAL—
JANDAL-ZOGG
IS...
YELISHA !
YELISHA !!
SPASM
SPASM
ARRRGGHH
COME BACK!
AREN'T YOU THE MAN PURSUED BY DOAL? STEADY!
YELISHA

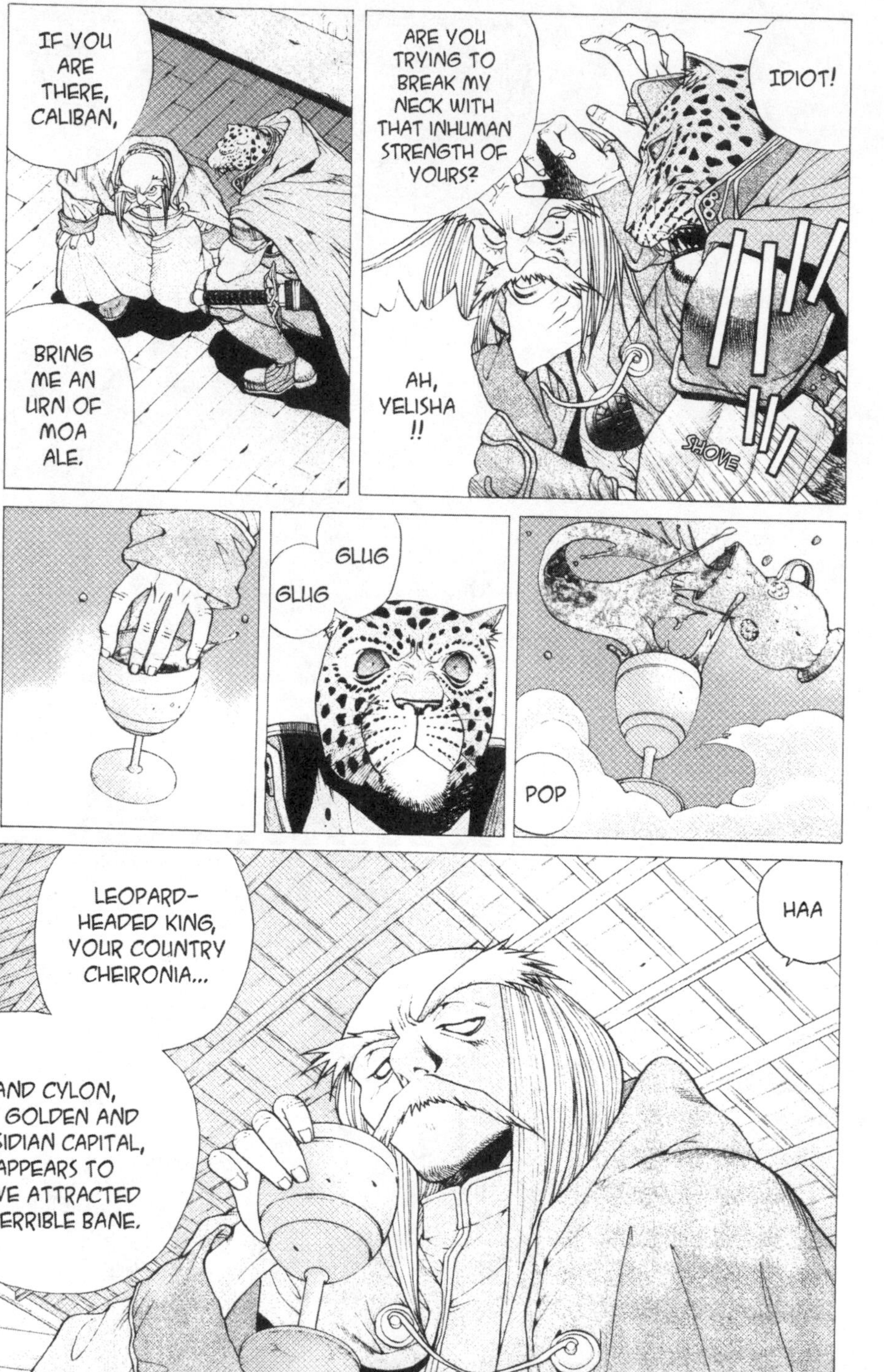
IDIOT!
ARE YOU TRYING TO BREAK MY NECK WITH THAT INHUMAN STRENGTH OF YOURS?
SHOVE
AH, YELISHA !!
IF YOU ARE THERE, CALIBAN,
BRING ME AN URN OF MOA ALE.
POP
GLUG
GLUG
HAA
LEOPARD-HEADED KING, YOUR COUNTRY CHEIRONIA...
AND CYLON, ITS GOLDEN AND OBSIDIAN CAPITAL, APPEARS TO HAVE ATTRACTED A TERRIBLE BANE.

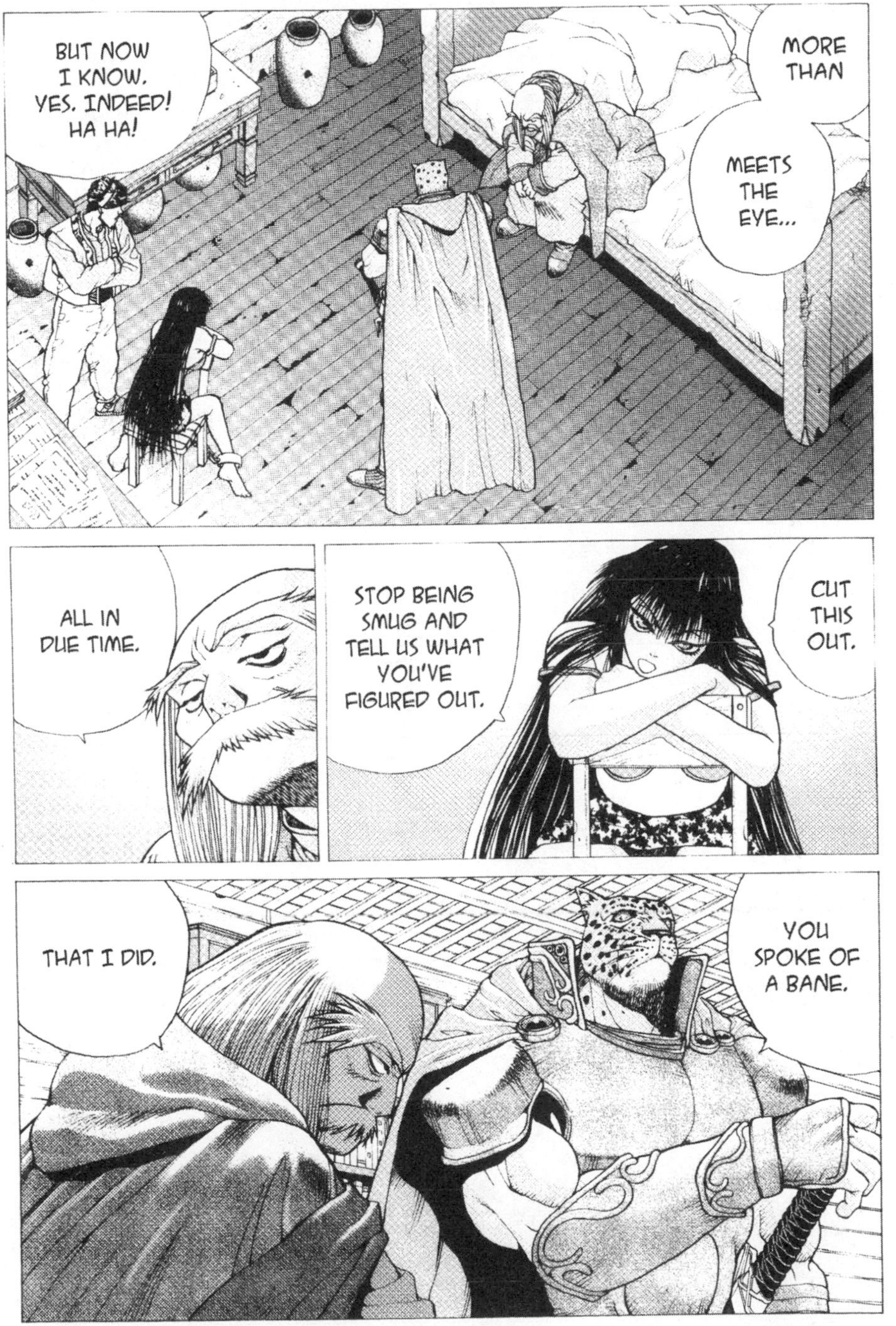
MORE THAN
MEETS THE EYE...
BUT NOW I KNOW. YES. INDEED! HA HA!
CUT THIS OUT.
STOP BEING SMUG AND TELL US WHAT YOU'VE FIGURED OUT.
ALL IN DUE TIME.
YOU SPOKE OF A BANE.
THAT I DID.

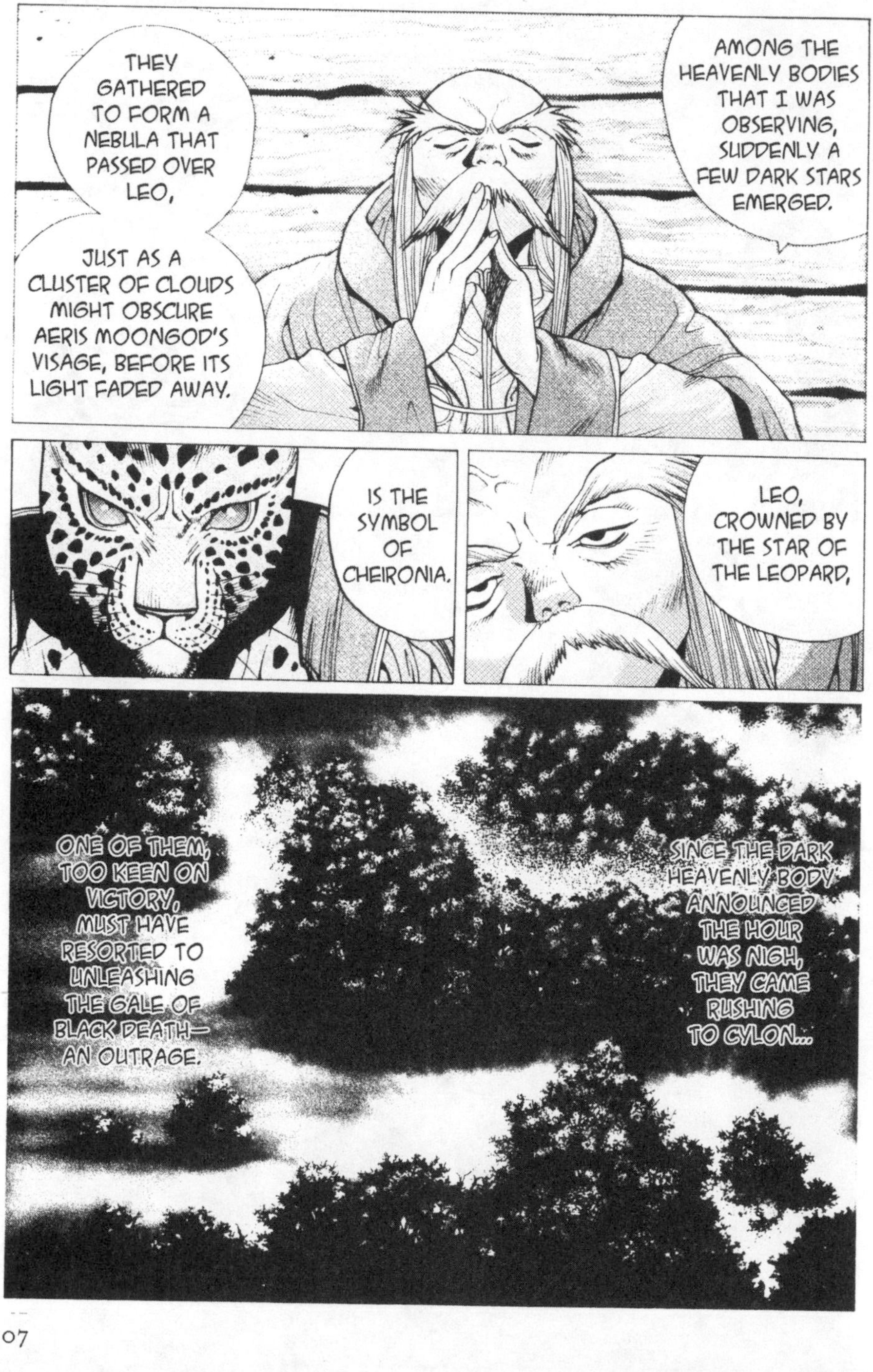
AMONG THE HEAVENLY BODIES THAT I WAS OBSERVING, SUDDENLY A FEW DARK STARS EMERGED.
THEY GATHERED TO FORM A NEBULA THAT PASSED OVER LEO,
JUST AS A CLUSTER OF CLOUDS MIGHT OBSCURE AERIS MOONGOD'S VISAGE, BEFORE ITS LIGHT FADED AWAY.
LEO, CROWNED BY THE STAR OF THE LEOPARD,
IS THE SYMBOL OF CHEIRONIA.
SINCE THE DARK HEAVENLY BODY ANNOUNCED THE HOUR WAS NIGH, THEY CAME RUSHING TO CYLON...
ONE OF THEM, TOO KEEN ON VICTORY, MUST HAVE RESORTED TO UNLEASHING THE GALE OF BLACK DEATH—AN OUTRAGE.

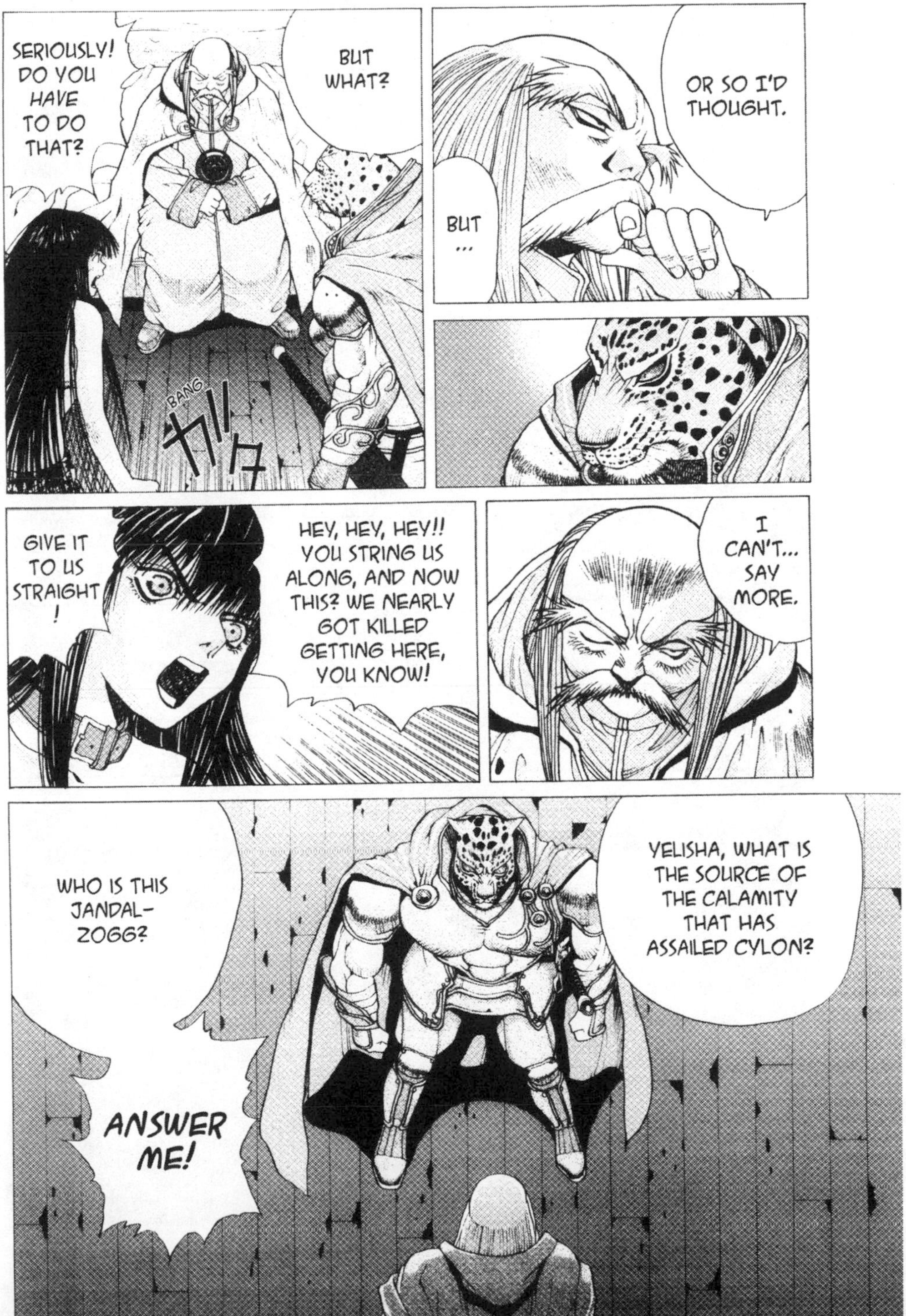
OR SO I'D THOUGHT.
BUT ...
BUT WHAT?
SERIOUSLY! DO YOU HAVE TO DO THAT?
BANG
I CAN'T... SAY MORE.
HEY, HEY, HEY!! YOU STRING US ALONG, AND NOW THIS? WE NEARLY GOT KILLED GETTING HERE, YOU KNOW!
GIVE IT TO US STRAIGHT!
YELISHA, WHAT IS THE SOURCE OF THE CALAMITY THAT HAS ASSAILED CYLON?
WHO IS THIS JANDAL-ZOGG?
ANSWER ME!

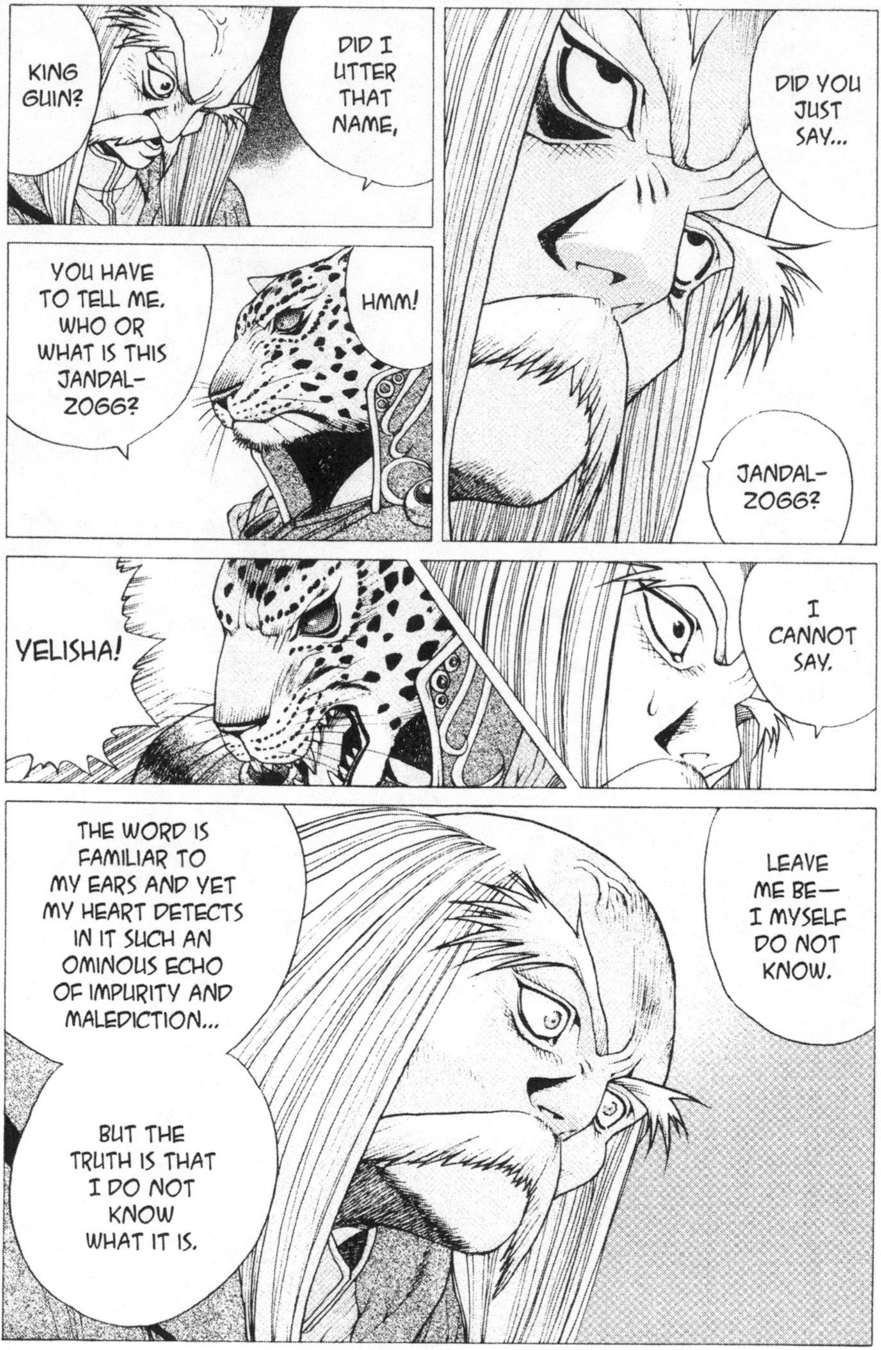
DID YOU JUST SAY...
JANDAL-ZOGG?
DID I UTTER THAT NAME,
KING GUIN?
HMM!
YOU HAVE TO TELL ME. WHO OR WHAT IS THIS JANDAL-ZOGG?
I CANNOT SAY.
YELISHA!
LEAVE ME BE— I MYSELF DO NOT KNOW.
THE WORD IS FAMILIAR TO MY EARS AND YET MY HEART DETECTS IN IT SUCH AN OMINOUS ECHO OF IMPURITY AND MALEDICTION...
BUT THE TRUTH IS THAT I DO NOT KNOW WHAT IT IS.

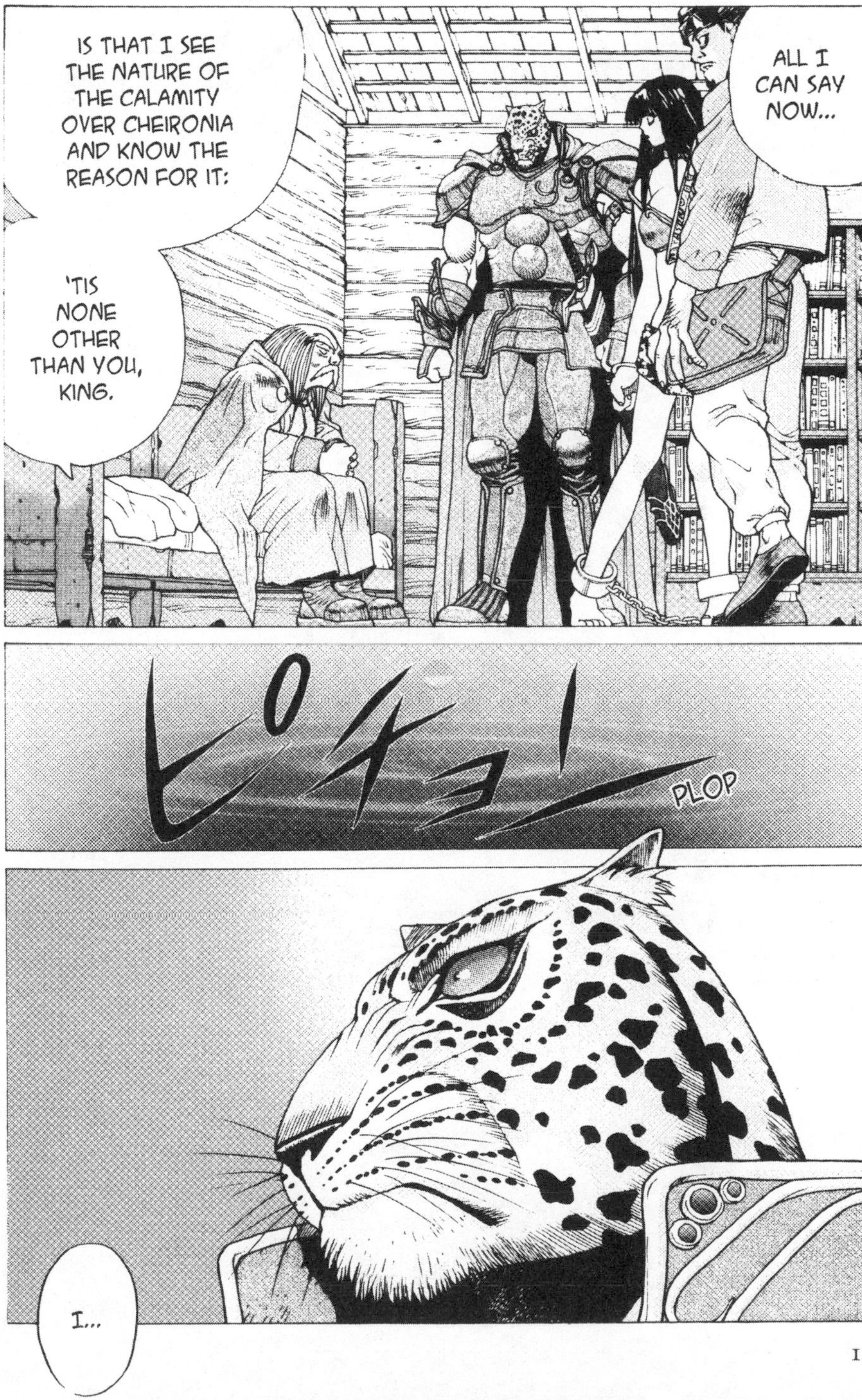
ALL I CAN SAY NOW...
IS THAT I SEE THE NATURE OF THE CALAMITY OVER CHEIRONIA AND KNOW THE REASON FOR IT:
'TIS NONE OTHER THAN YOU, KING.
PLOP
I...

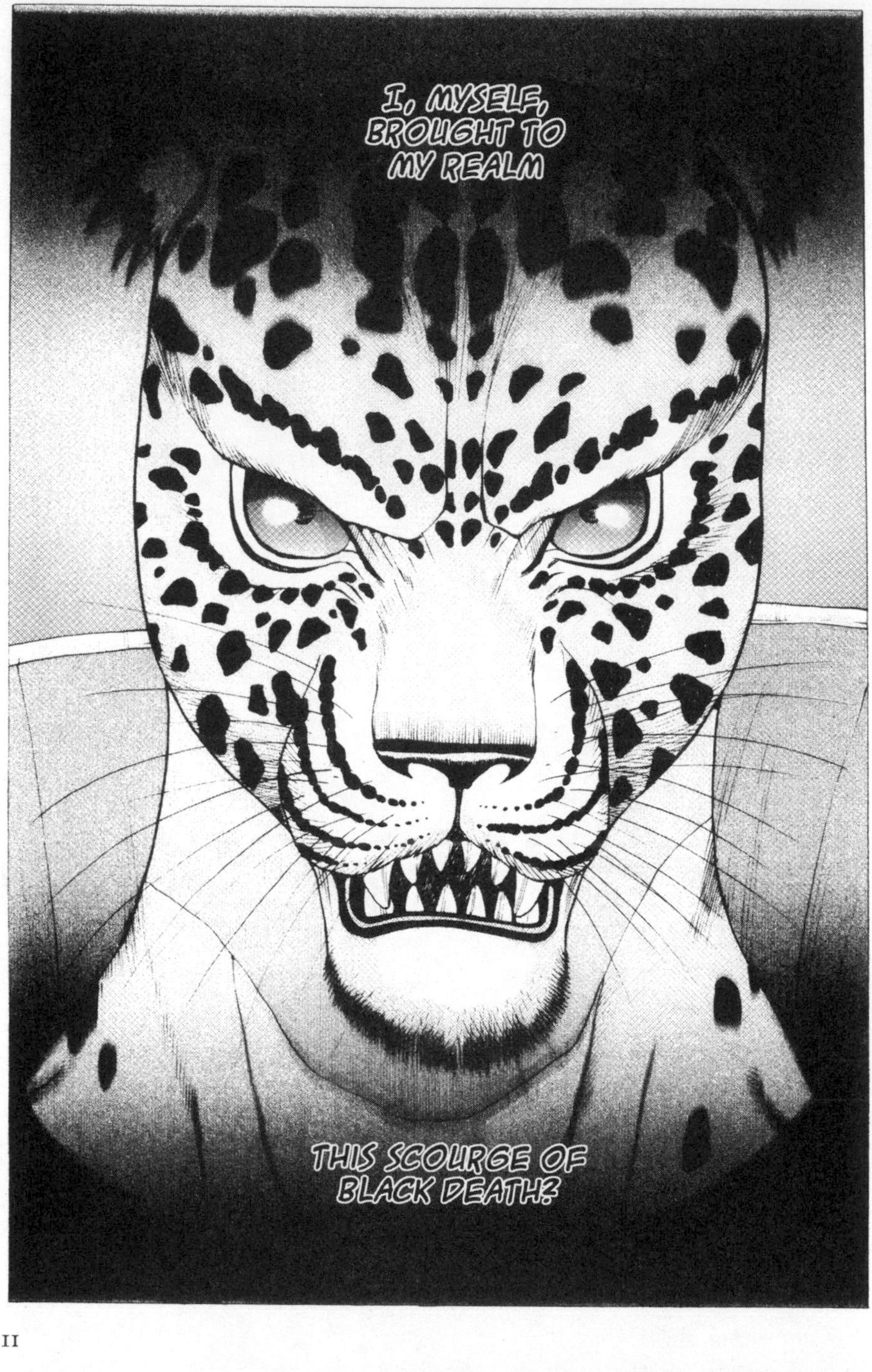
I, MYSELF, BROUGHT TO MY REALM
THIS SCOURGE OF BLACK DEATH?

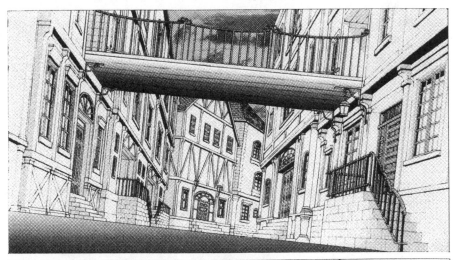

I AM NOT SAYING THAT YOU OPENED THE GATES OF DEATH WITH YOUR OWN HANDS TO UNLEASH THE FATAL GALE.
LEOPARD-HEADED KING...
YOUR BEING, YOUR RARE SOUL SUMMONS THE EXTRAORDINARY
TO YOUR ENVIRONS—GOOD AND ILL FORTUNE.
THAT IS WHO YOU ARE.

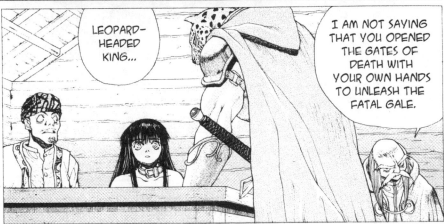

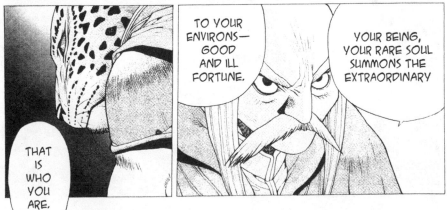

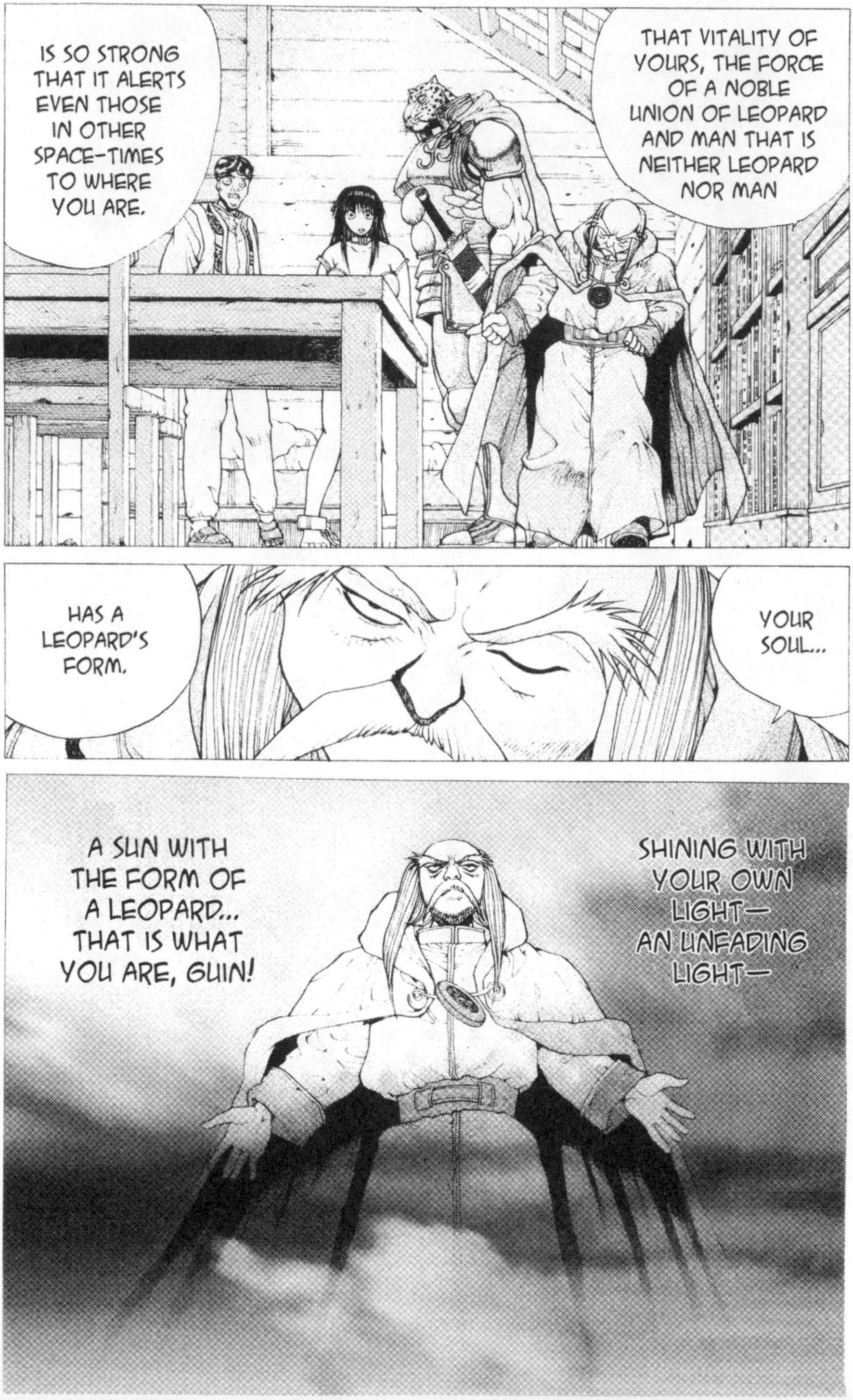
THAT VITALITY OF YOURS, THE FORCE OF A NOBLE UNION OF LEOPARD AND MAN THAT IS NEITHER LEOPARD NOR MAN
IS SO STRONG THAT IT ALERTS EVEN THOSE IN OTHER SPACE-TIMES TO WHERE YOU ARE.
YOUR SOUL...
HAS A LEOPARD'S FORM.
SHINING WITH YOUR OWN LIGHT— AN UNFADING LIGHT—
A SUN WITH THE FORM OF A LEOPARD... THAT IS WHAT YOU ARE, GUIN!

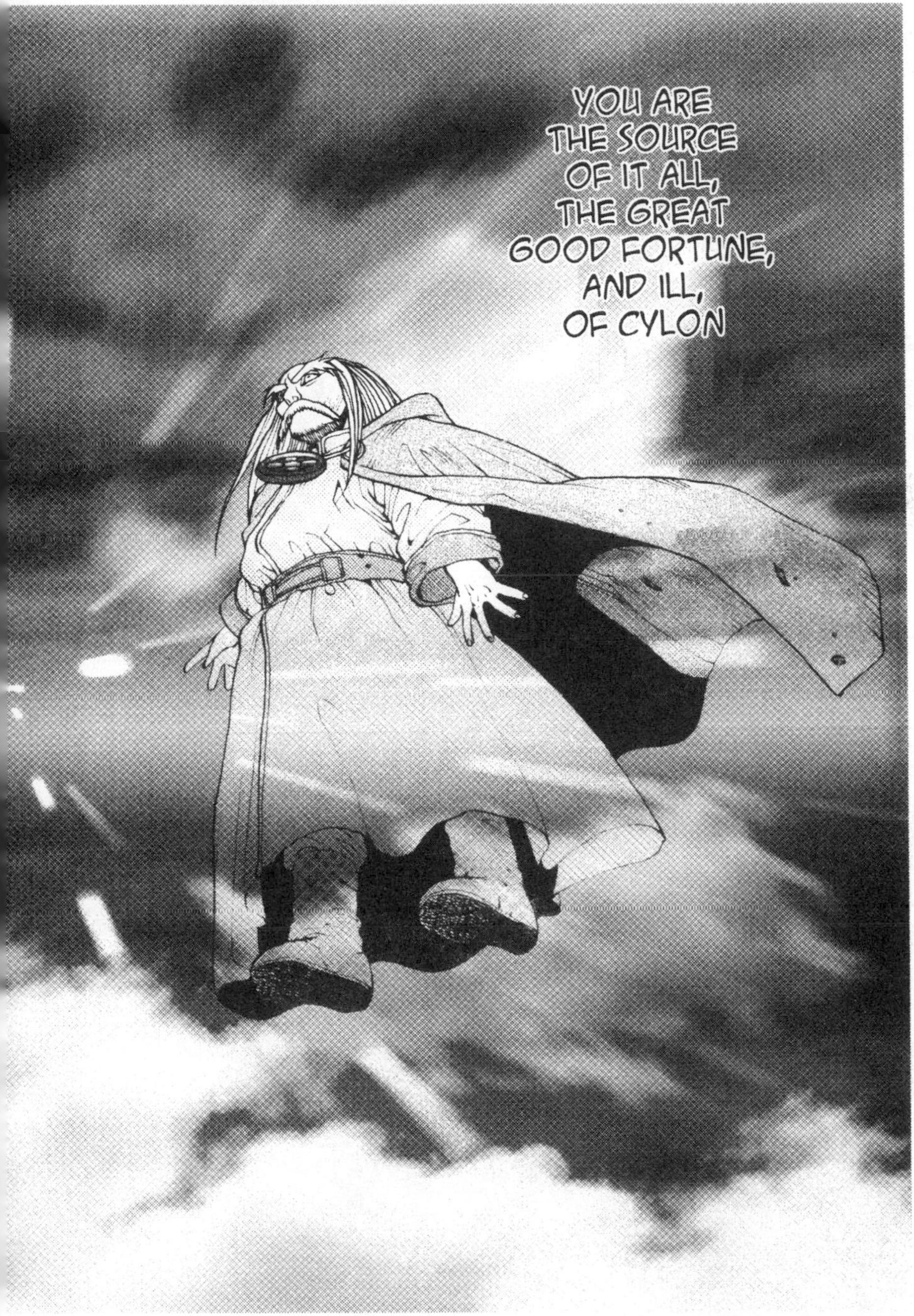
YOU ARE THE SOURCE OF IT ALL, THE GREAT GOOD FORTUNE, AND ILL, OF CYLON

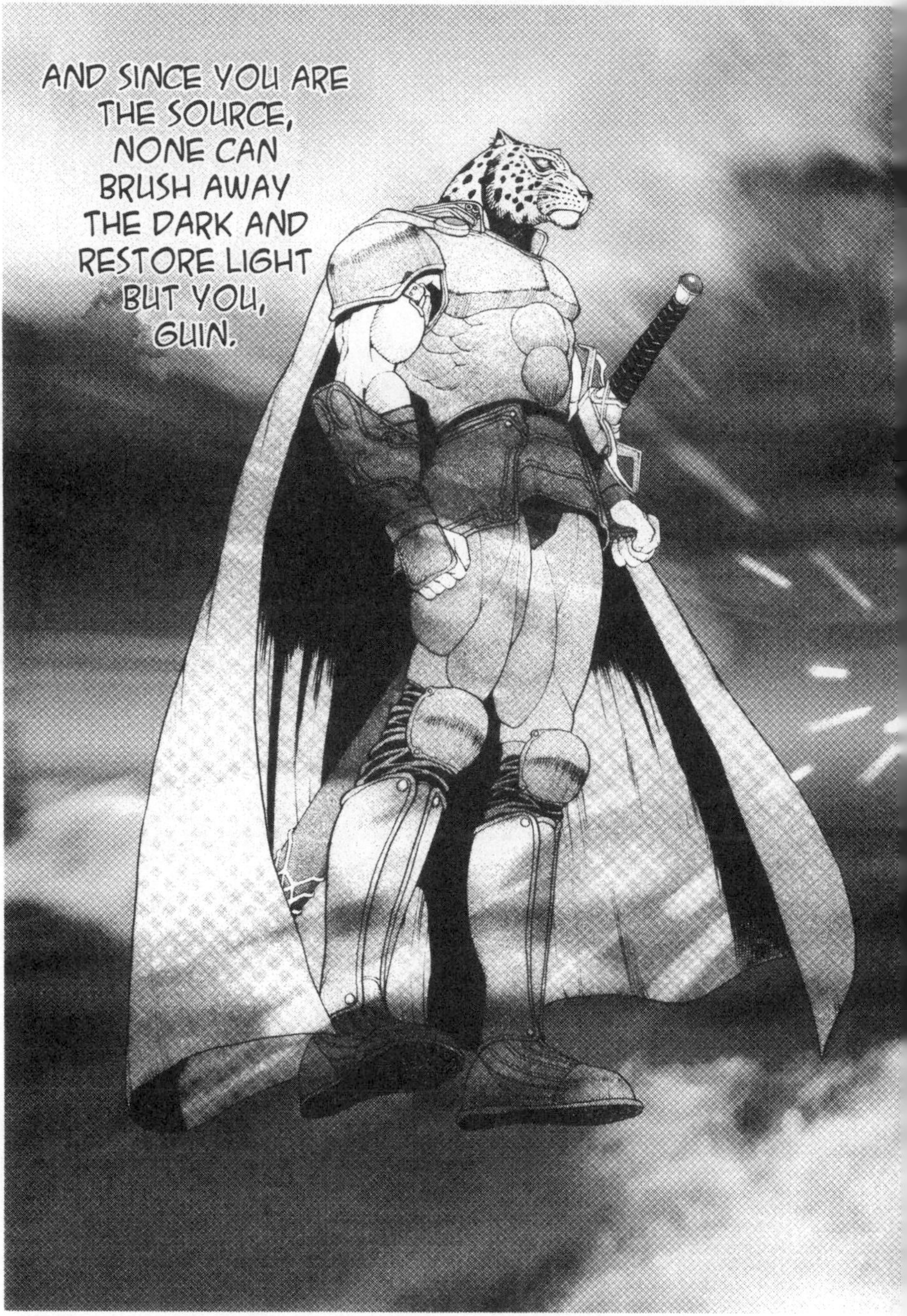
AND SINCE YOU ARE THE SOURCE, NONE CAN BRUSH AWAY THE DARK AND RESTORE LIGHT BUT YOU, GUIN.

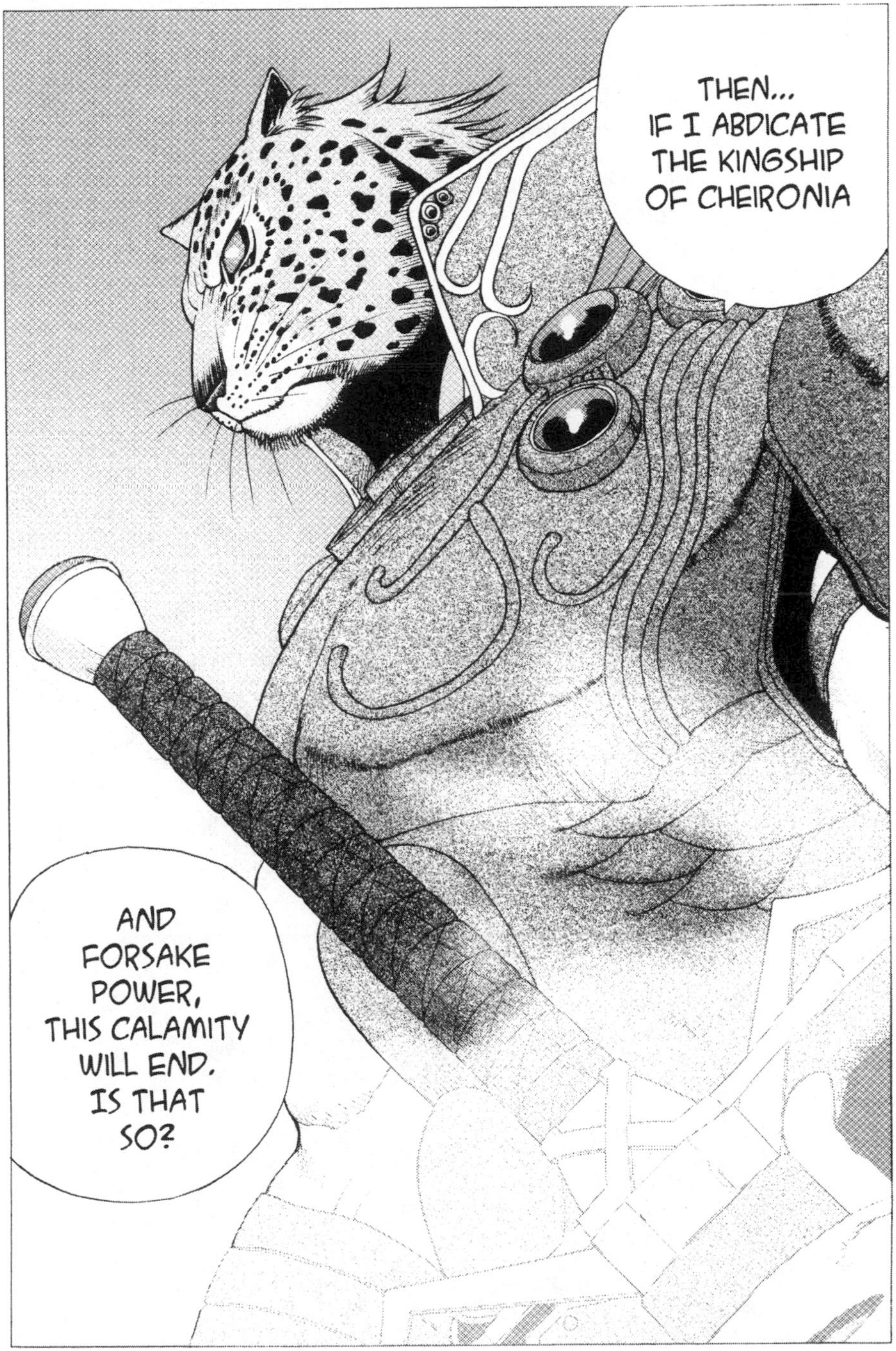
THEN... IF I ABDICATE THE KINGSHIP OF CHEIRONIA
AND FORSAKE POWER, THIS CALAMITY WILL END. IS THAT SO?

CHAPTER 6

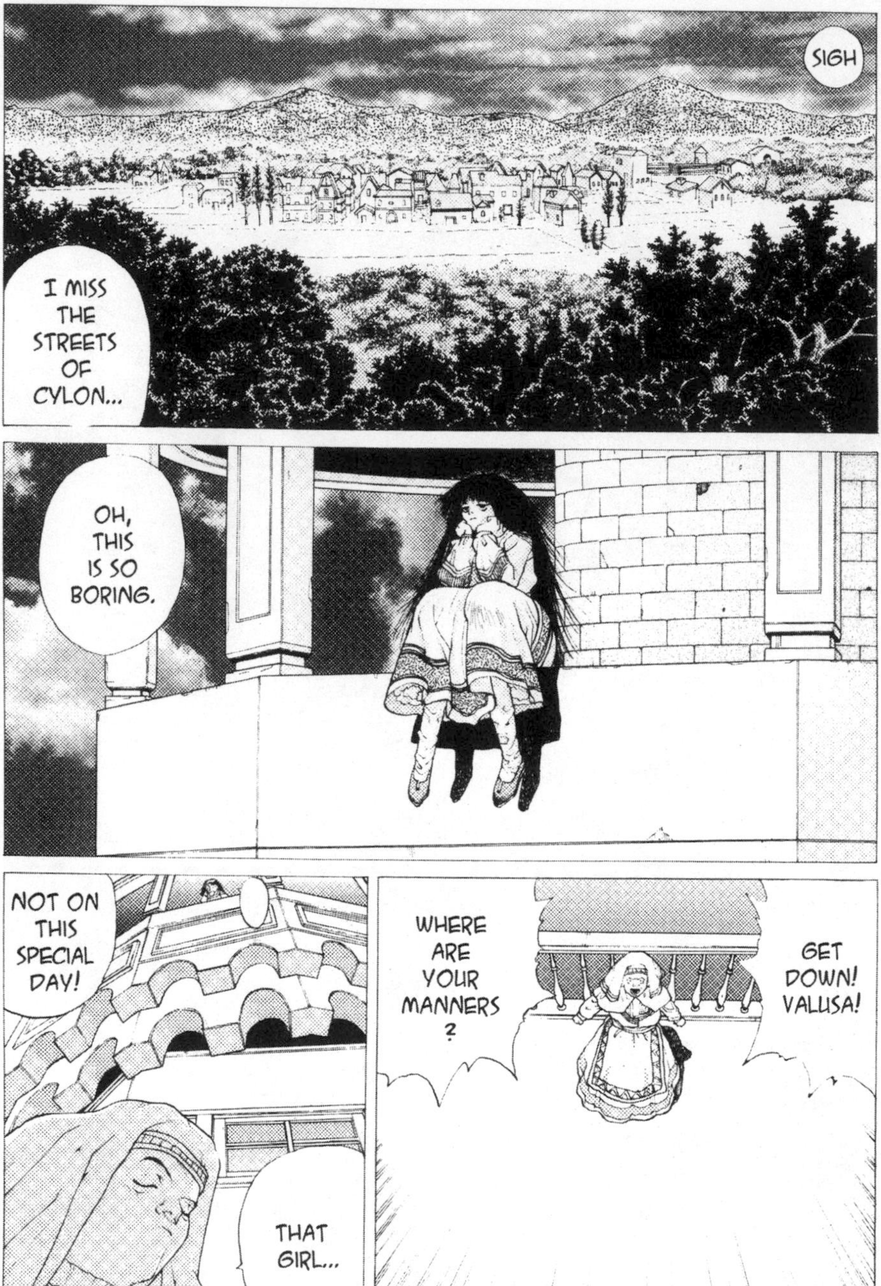
SIGH
I MISS THE STREETS OF CYLON...
OH, THIS IS SO BORING.
GET DOWN! VALUSA!
WHERE ARE YOUR MANNERS?
NOT ON THIS SPECIAL DAY!
THAT GIRL...

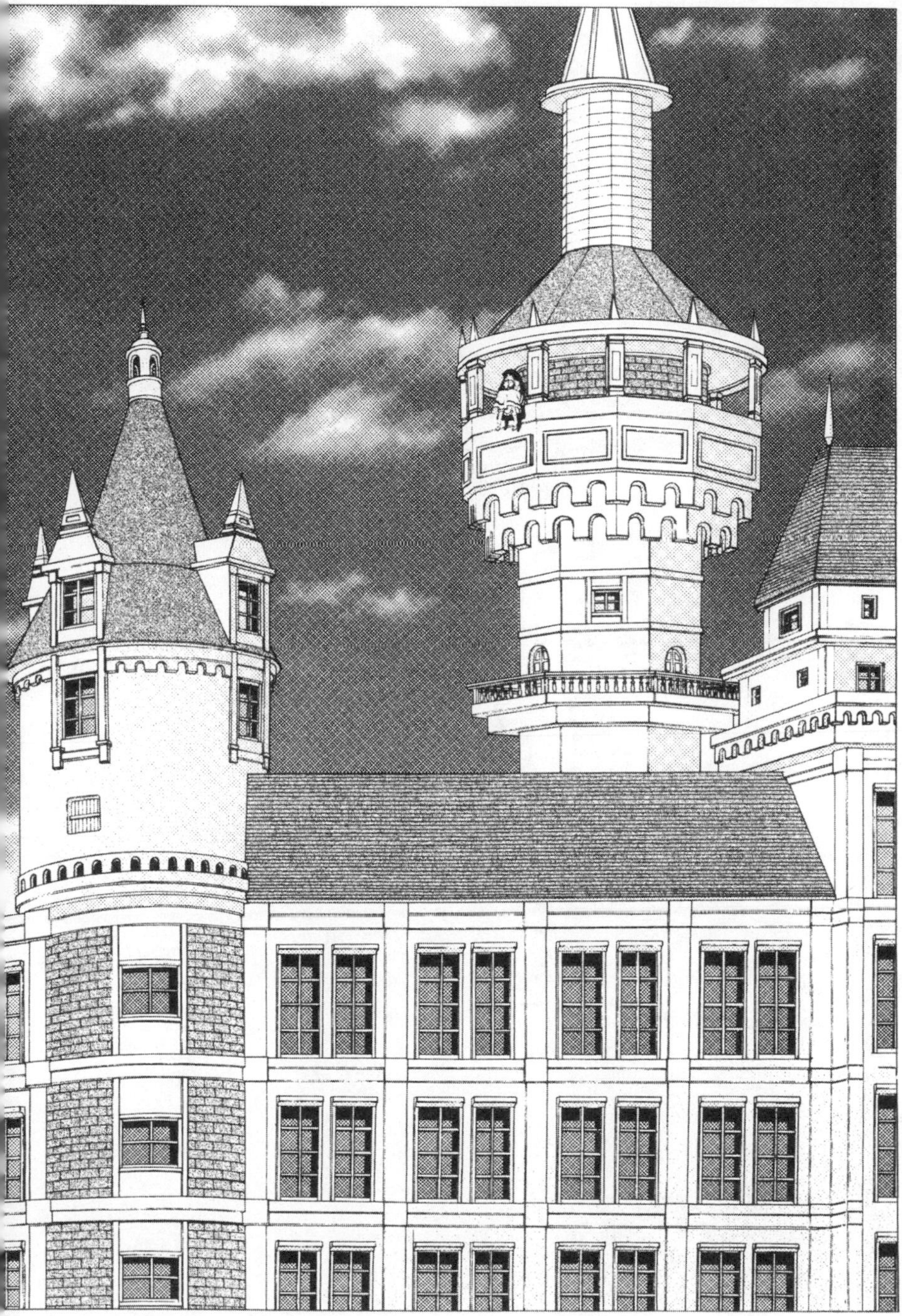

Chapter 6

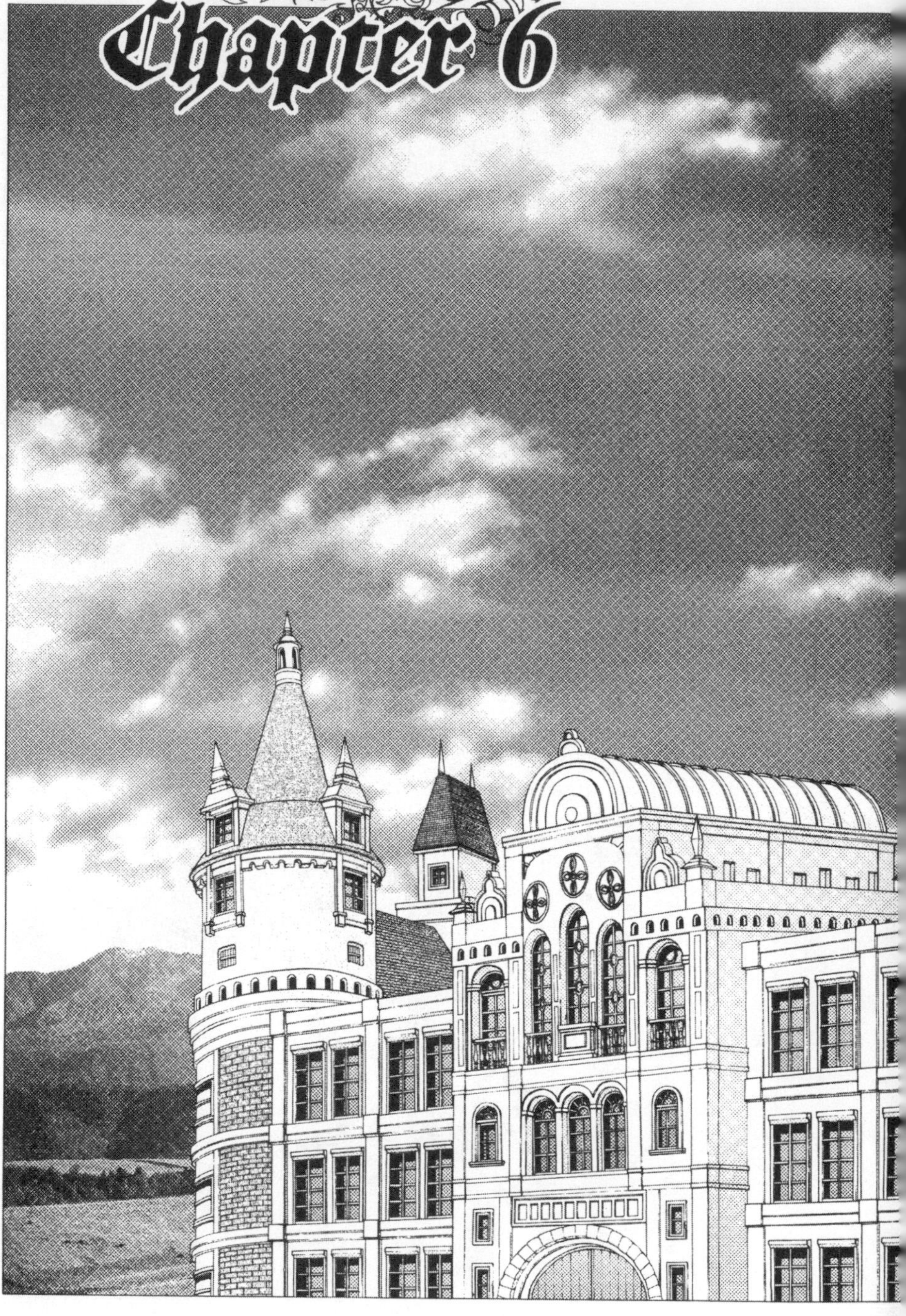

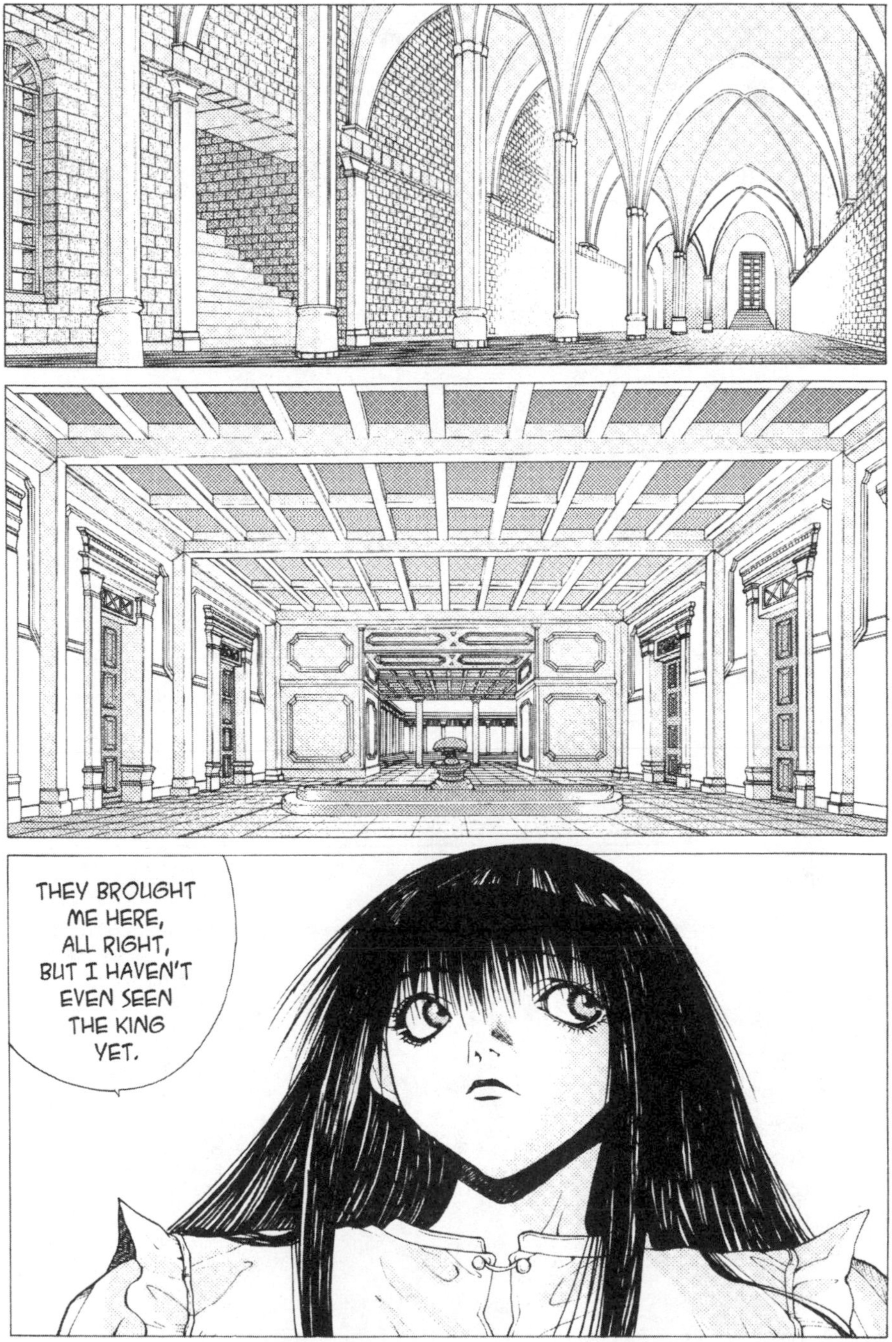
THEY BROUGHT ME HERE, ALL RIGHT, BUT I HAVEN'T EVEN SEEN THE KING YET.

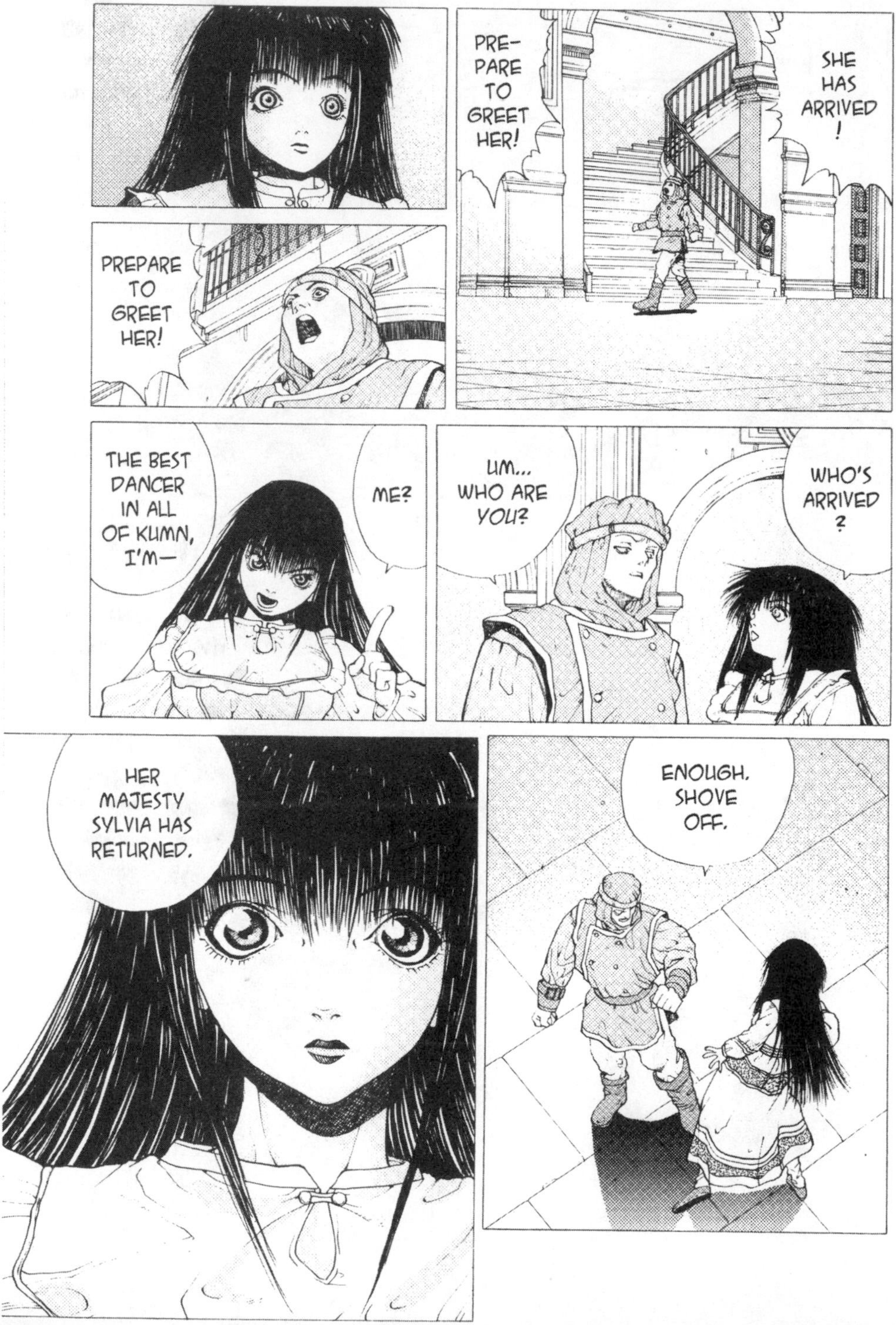
SHE HAS ARRIVED!
PRE-PARE TO GREET HER!
PREPARE TO GREET HER!
WHO'S ARRIVED?
UM... WHO ARE YOU?
ME?
THE BEST DANCER IN ALL OF KUMN, I'M—
ENOUGH. SHOVE OFF.
HER MAJESTY SYLVIA HAS RETURNED.

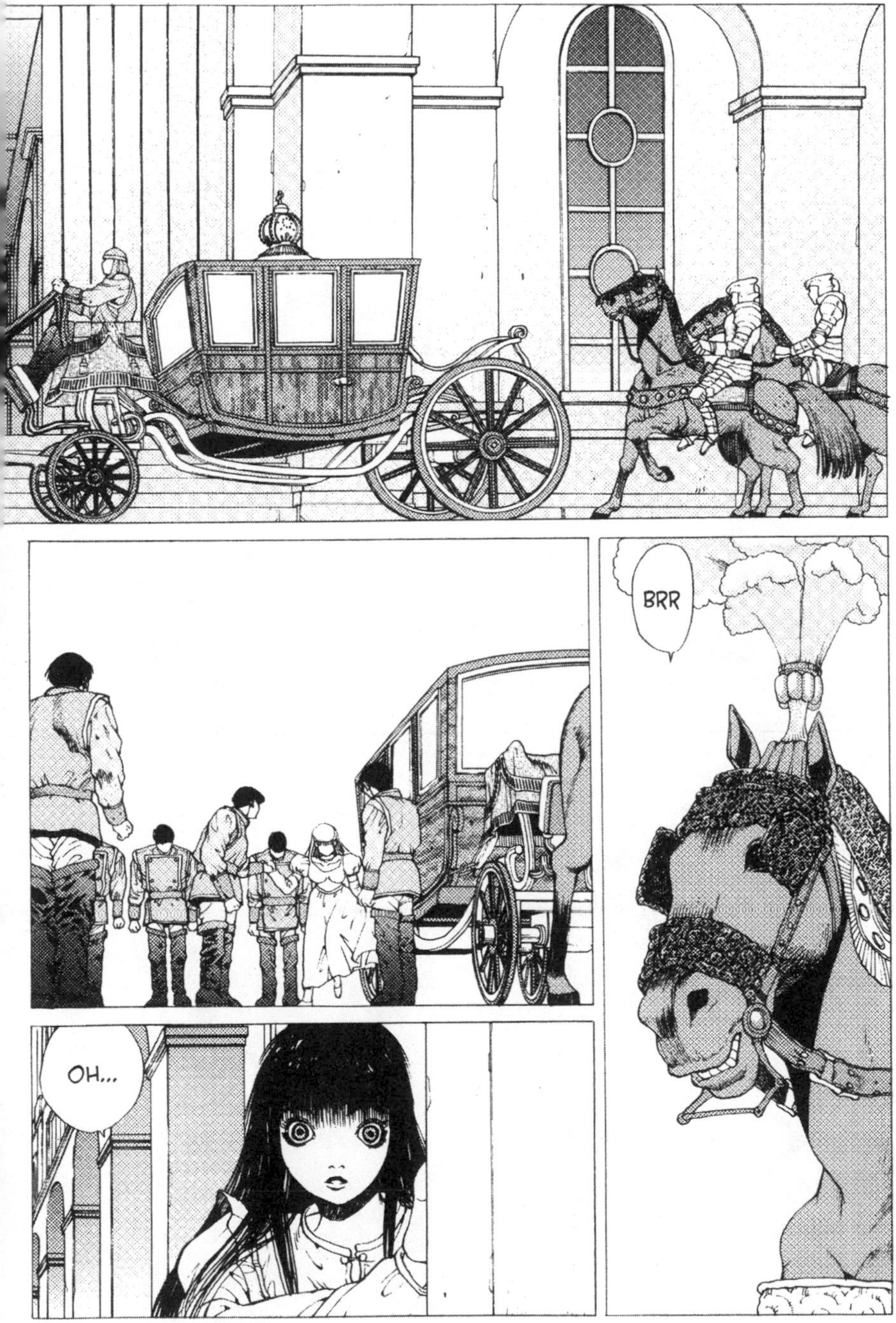
BRR
OH...

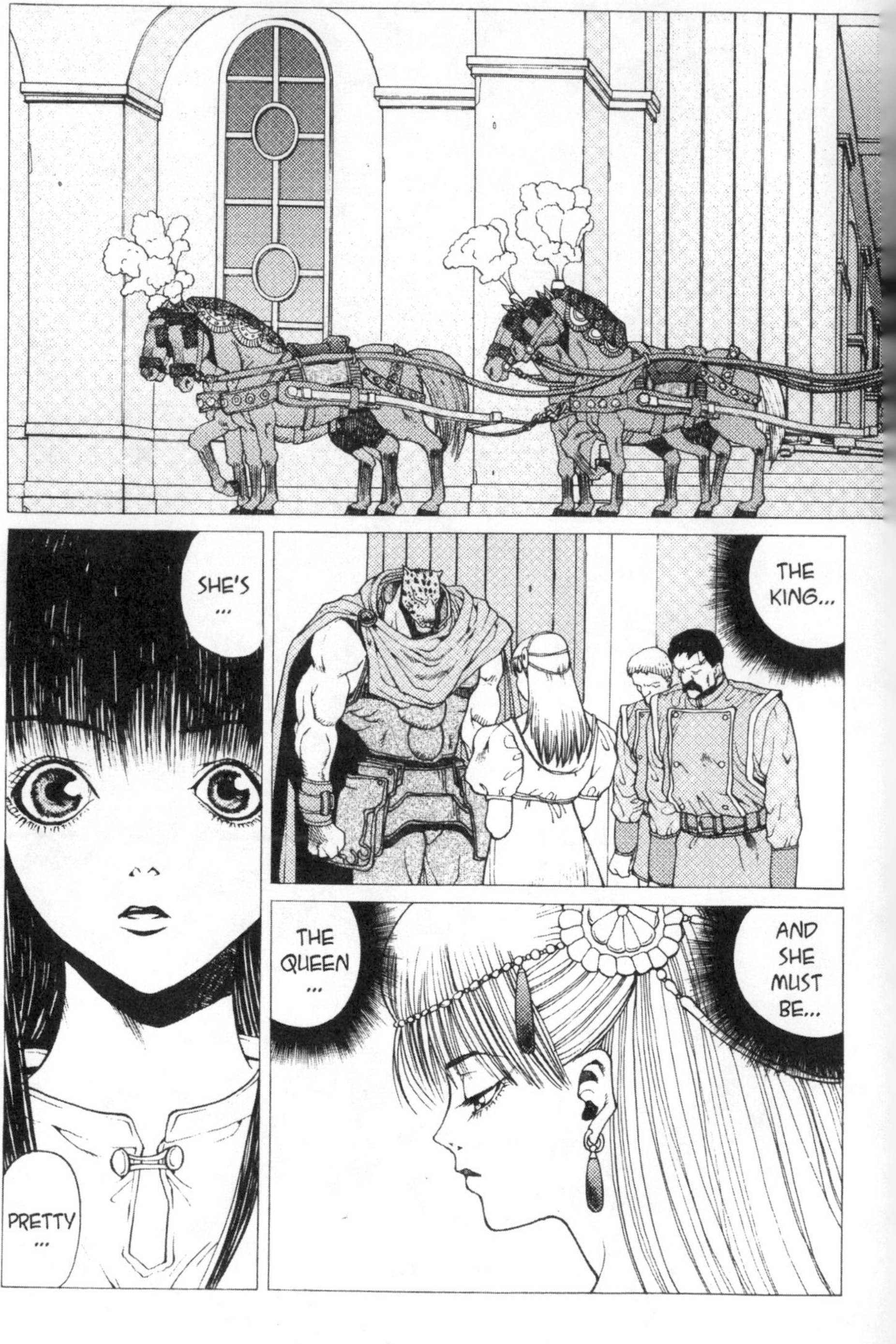
THE KING...
AND SHE MUST BE...
THE QUEEN ...
SHE'S ...
PRETTY ...

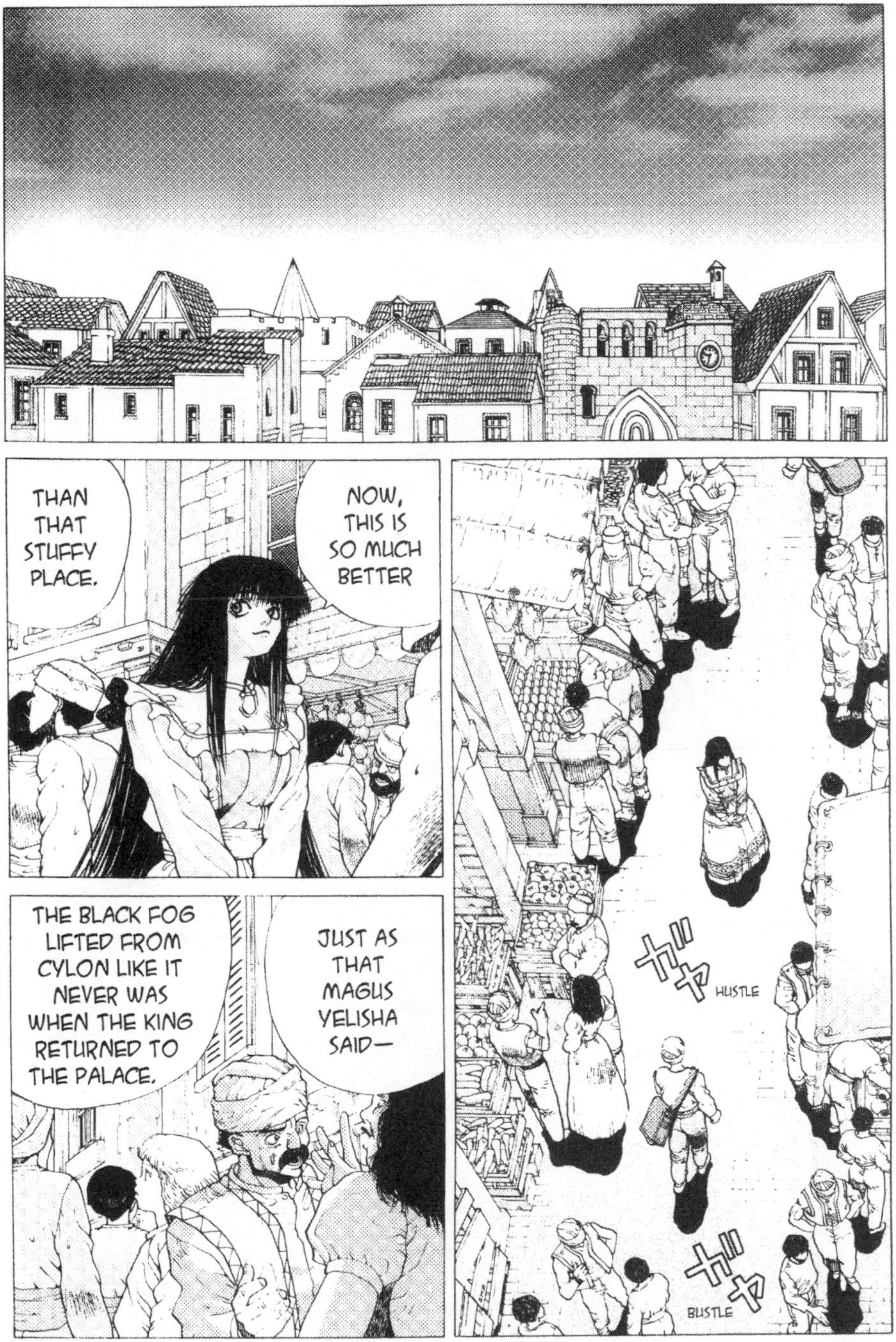
ガヤ
HUSTLE
ガヤ
BUSTLE
NOW, THIS IS SO MUCH BETTER
THAN THAT STUFFY PLACE.
JUST AS THAT MAGUS YELISHA SAID—
THE BLACK FOG LIFTED FROM CYLON LIKE IT NEVER WAS WHEN THE KING RETURNED TO THE PALACE.

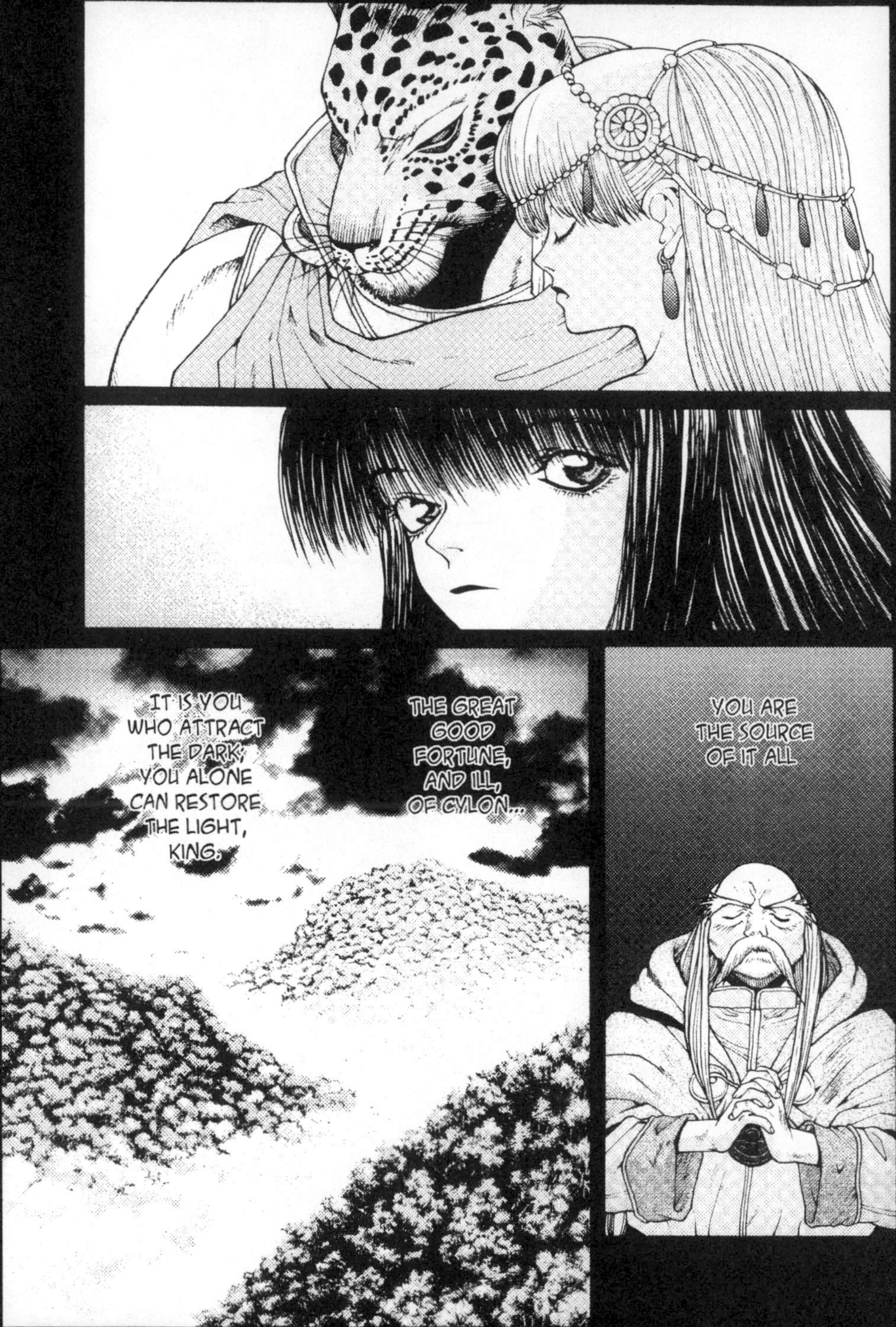
YOU ARE THE SOURCE OF IT ALL
THE GREAT GOOD FORTUNE, AND ILL, OF CYLON...
IT IS YOU WHO ATTRACT THE DARK; YOU ALONE CAN RESTORE THE LIGHT, KING.

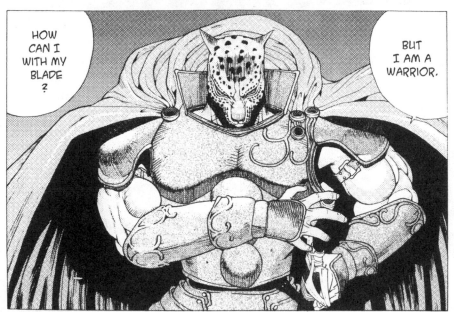

BUT I AM A WARRIOR.
HOW CAN I WITH MY BLADE ?
WORRY NOT.
THEY MUST HAVE SENSED THEIR TIME WAS NIGH WHEN YOU APPEARED IN TALIDD.
LEAVE THIS HOUSE TO FIND A COOL BREEZE FROM THE WEST BLOWING AWAY THE WINDS OF BLACK DEATH,

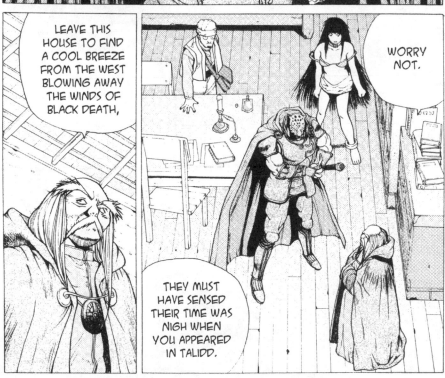

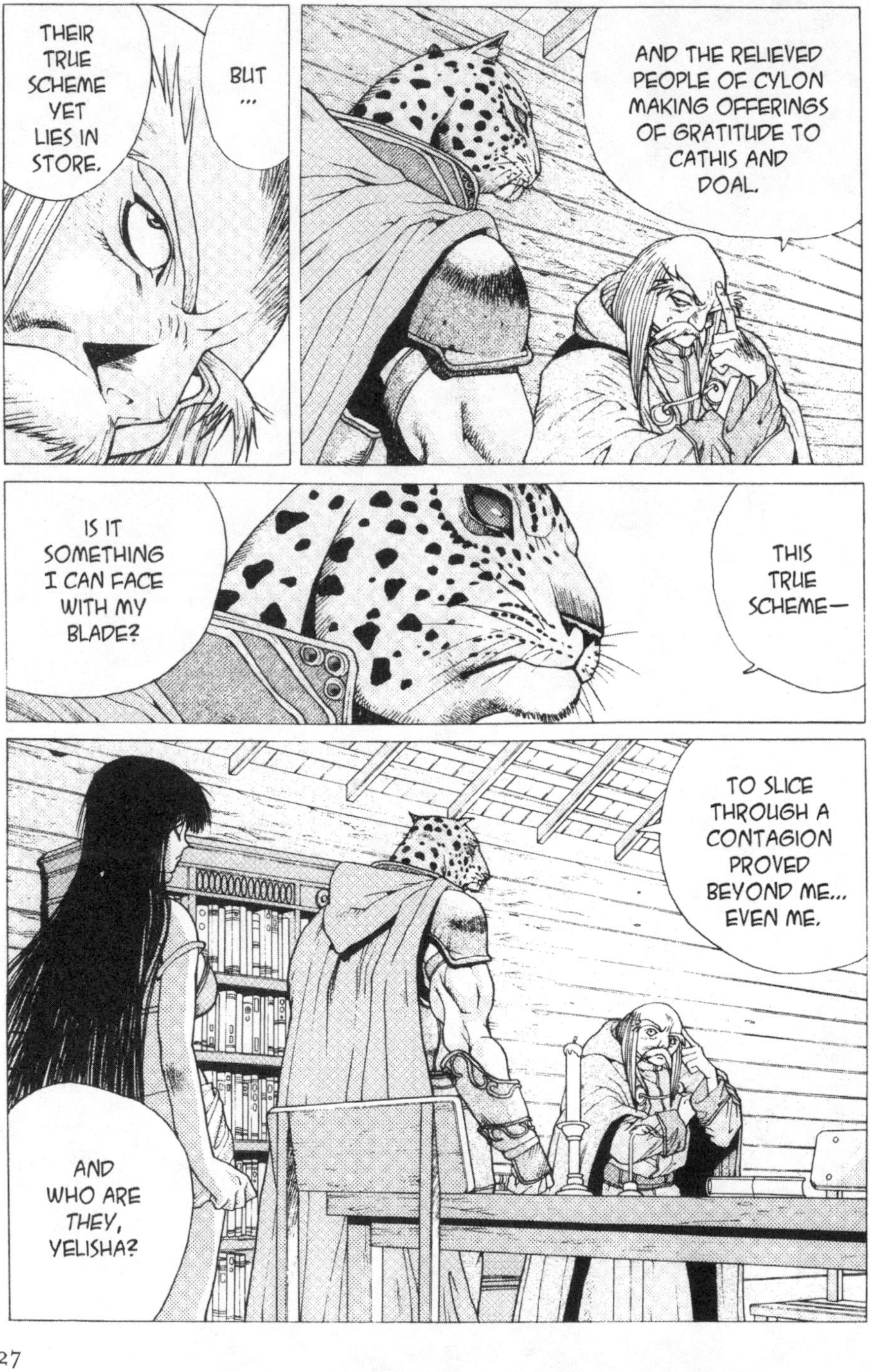
AND THE RELIEVED PEOPLE OF CYLON MAKING OFFERINGS OF GRATITUDE TO CATHIS AND DOAL.
BUT ...
THEIR TRUE SCHEME YET LIES IN STORE.
THIS TRUE SCHEME—
IS IT SOMETHING I CAN FACE WITH MY BLADE?
TO SLICE THROUGH A CONTAGION PROVED BEYOND ME... EVEN ME.
AND WHO ARE THEY, YELISHA?

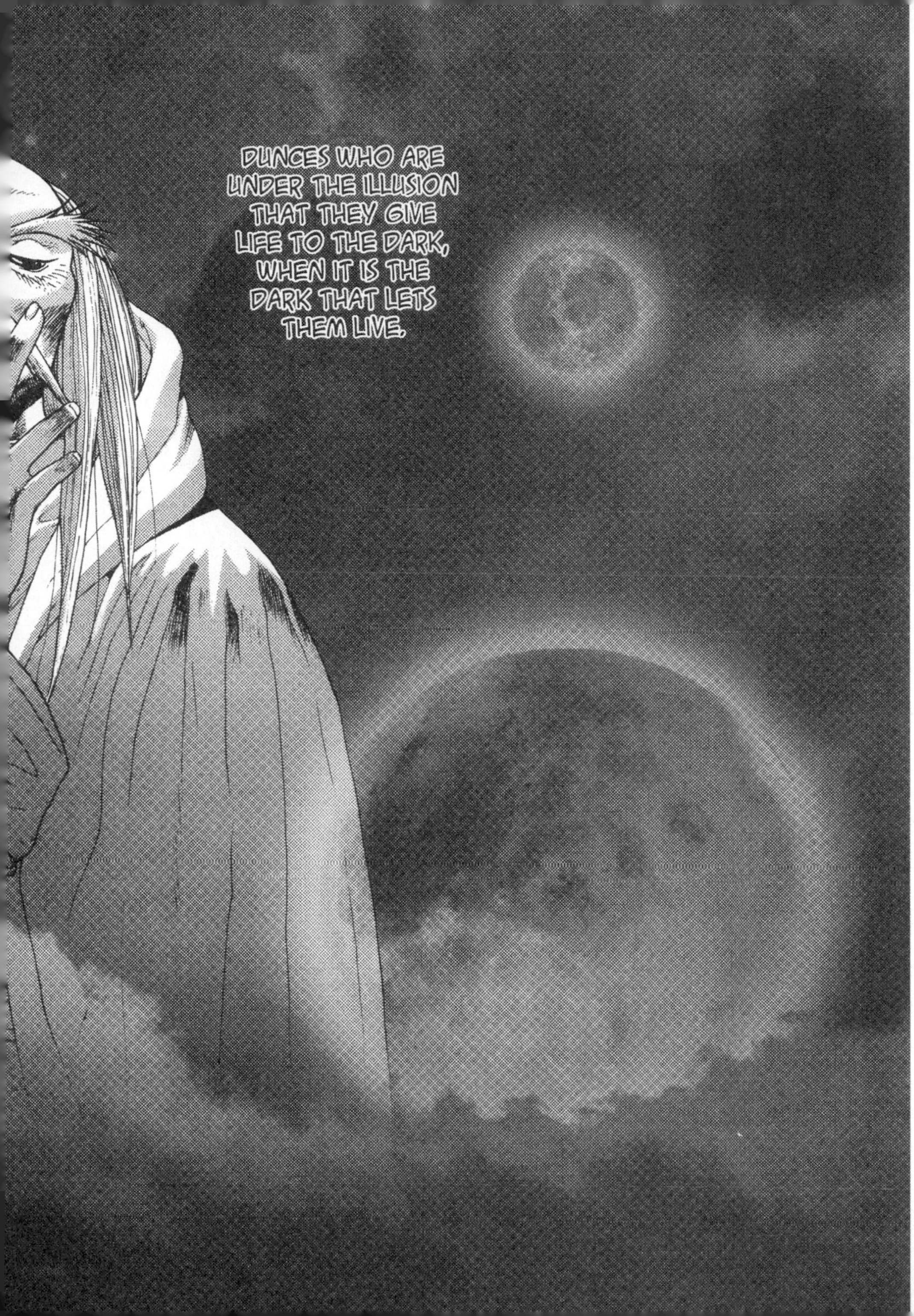
DUNCES WHO ARE UNDER THE ILLUSION THAT THEY GIVE LIFE TO THE DARK, WHEN IT IS THE DARK THAT LETS THEM LIVE.

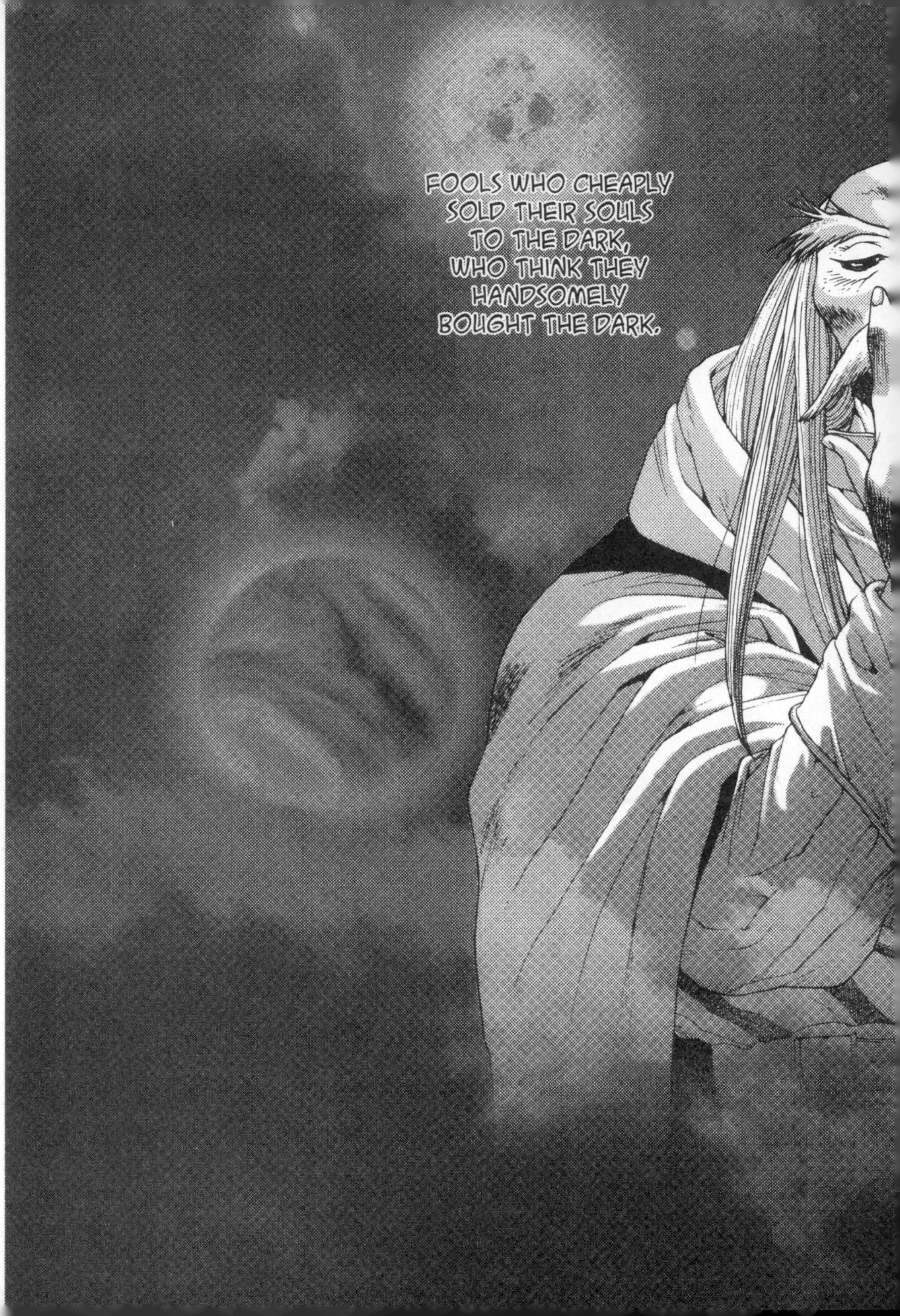
FOOLS WHO CHEAPLY SOLD THEIR SOULS TO THE DARK, WHO THINK THEY HANDSOMELY BOUGHT THE DARK.

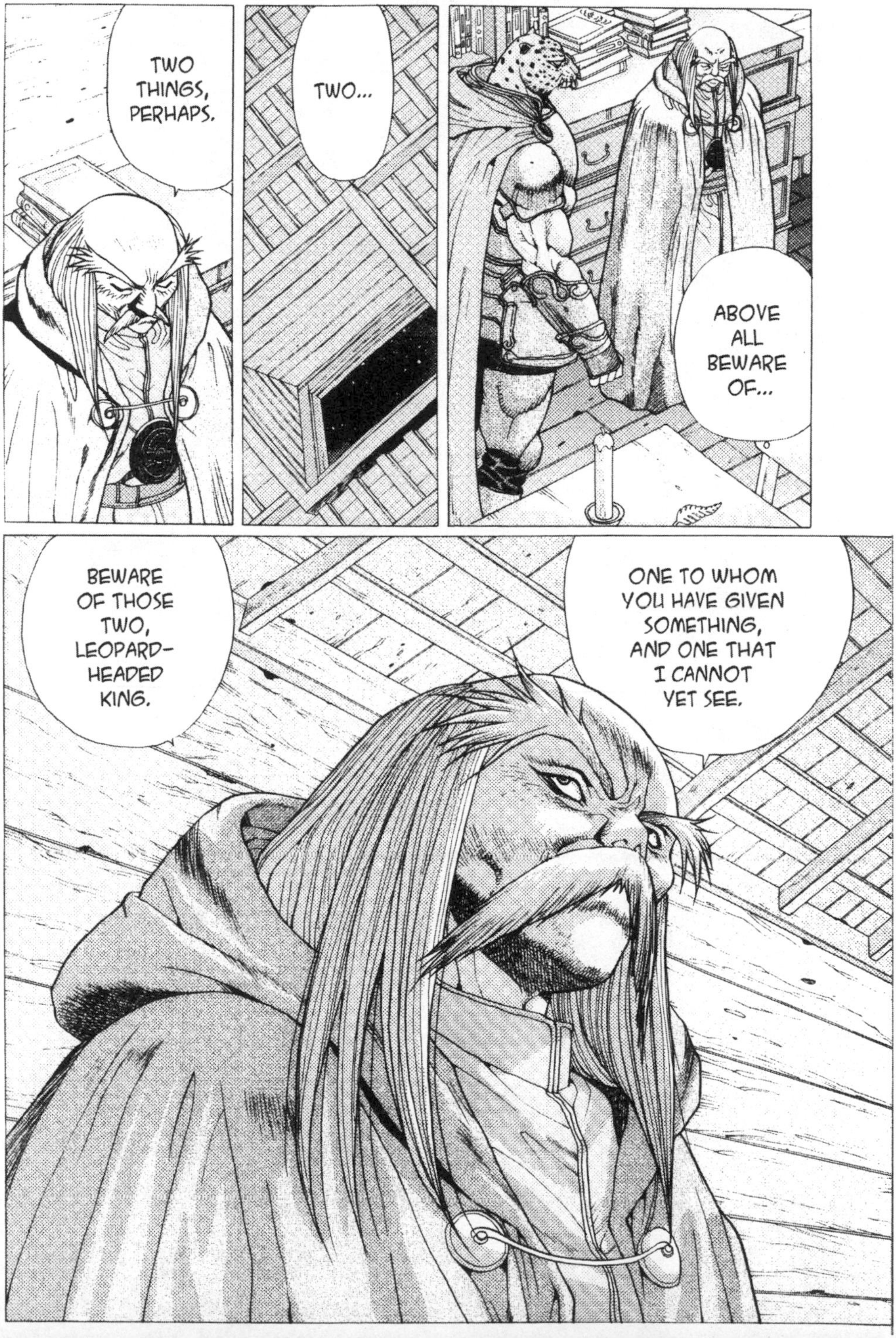
TWO THINGS, PERHAPS.
TWO...
ABOVE ALL BEWARE OF...
BEWARE OF THOSE TWO, LEOPARD-HEADED KING.
ONE TO WHOM YOU HAVE GIVEN SOMETHING, AND ONE THAT I CANNOT YET SEE.

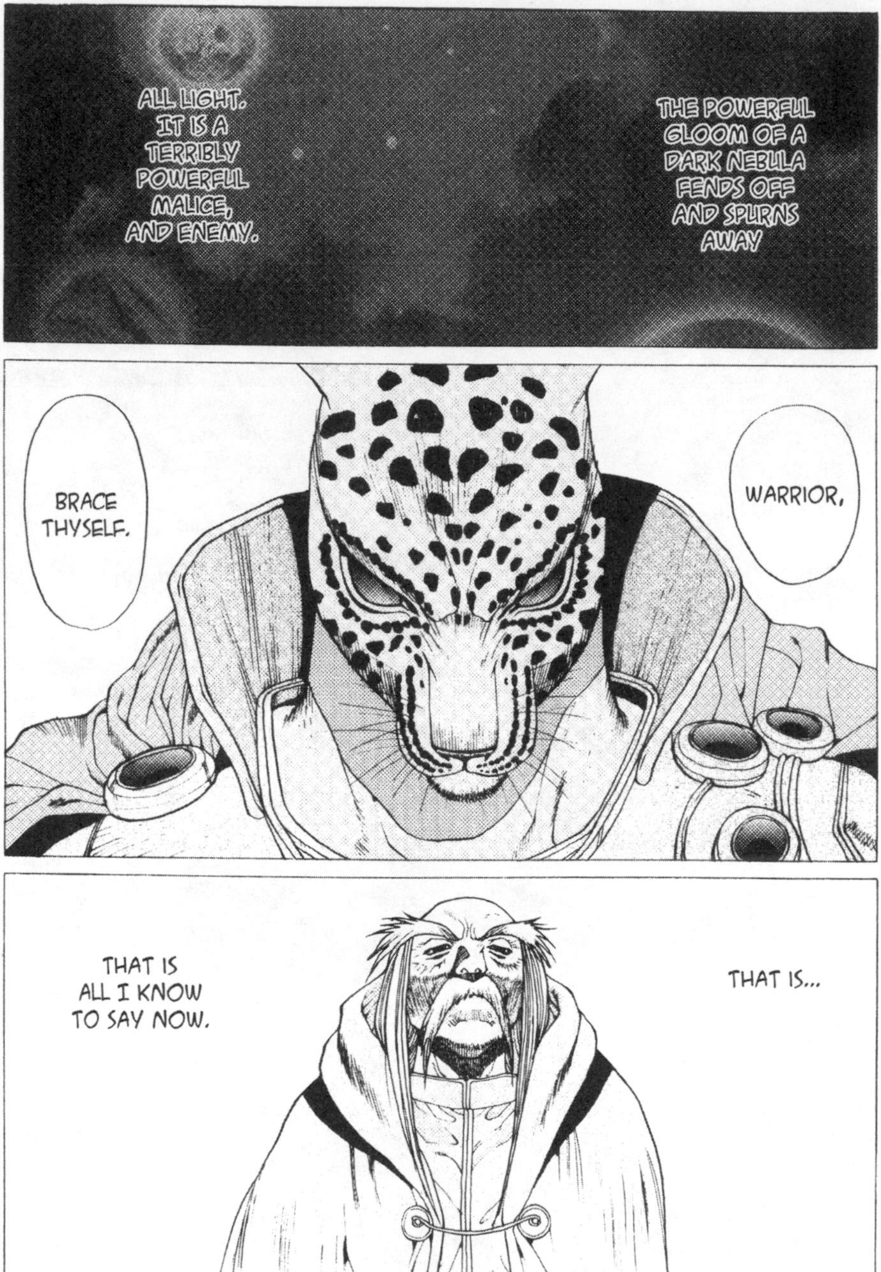
THE POWERFUL GLOOM OF A DARK NEBULA FENDS OFF AND SPURNS AWAY
ALL LIGHT. IT IS A TERRIBLY POWERFUL MALICE, AND ENEMY.
WARRIOR,
BRACE THYSELF.
THAT IS...
THAT IS ALL I KNOW TO SAY NOW.

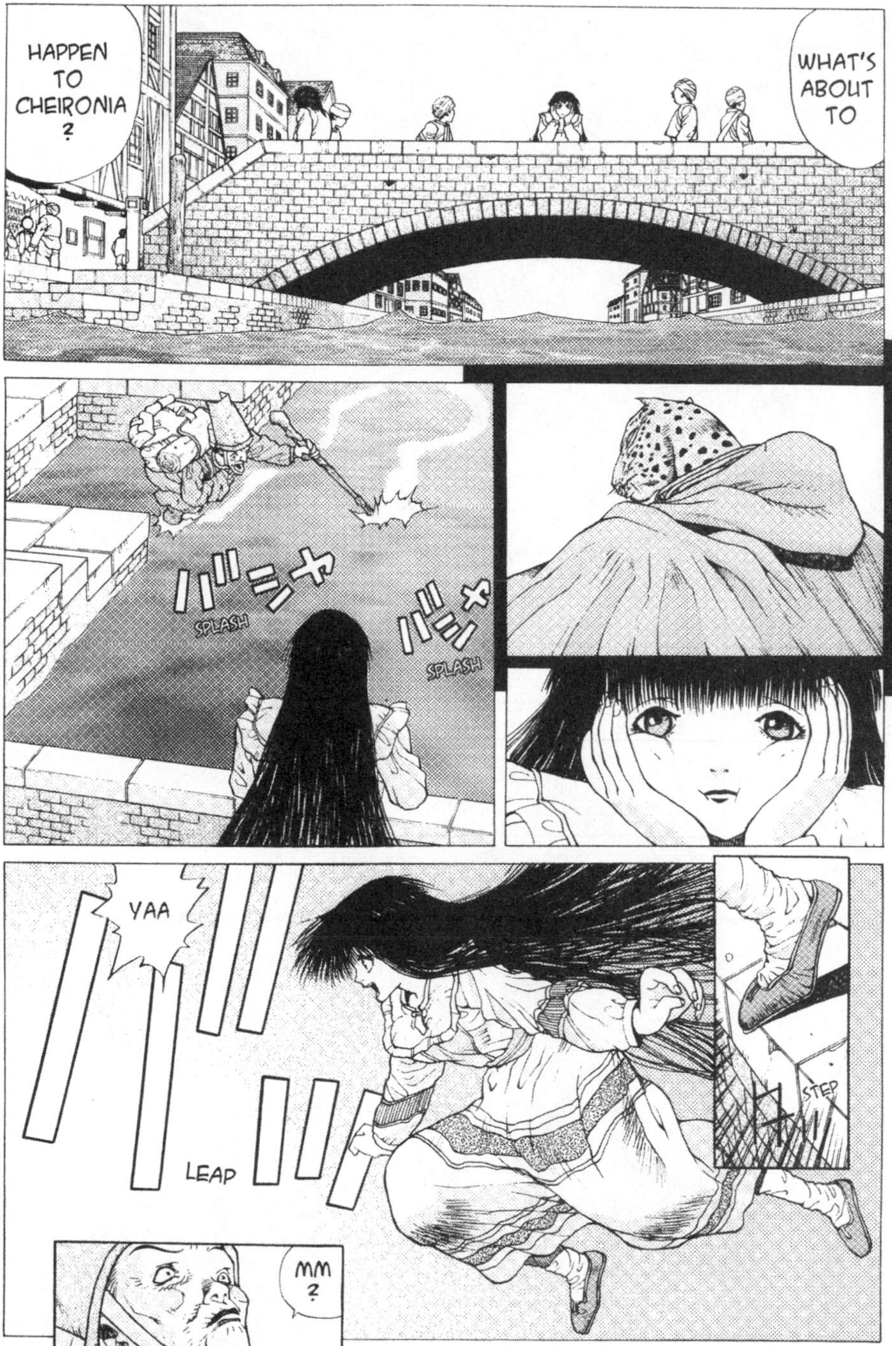
WHAT'S ABOUT TO
HAPPEN TO CHEIRONIA ?
バシャ
SPLASH
バシャ
SPLASH
STEP
YAA
LEAP
MM ?

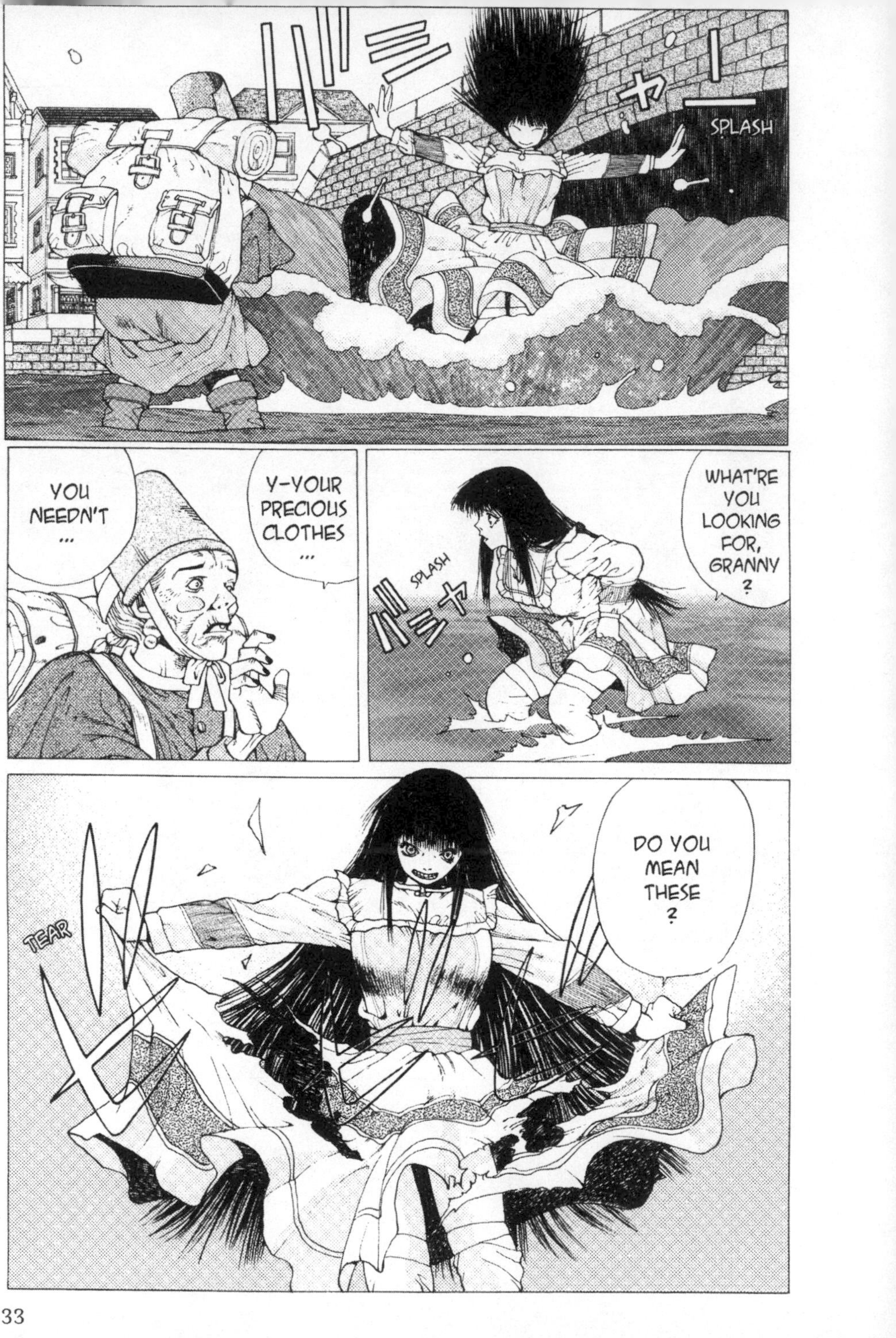
SPLASH
WHAT'RE YOU LOOKING FOR, GRANNY?
SPLASH
Y-YOUR PRECIOUS CLOTHES ...
YOU NEEDN'T ...
DO YOU MEAN THESE?
TEAR

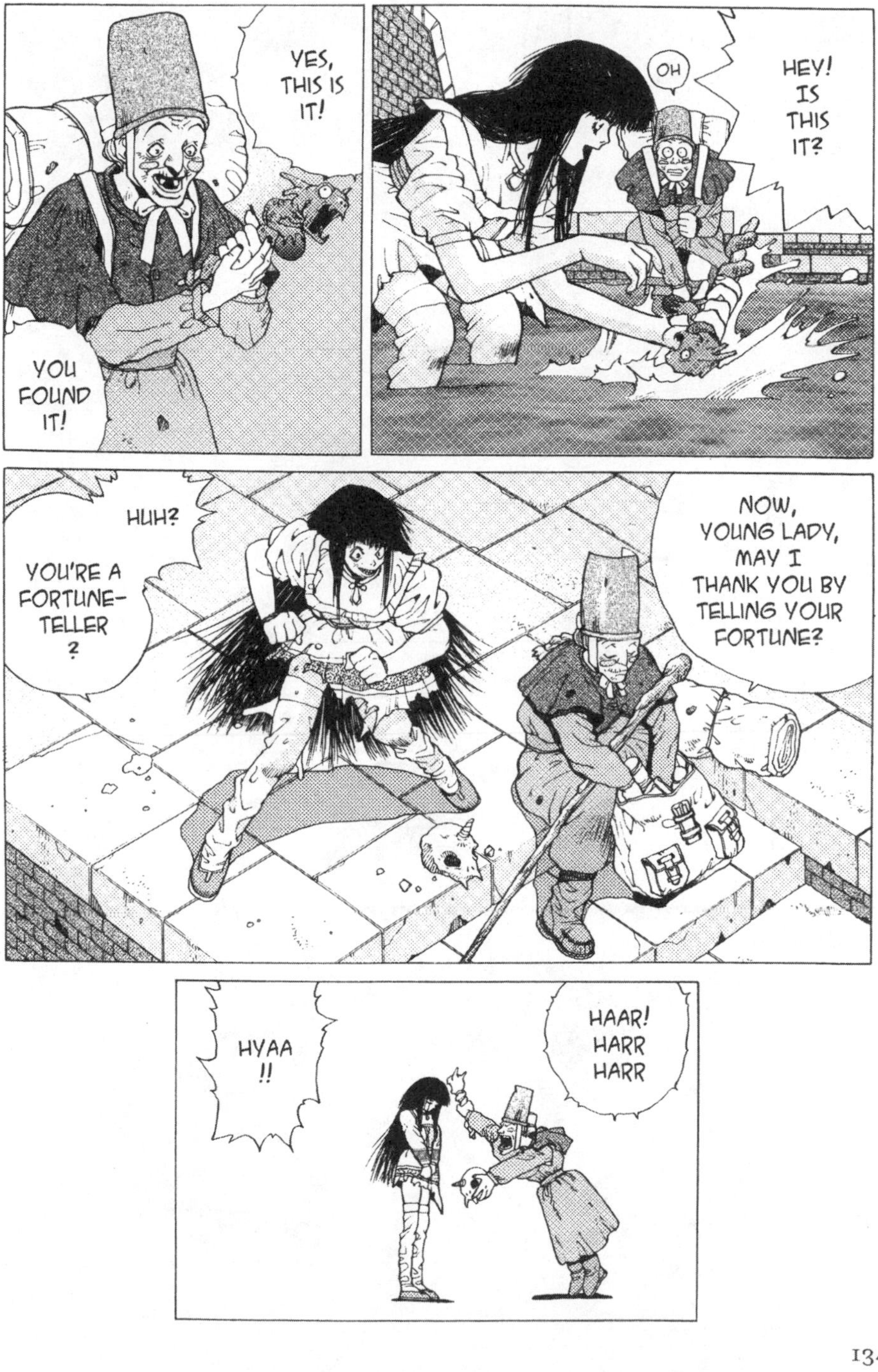
HEY! IS THIS IT?
OH
YES, THIS IS IT!
YOU FOUND IT!
NOW, YOUNG LADY, MAY I THANK YOU BY TELLING YOUR FORTUNE?
HUH?
YOU'RE A FORTUNE-TELLER?
HAAR! HARR HARR
HYAA!!

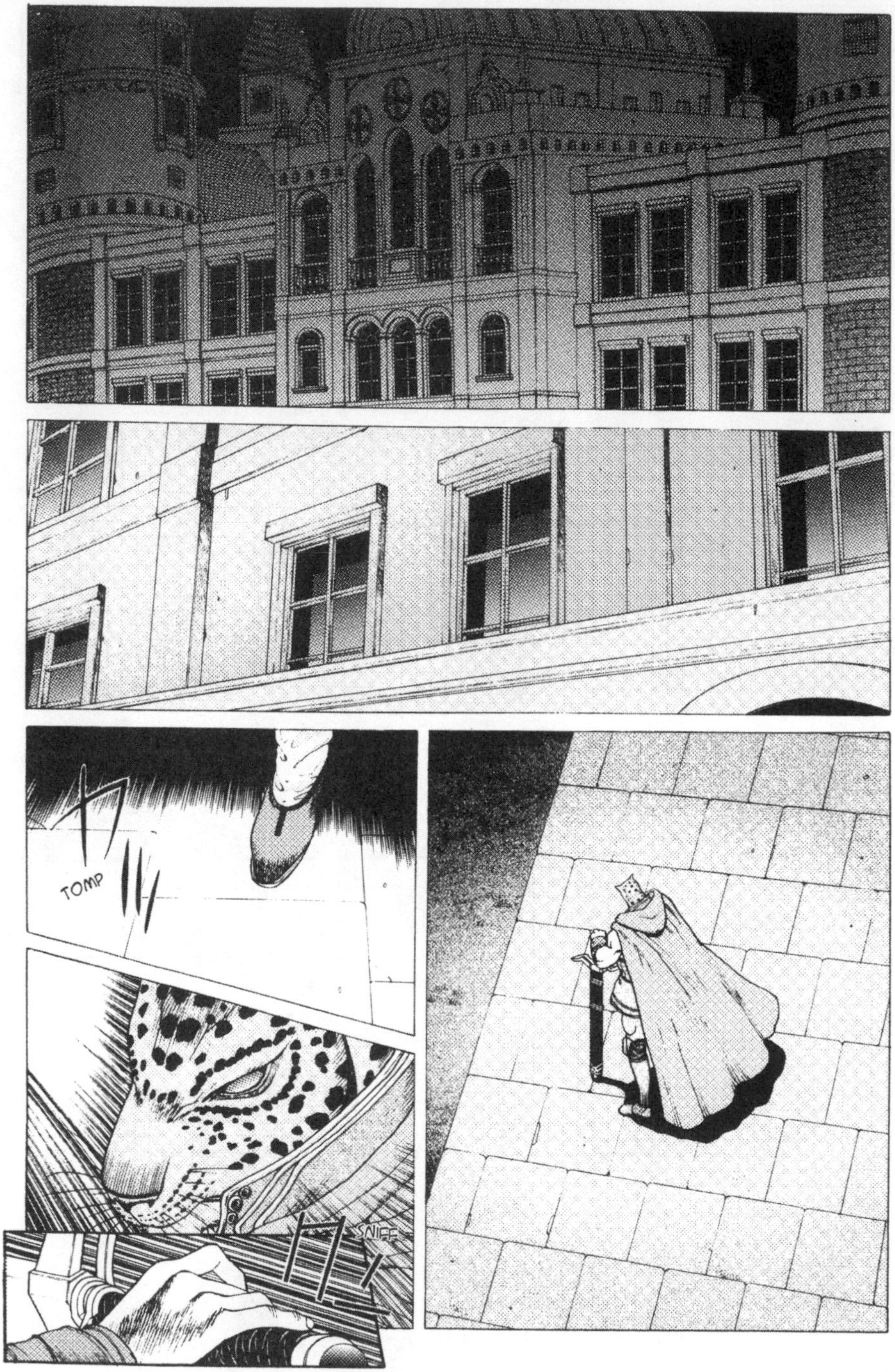
TOMP
SNIFF

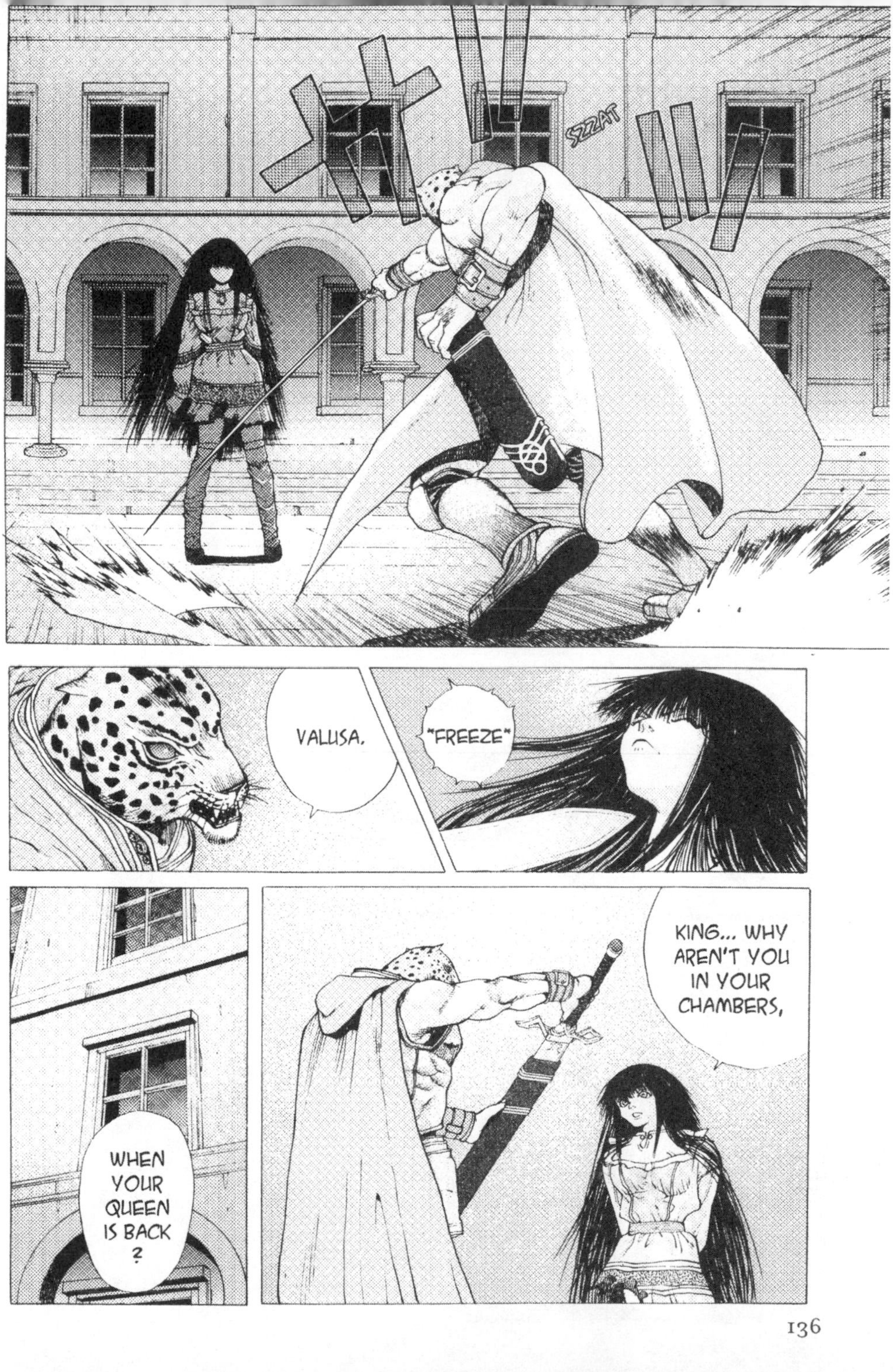
SZZAT
"FREEZE"
VALUSA.
KING... WHY AREN'T YOU IN YOUR CHAMBERS,
WHEN YOUR QUEEN IS BACK ?

I JUST DON'T GET IT.

I MEAN,

...

LUCKY ME...

YOU BRING A LOST GIRL LIKE ME TO THE WINDY HILL AND GIVE ME A PLACE. WHY?

HMM.

WOULD YOU LIKE TO SEE VALUSA'S— KUMN'S BEST DANCER'S—DANCE OF CURSES? A DANCE TO DISPEL CURSES?

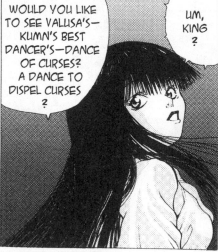

UM, KING?

YOU DON'T LIKE TO WATCH?

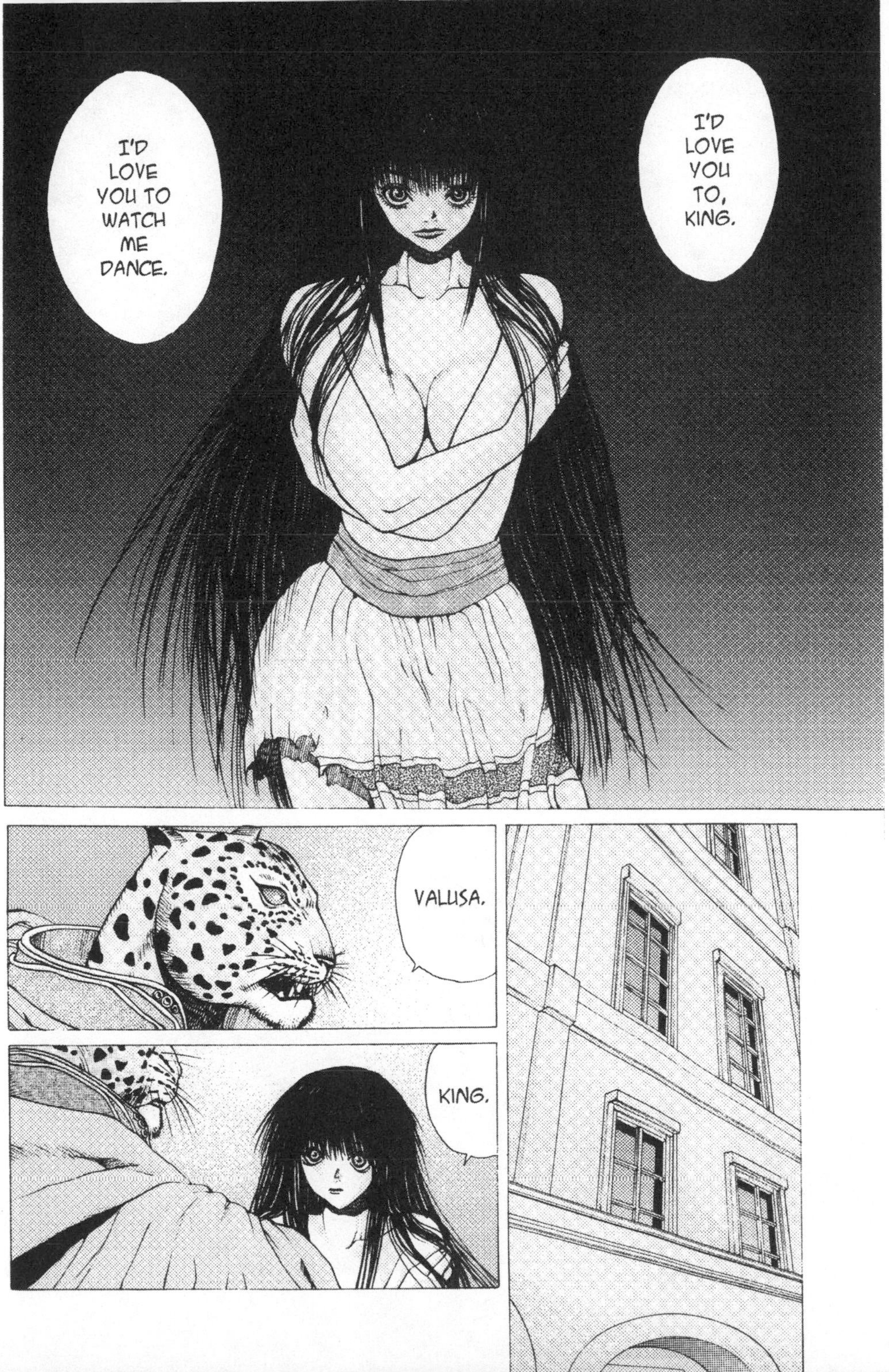
I'D LOVE YOU TO, KING.
I'D LOVE YOU TO WATCH ME DANCE.
VALUSA.
KING.

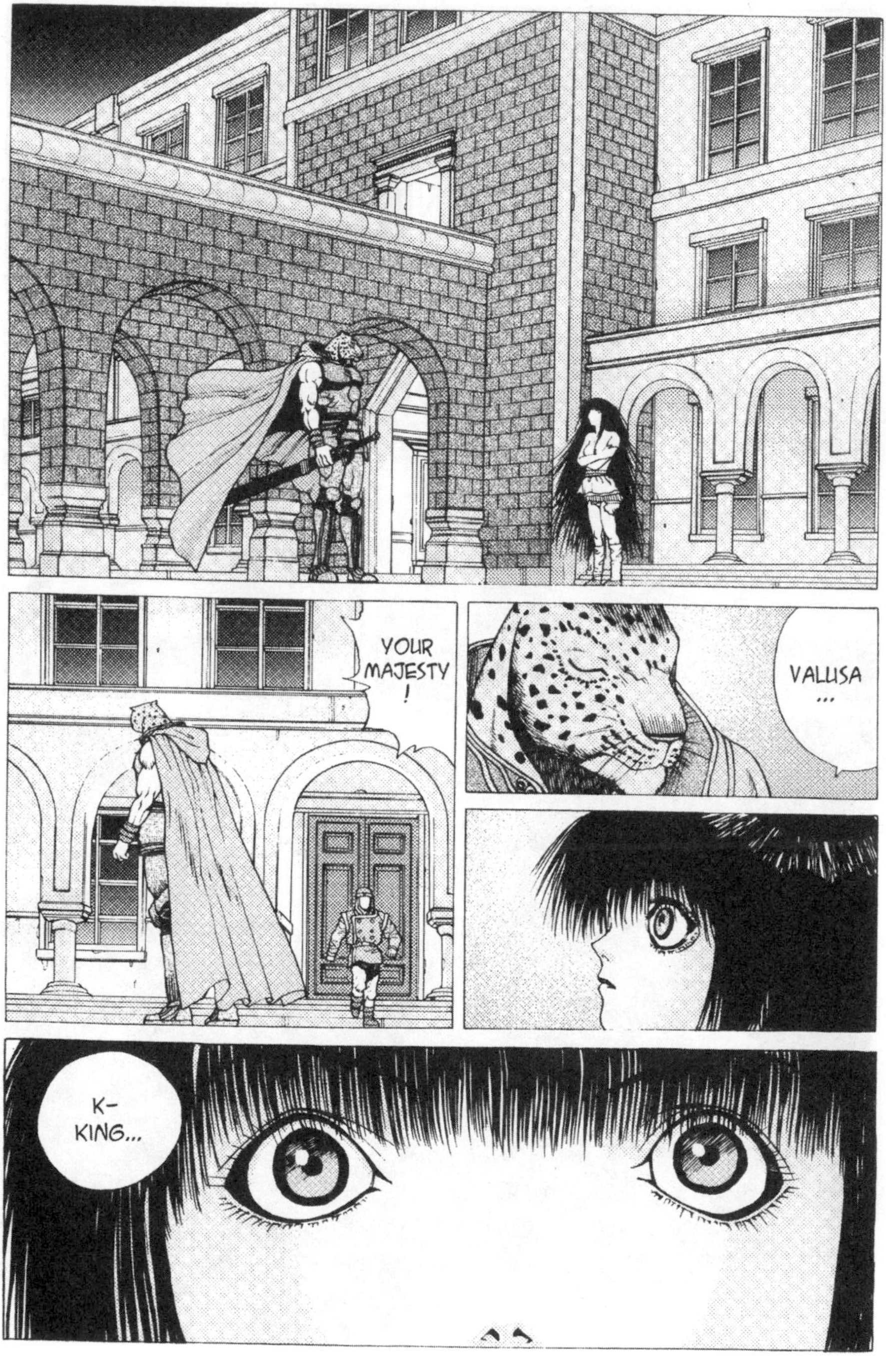
VALUSA ...
YOUR MAJESTY !
K- KING...

Chapter 7

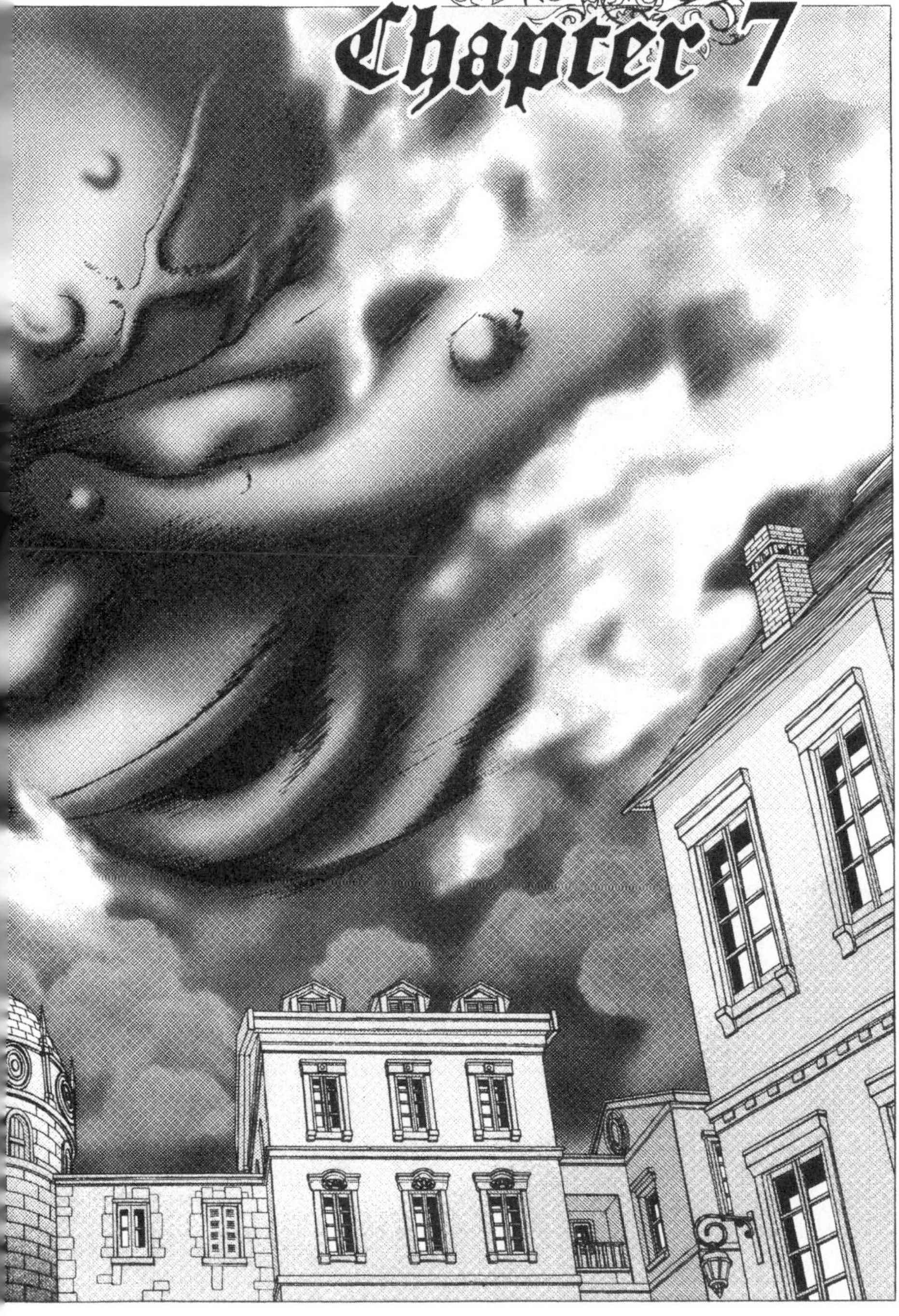

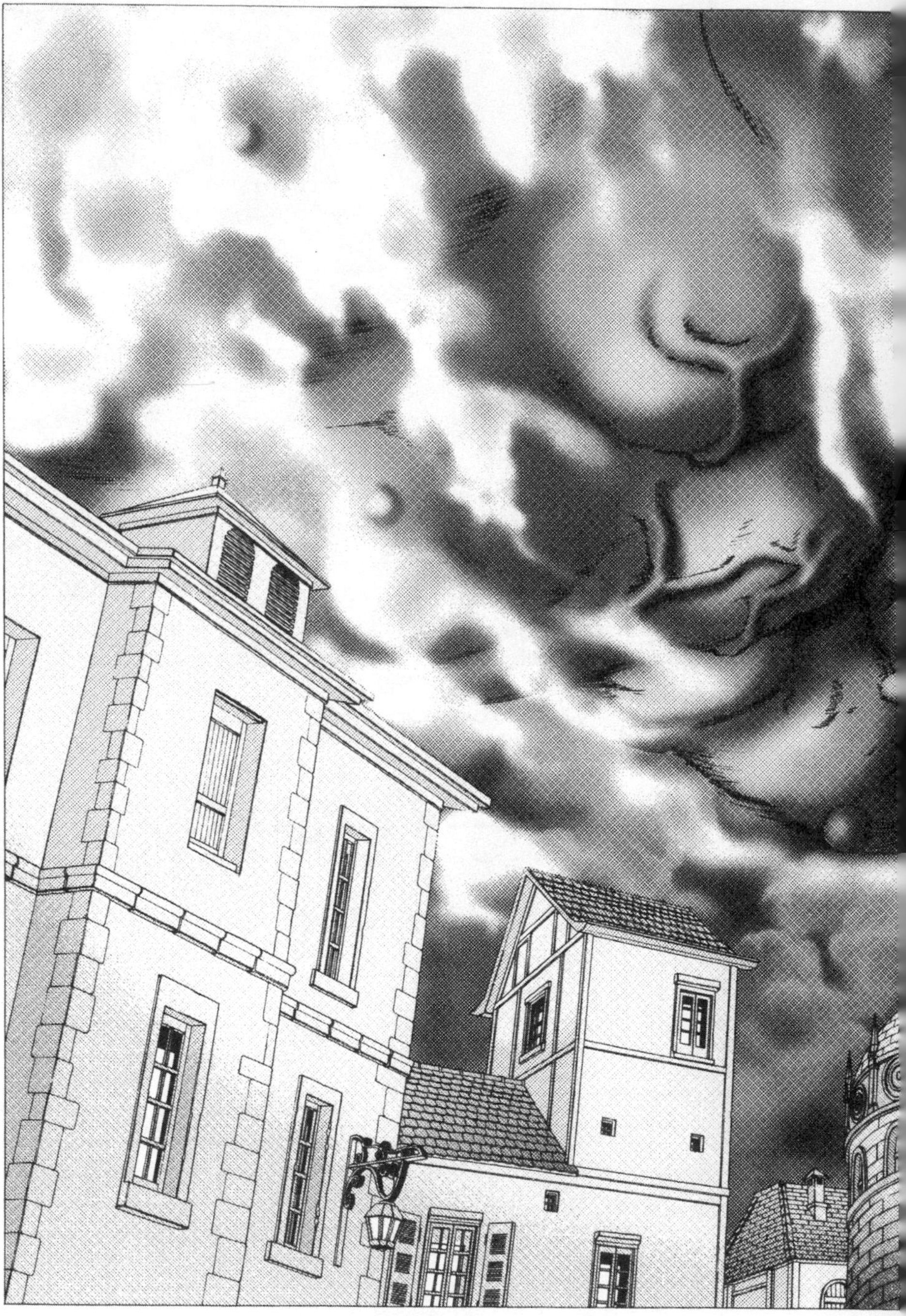

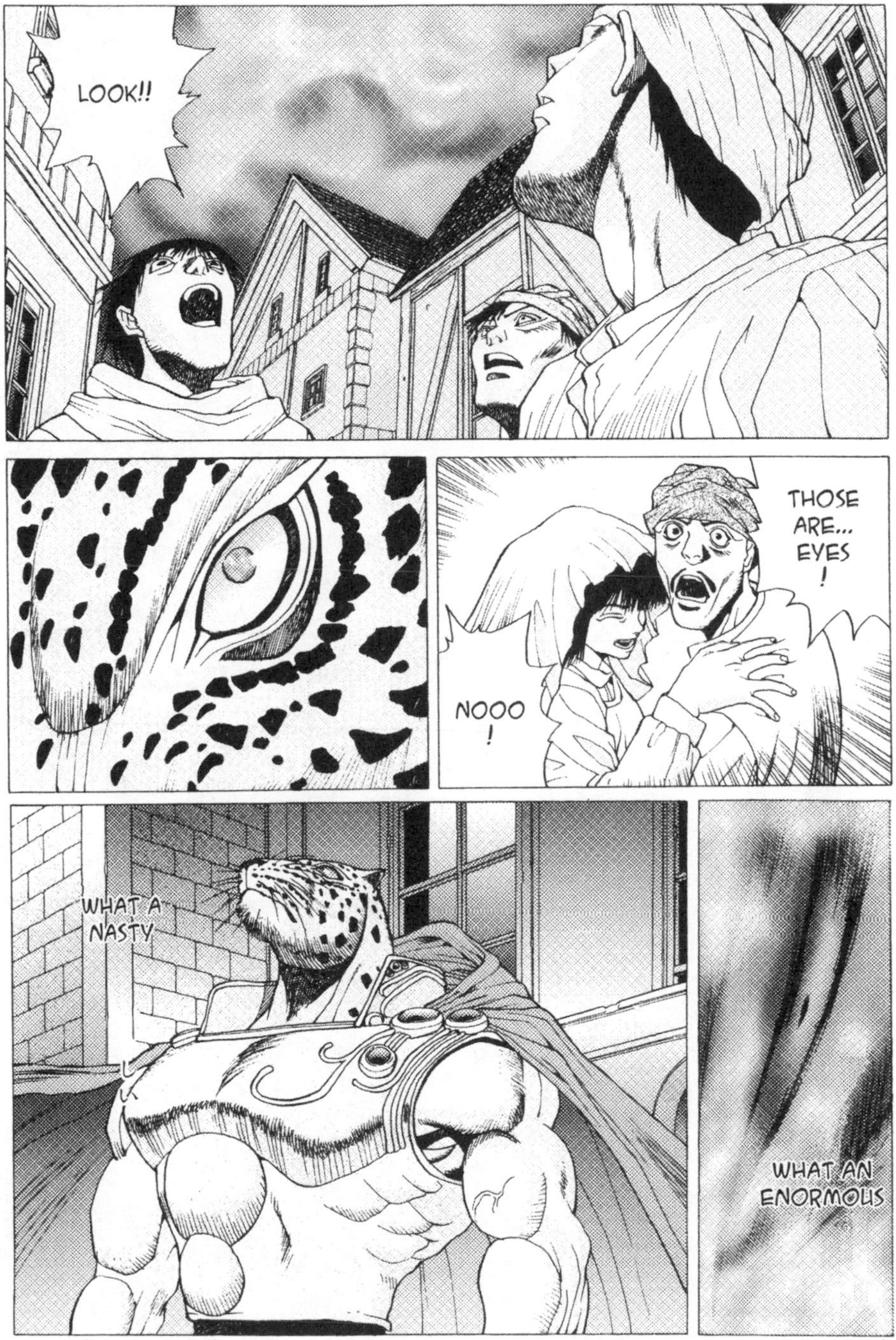
LOOK!!
THOSE ARE... EYES!
NOOO!
WHAT AN ENORMOUS
WHAT A NASTY

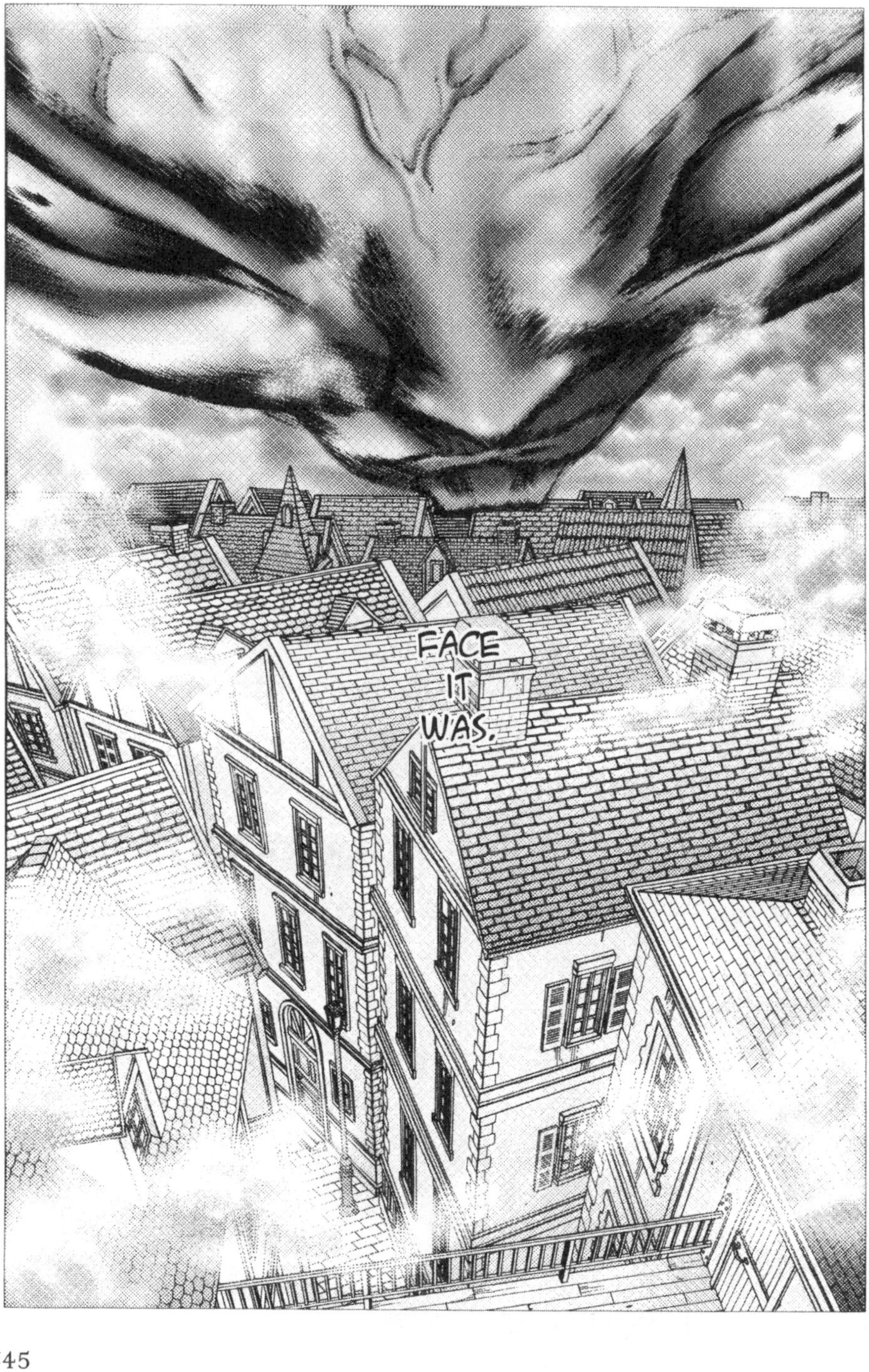
FACE IT WAS.

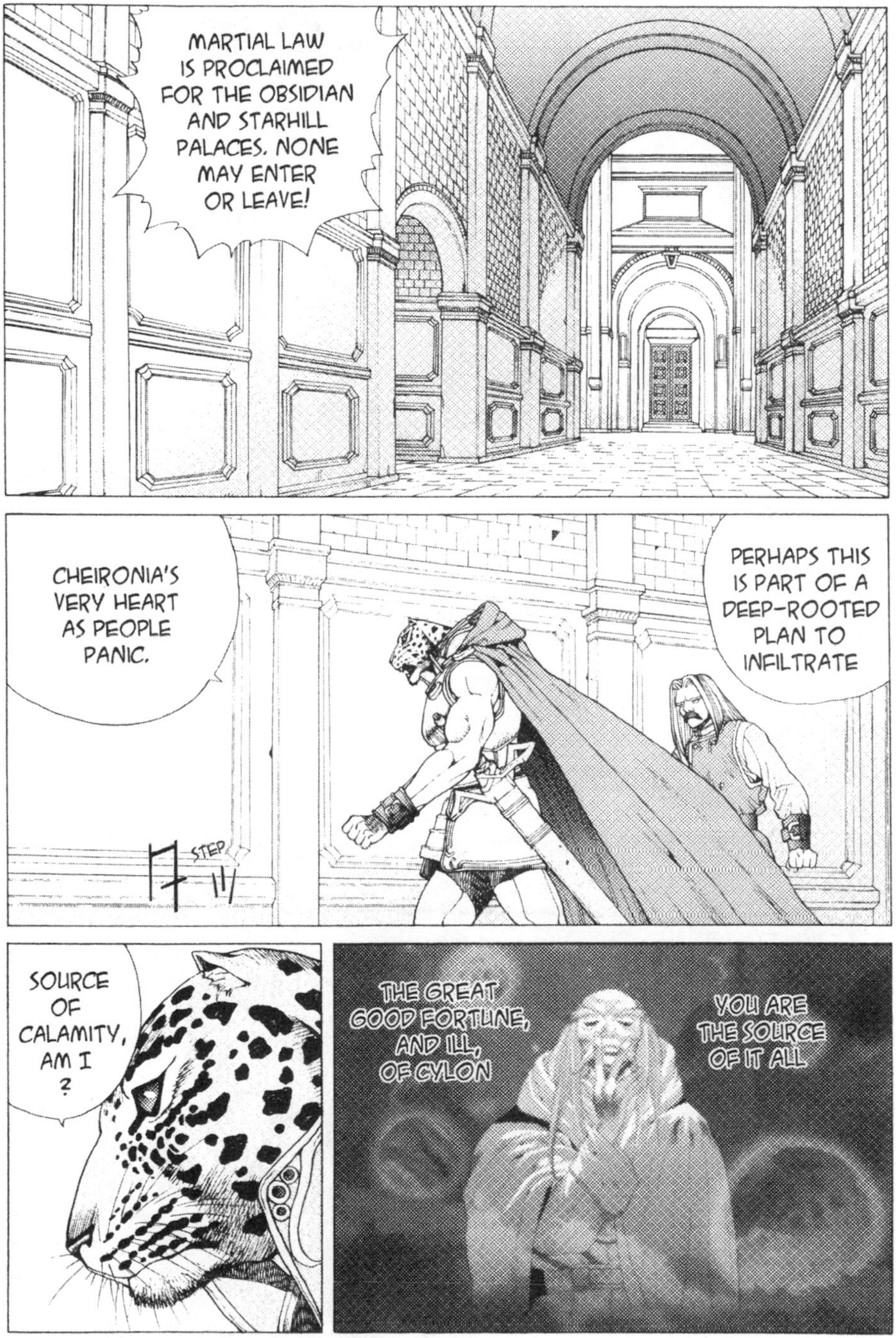
MARTIAL LAW IS PROCLAIMED FOR THE OBSIDIAN AND STARHILL PALACES. NONE MAY ENTER OR LEAVE!
PERHAPS THIS IS PART OF A DEEP-ROOTED PLAN TO INFILTRATE
CHEIRONIA'S VERY HEART AS PEOPLE PANIC.
STEP
YOU ARE THE SOURCE OF IT ALL
THE GREAT GOOD FORTUNE, AND ILL, OF CYLON
SOURCE OF CALAMITY, AM I ?

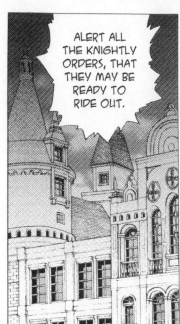

SIRE?
I WAS
TALKING TO MYSELF.
ALERT ALL THE KNIGHTLY ORDERS, THAT THEY MAY BE READY TO RIDE OUT.

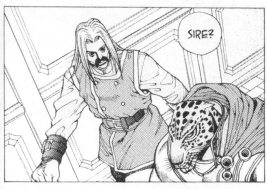

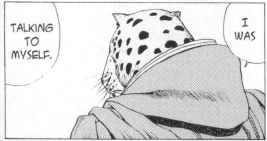

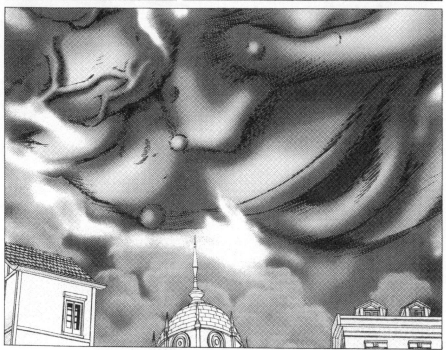

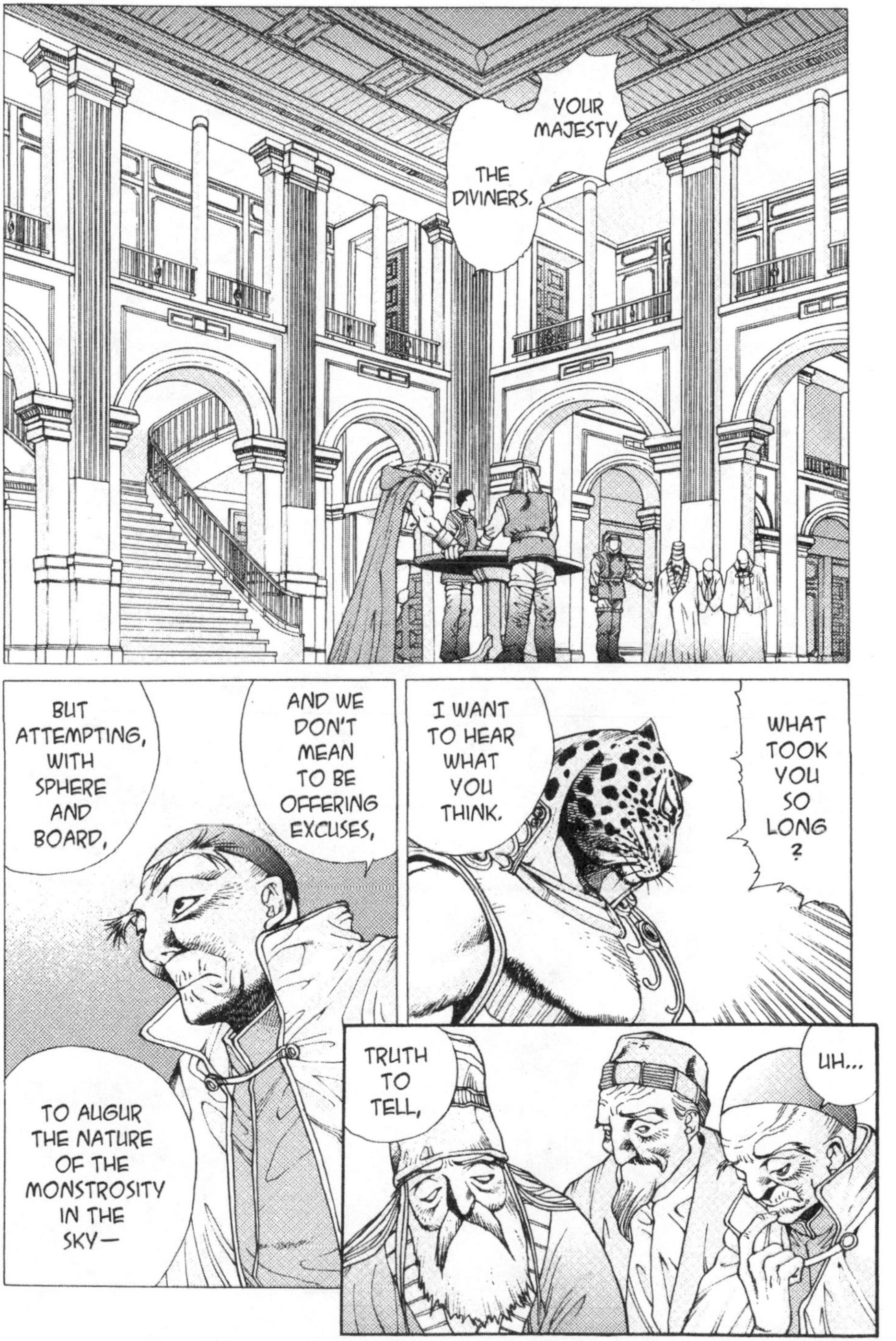
YOUR MAJESTY
THE DIVINERS.
WHAT TOOK YOU SO LONG?
I WANT TO HEAR WHAT YOU THINK.
UH...
TRUTH TO TELL,
AND WE DON'T MEAN TO BE OFFERING EXCUSES,
BUT ATTEMPTING, WITH SPHERE AND BOARD,
TO AUGUR THE NATURE OF THE MONSTROSITY IN THE SKY—

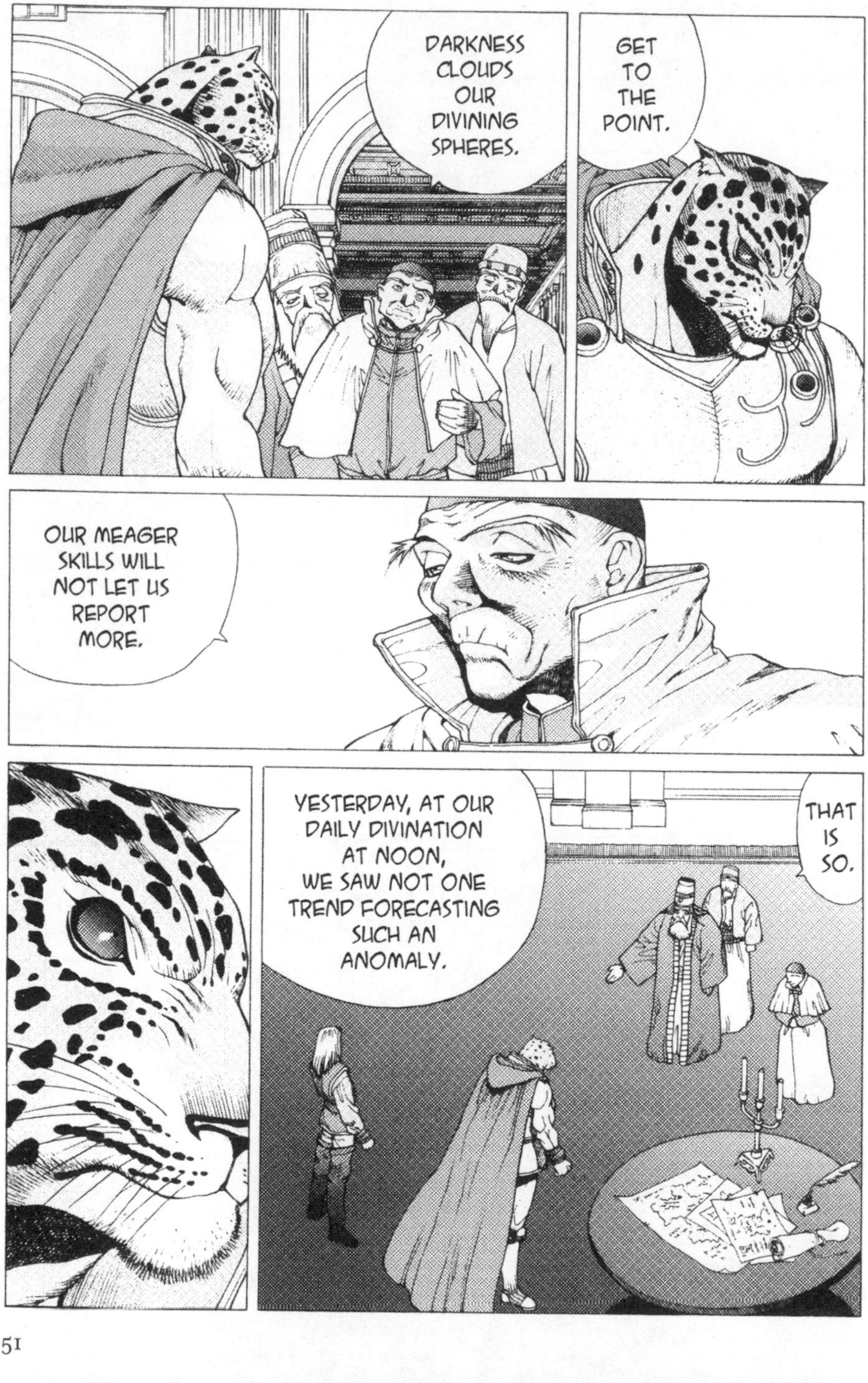
DARKNESS CLOUDS OUR DIVINING SPHERES.
GET TO THE POINT.
OUR MEAGER SKILLS WILL NOT LET US REPORT MORE.
YESTERDAY, AT OUR DAILY DIVINATION AT NOON, WE SAW NOT ONE TREND FORECASTING SUCH AN ANOMALY.
THAT IS SO.

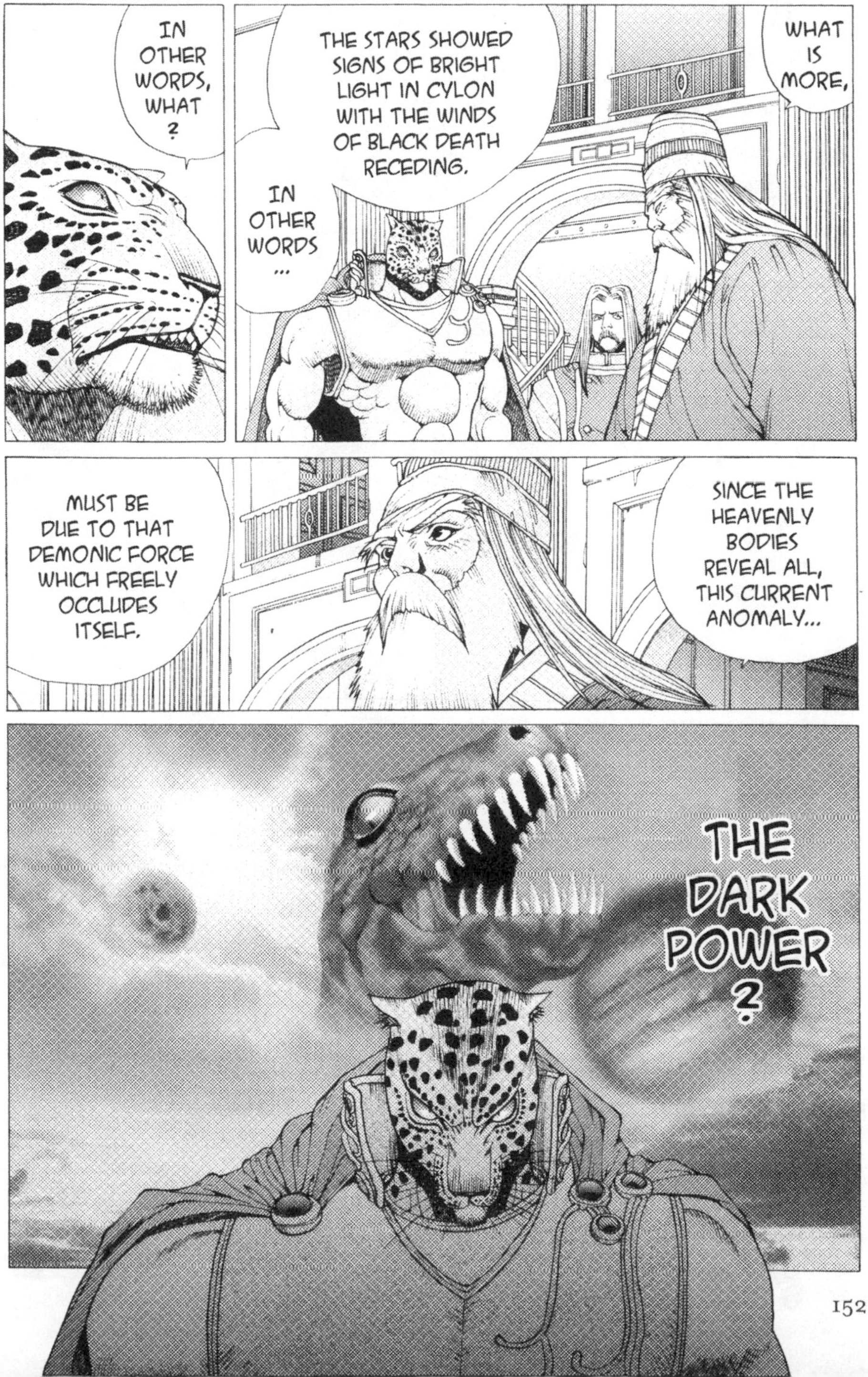
WHAT IS MORE,
THE STARS SHOWED SIGNS OF BRIGHT LIGHT IN CYLON WITH THE WINDS OF BLACK DEATH RECEDING.
IN OTHER WORDS ...
IN OTHER WORDS, WHAT ?
SINCE THE HEAVENLY BODIES REVEAL ALL, THIS CURRENT ANOMALY...
MUST BE DUE TO THAT DEMONIC FORCE WHICH FREELY OCCLUDES ITSELF.
THE DARK POWER ?

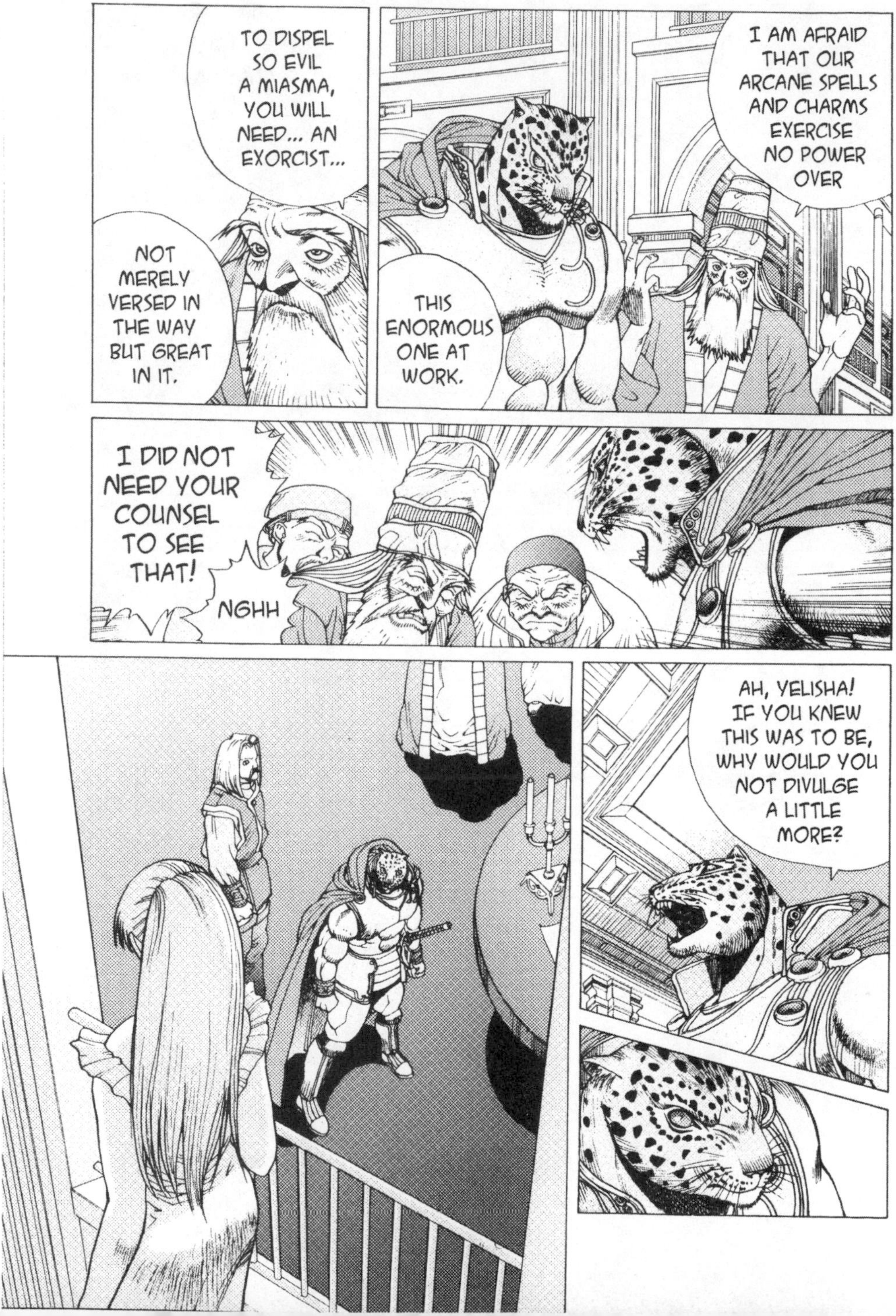
I AM AFRAID THAT OUR ARCANE SPELLS AND CHARMS EXERCISE NO POWER OVER
THIS ENORMOUS ONE AT WORK.
TO DISPEL SO EVIL A MIASMA, YOU WILL NEED... AN EXORCIST...
NOT MERELY VERSED IN THE WAY BUT GREAT IN IT.
I DID NOT NEED YOUR COUNSEL TO SEE THAT!
NGHH
AH, YELISHA! IF YOU KNEW THIS WAS TO BE, WHY WOULD YOU NOT DIVULGE A LITTLE MORE?

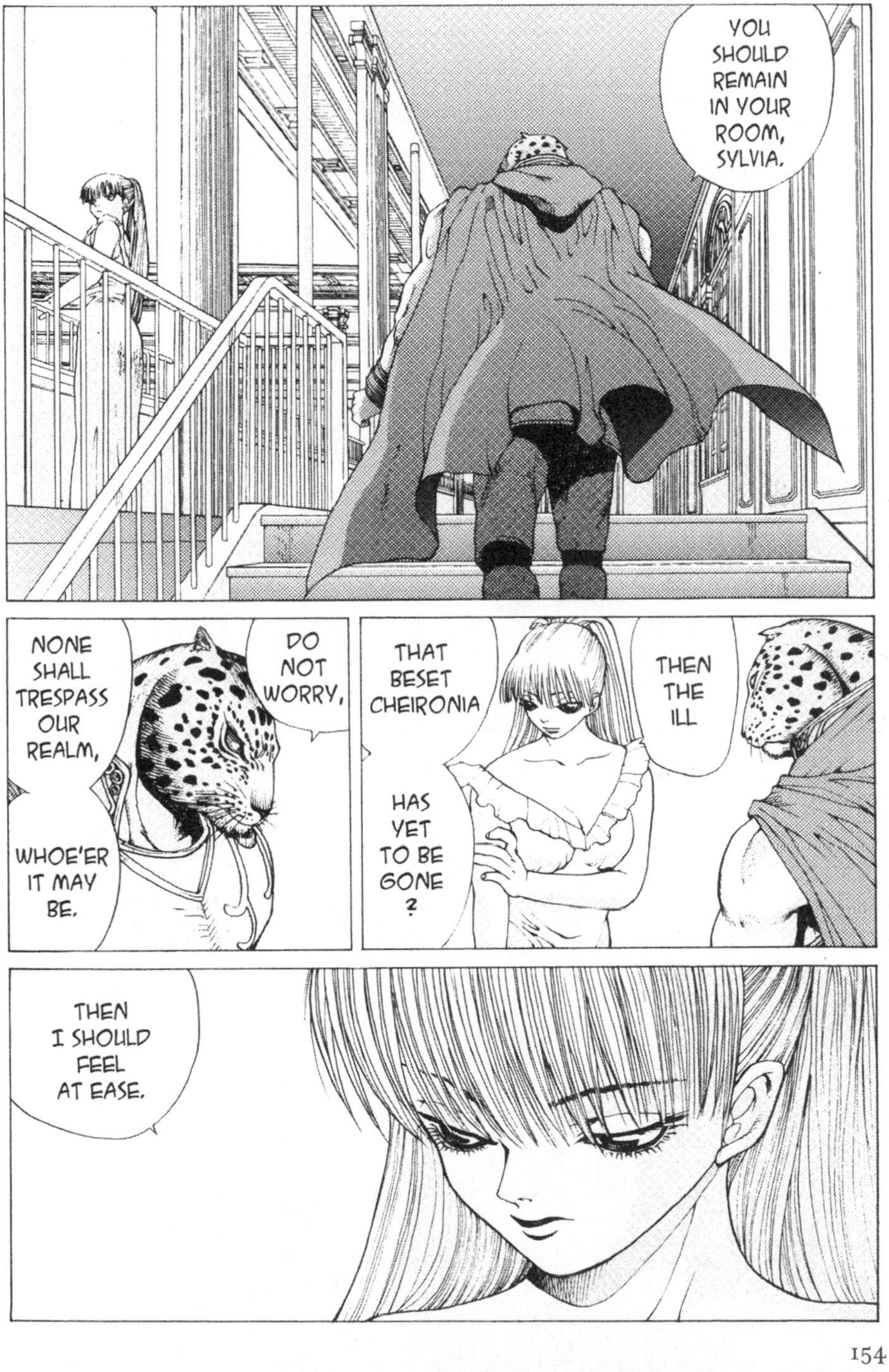
YOU SHOULD REMAIN IN YOUR ROOM, SYLVIA.
THEN THE ILL
THAT BESET CHEIRONIA
HAS YET TO BE GONE?
DO NOT WORRY,
NONE SHALL TRESPASS OUR REALM,
WHOE'ER IT MAY BE.
THEN I SHOULD FEEL AT EASE.

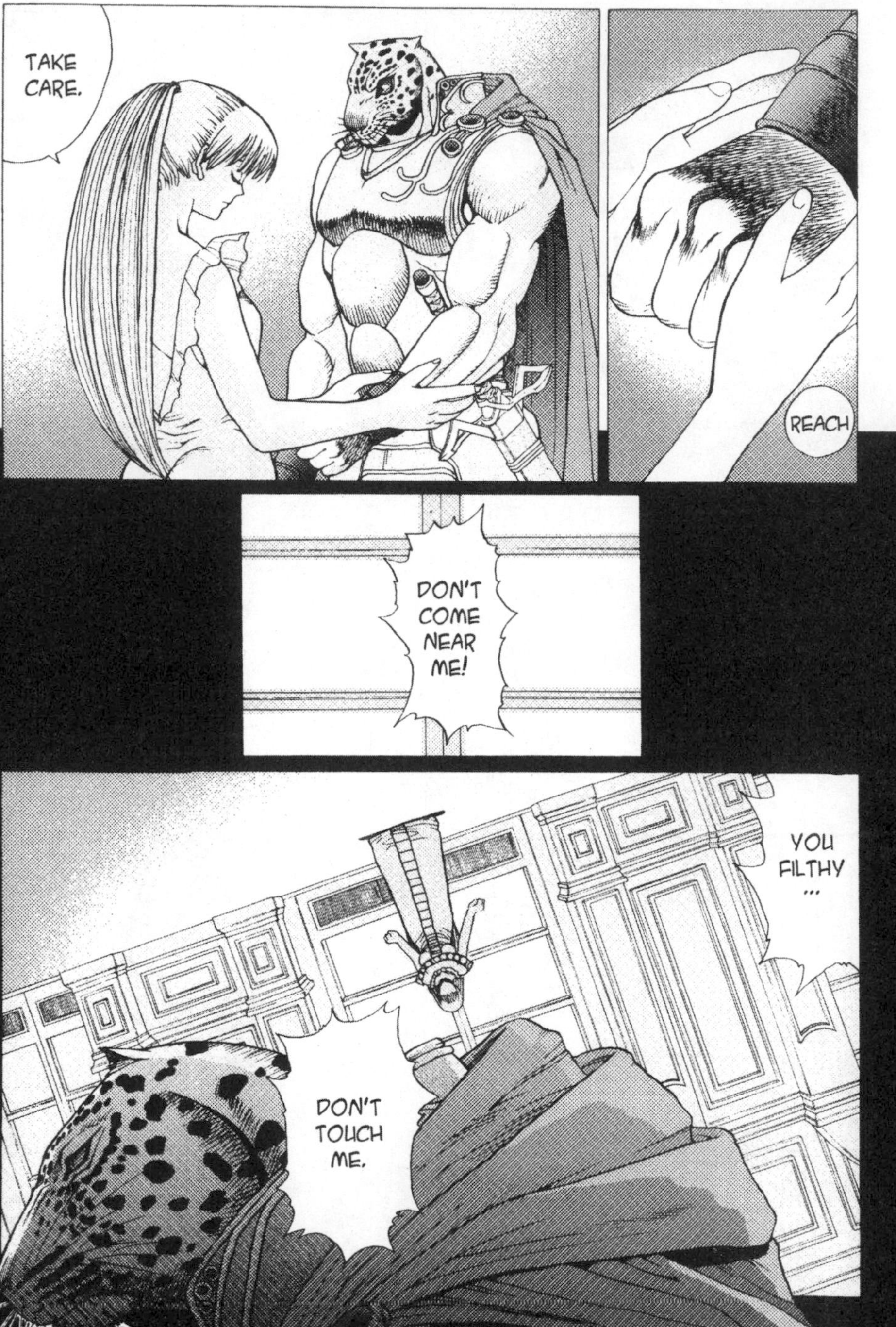
REACH
TAKE CARE.
DON'T COME NEAR ME!
YOU FILTHY ...
DON'T TOUCH ME.

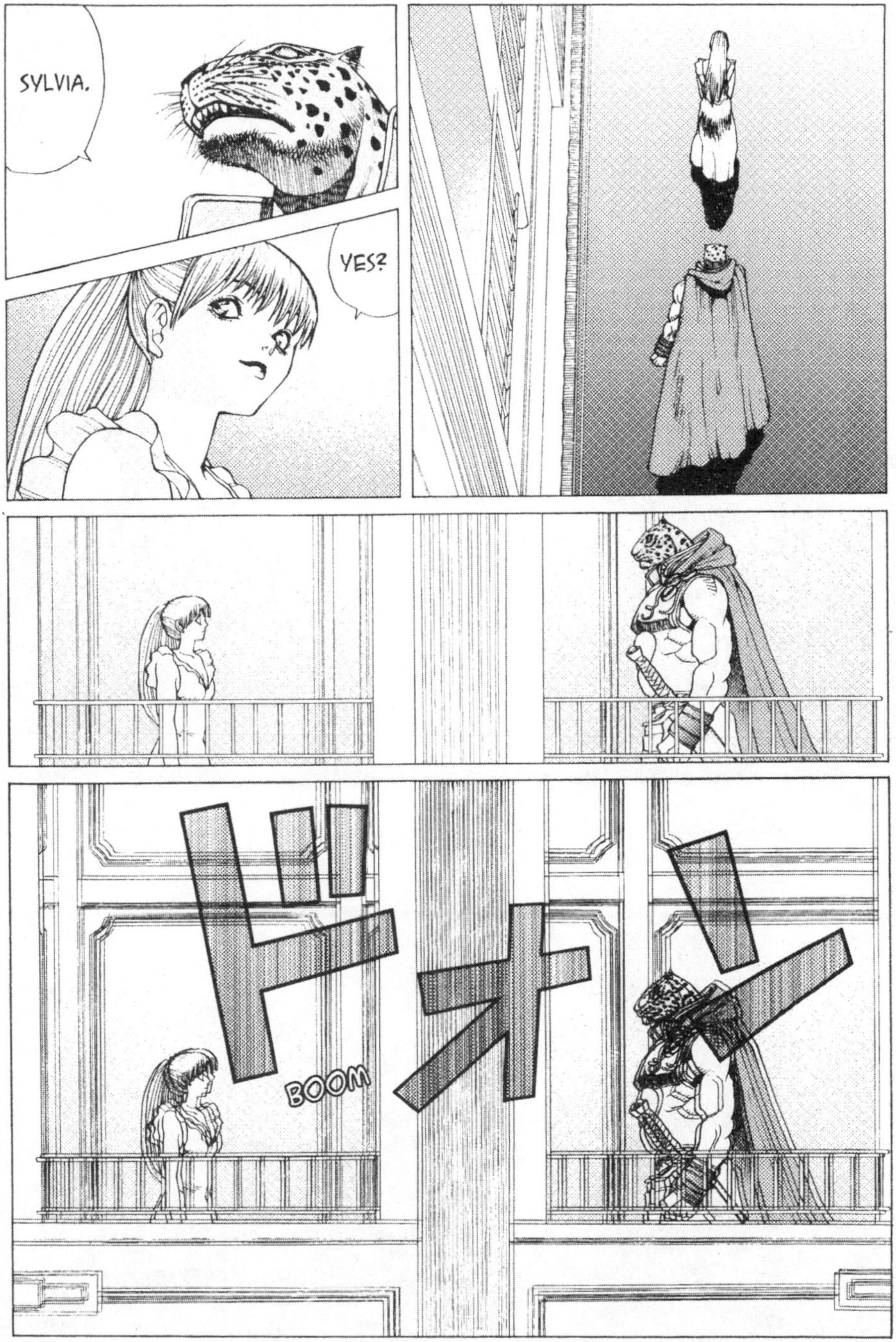
SYLVIA.
YES?
ドォン
BOOM

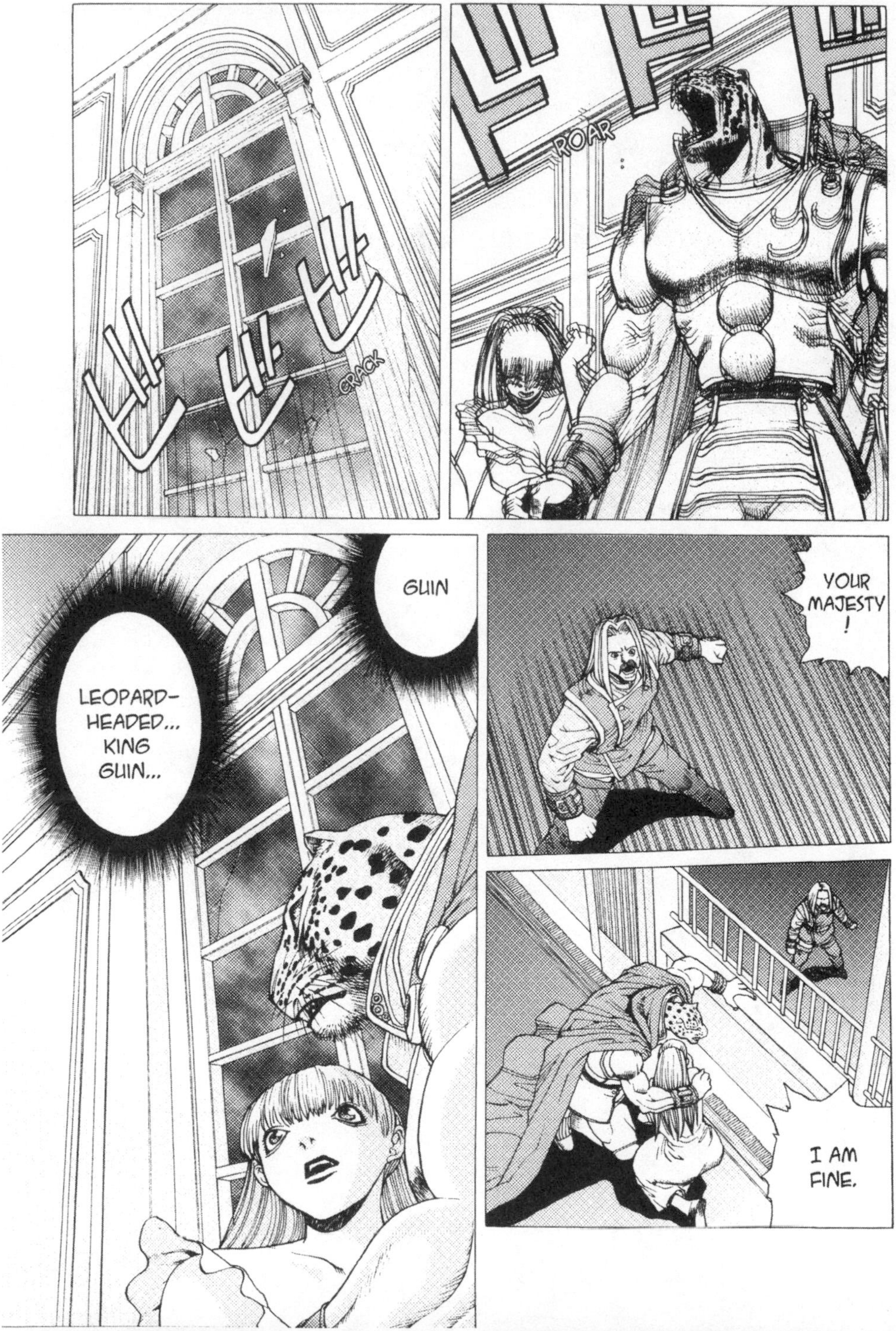
ROAR
CRACK
YOUR MAJESTY!
I AM FINE.
GUIN
LEOPARD-HEADED... KING GUIN...

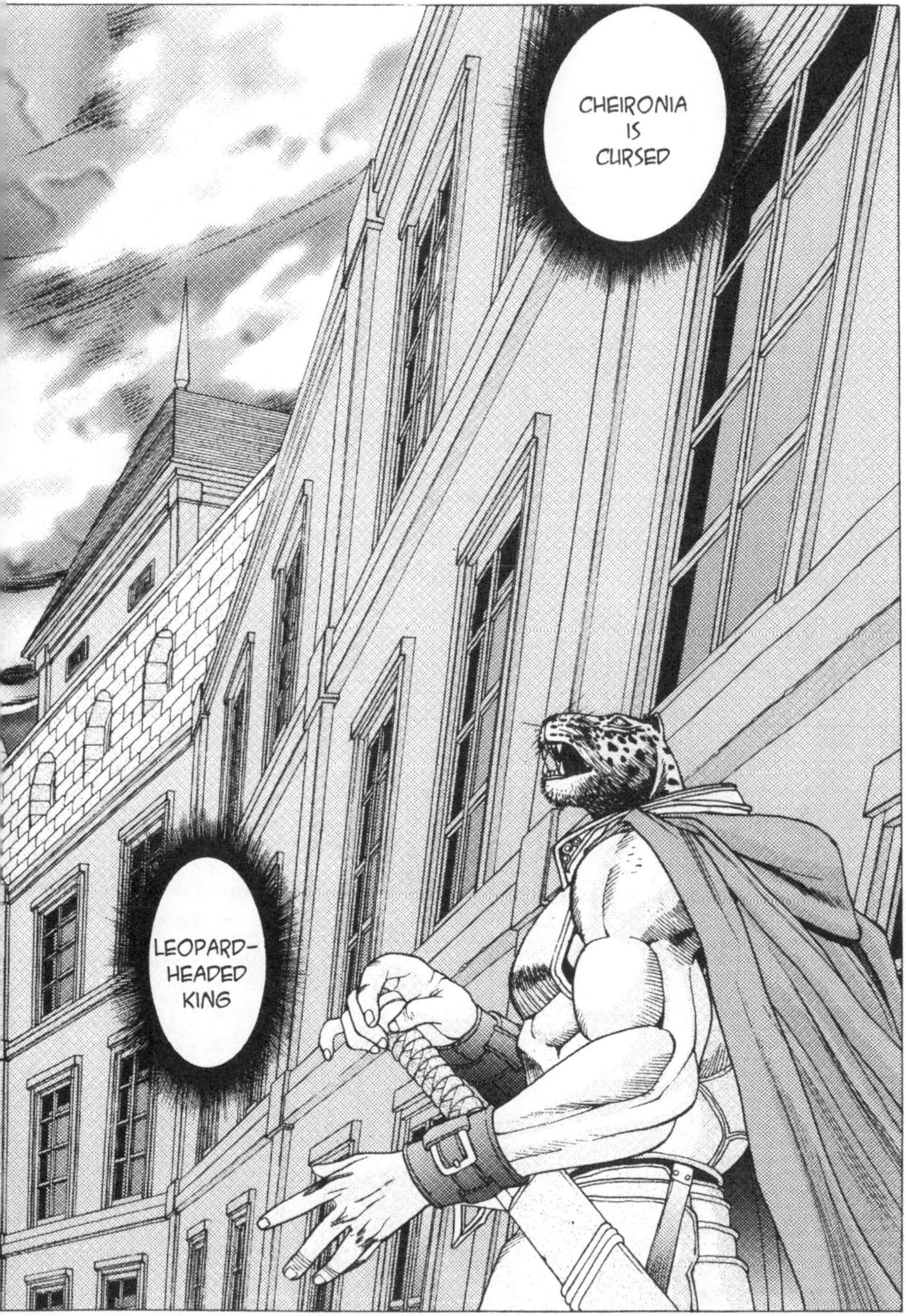
CHEIRONIA IS CURSED
LEOPARD-HEADED KING

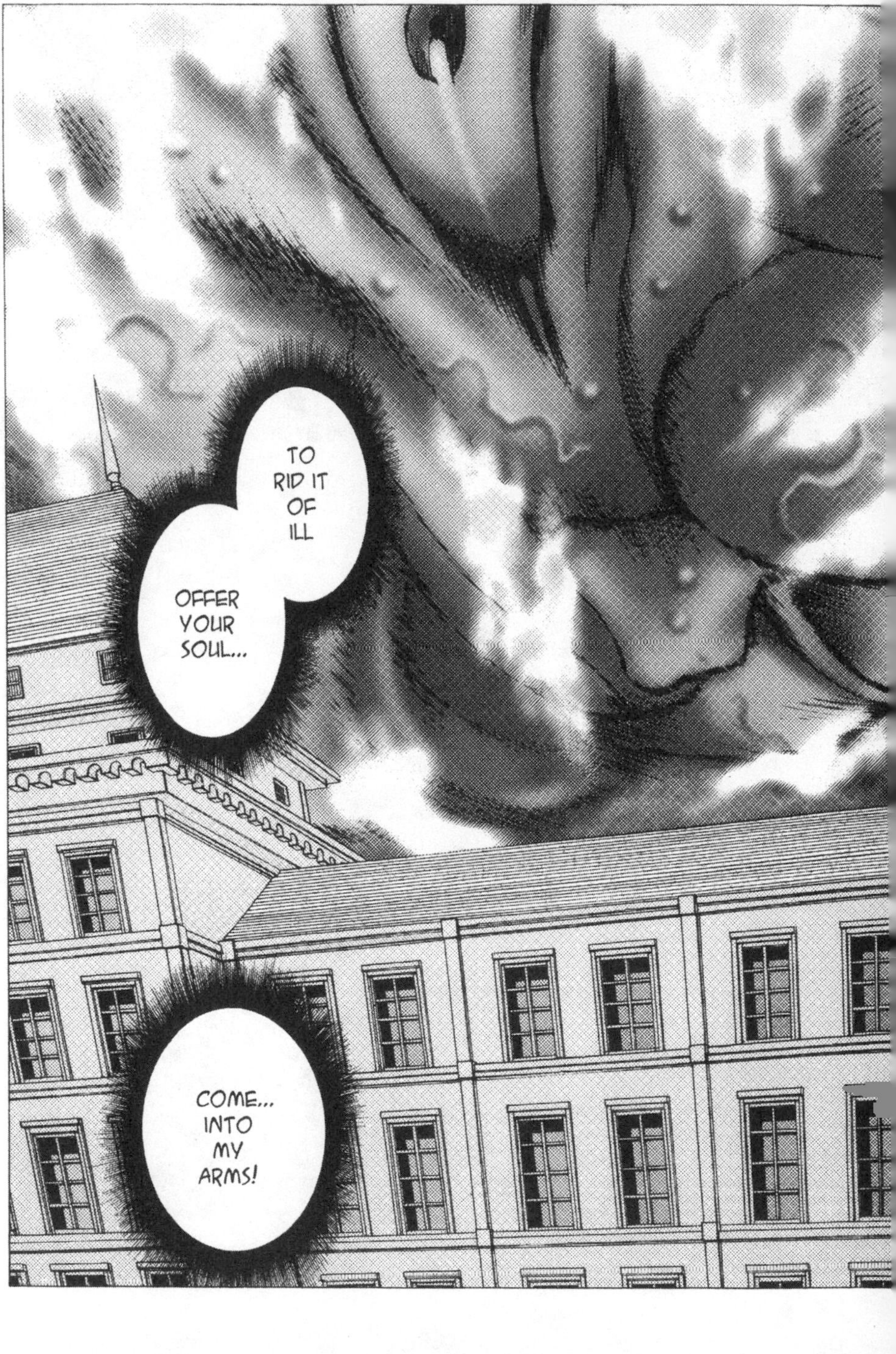
TO RID IT OF ILL
OFFER YOUR SOUL...
COME... INTO MY ARMS!

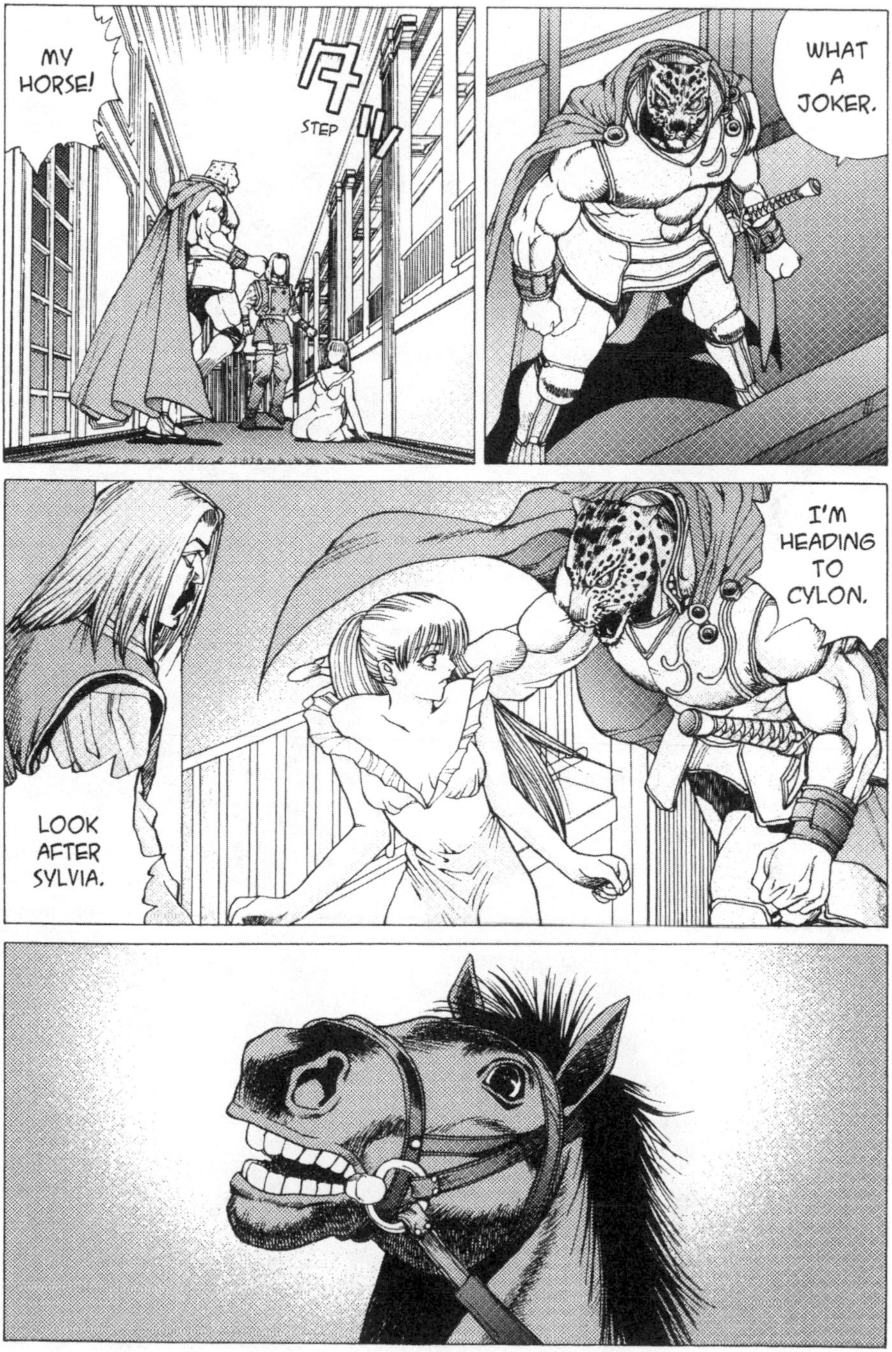
WHAT A JOKER.
MY HORSE!
STEP
I'M HEADING TO CYLON.
LOOK AFTER SYLVIA.

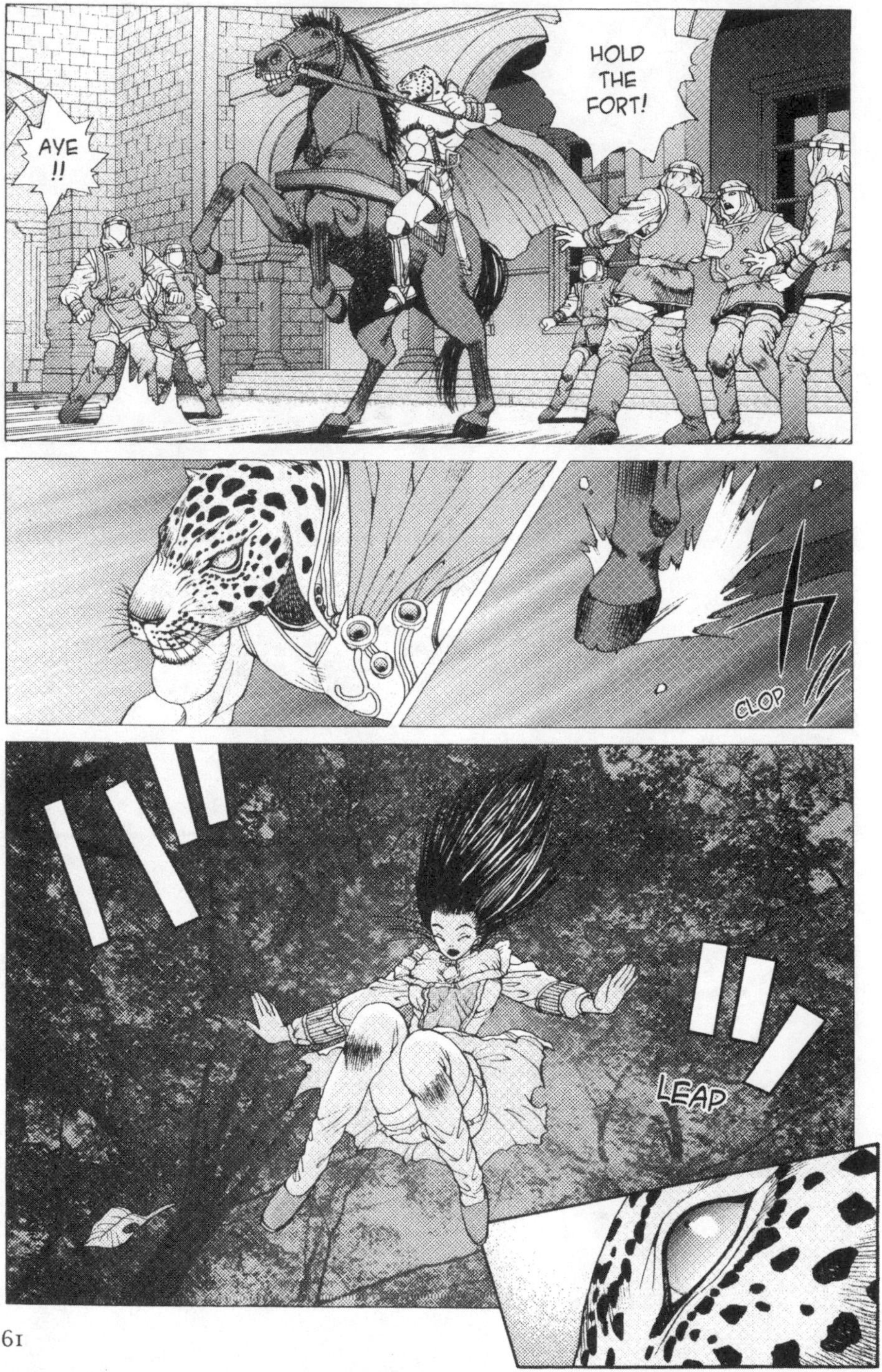
HOLD THE FORT!
AYE !!
CLOP
LEAP

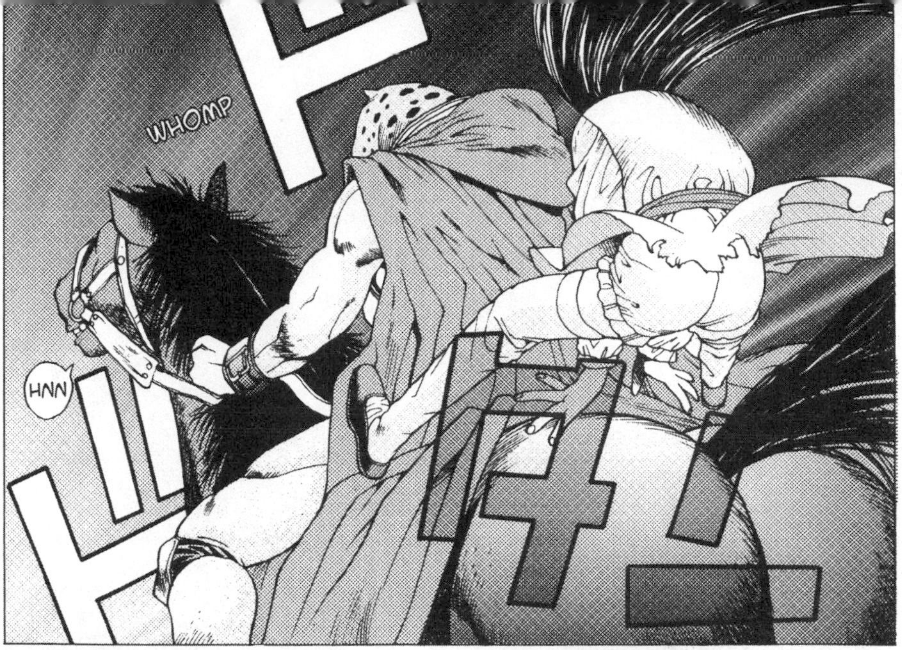
WHOMP
HNN
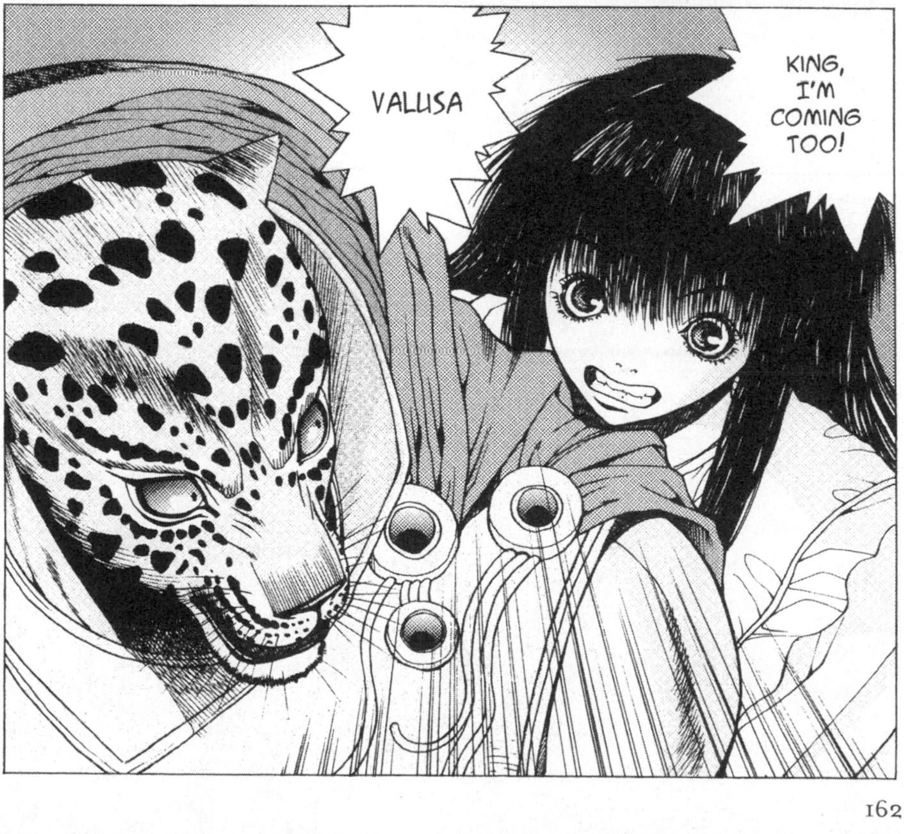
KING, I'M COMING TOO!
VALUSA

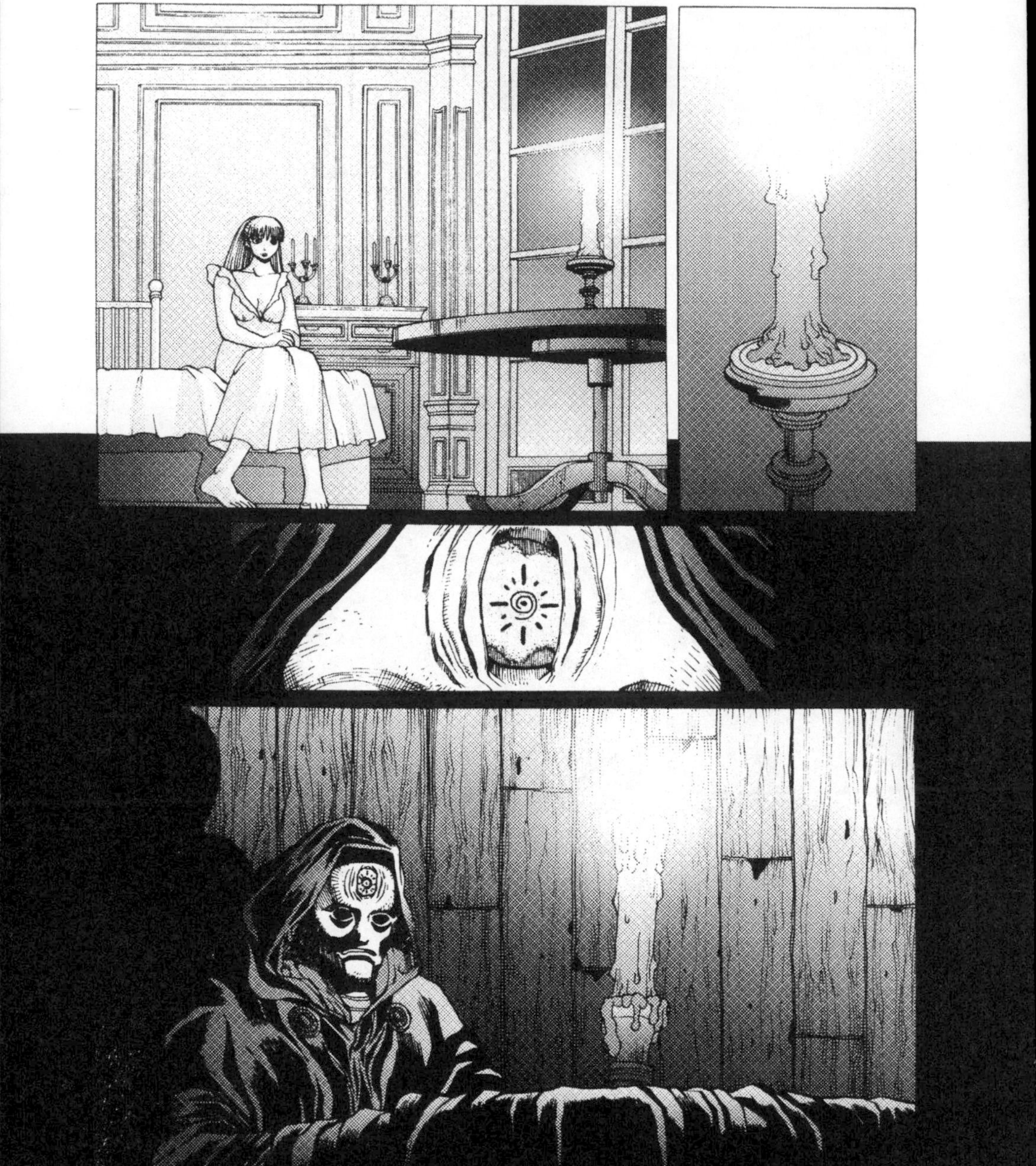

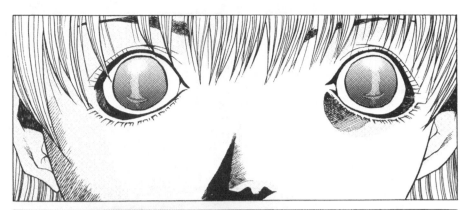

IS
MINE.

THE
KING...

To Be Continued

About the Authors

Comics artist **Kazuaki Yanagisawa** is renowned for his fine pen-touch and excellence at adapting sophisticated source material. Other works by Yanagisawa include *Paparazzi* (story by *Lone Wolf and Club*'s Kazuo Koike), a *Megami Tensei* comic based on the hit videogame cycle, and *The Summer of the Ocelot*, adapted from the novel by former *Golgo 13* storywriter Yoichi Funado.

The Guin Saga is the lifework of multi-talented **Kaoru Kurimoto**, who has written musicals based on her creation in addition to the bestselling novels. *The Seven Magi* first appeared in novel form in 1979 to great acclaim. The five-book opening episode of the saga proper is also being published by Vertical.

THE GUIN SAGA *Manga*

The Seven Magi

ILLUSTRATED BY
KAZUAKI YANAGISAWA

STORY BY
KAORU KURIMOTO

The bestselling Japanese heroic fantasy, reborn as manga, continues in Vols. 2 & 3!

Never has a story been more suited to the form than the pulse-pounding saga of the leopard-masked warrior.

In the concluding two installments, King Guin is pursued by and battles magi who desire to control his immense life-force.

Volume 2
January 2008

Volume 3
March 2008

THE GUIN SAGA

BY KAORU KURIMOTO

"Japan's answer to *The Lord of the Rings*" —*The Globe and Mail*

BOOK ONE:
The Leopard Mask
November 2007

BOOK TWO:
Warrior in the Wilderness
January 2008

BOOK THREE:
The Battle of Nospherus
March 2008

It all began here: the inaugural novels of *The Guin Saga* which has sold more than 25 million copies in Japan. Each of these paperback installments features artwork by Naoyuki Kato from the original Japanese editions.

Long before the events of *The Seven Magi*, Guin, the mighty warrior, cannot remember his past. His only clue is a leopard mask mystically attached to his head. Joined by the royal twins of Parros, a simian-girl, and a mercenary, our hero must cross the treacherous River Kes and journey into the badlands of Nospherus. In hot pursuit is a vast Mongauli army, led by the beautiful and dangerous General Amnelis.

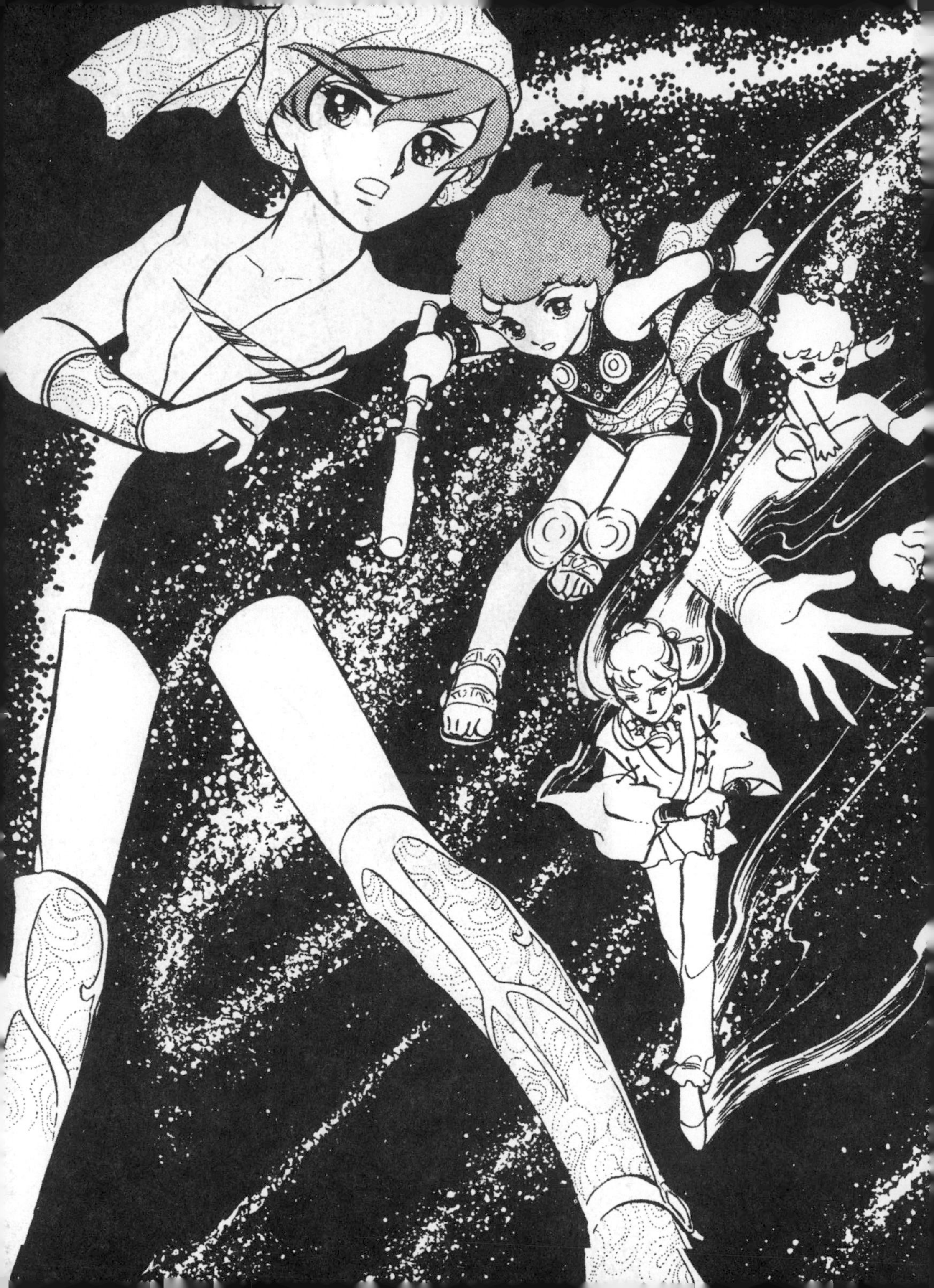

WRONG WAY!

Japanese books, including manga like this one,
are meant to be read from right to left.

So the front cover is actually the back cover, and vice-versa.

To read this book, please flip it over and start in the top right-hand corner.
Read the panels, and the bubbles in the panels, from right to left,
then drop down to the next row and repeat.

It may make you dizzy at first,
but forcing your brain to do things backwards makes you smarter in the long run.
We swear.